Aphra Behn: The

ANALYSING TEXTS

General Editor: Nicholas Marsh

Published

Chaucer: *The Canterbury Tales*   *Gail Ashton*

Aphra Behn: The Comedies   *Kate Aughterson*

Webster: The Tragedies   *Kate Aughterson*

John Keats   *John Blades*

Shakespeare: The Comedies   *R. P. Draper*

Charlotte Brontë: The Novels   *Mike Edwards*

E. M. Forster: The Novels   *Mike Edwards*

Shakespeare: The Tragedies   *Nicholas Marsh*

Shakespeare: Three Problem Plays   *Nicholas Marsh*

Jane Austen: The Novels   *Nicholas Marsh*

Emily Brontë: *Wuthering Heights*   *Nicholas Marsh*

Virginia Woolf: The Novels   *Nicholas Marsh*

D. H. Lawrence: The Novels   *Nicholas Marsh*

William Blake: The Poems   *Nicholas Marsh*

John Donne: The Poems   *Joe Nutt*

Thomas Hardy: The Novels   *Norman Page*

Marlowe: The Plays   *Stevie Simkin*

Analysing Texts
Series Standing Order ISBN 0–333–73260–X
(*outside North America only*)

You can receive future titles in this series as they are published by placing a standing order. Please contact your bookseller or, in case of difficulty, write to us at the address below with your name and address, the title of the series and the ISBN quoted above.

Customer Services Department, Palgrave Ltd
Houndmills, Basingstoke, Hampshire RG21 6XS, England

Aphra Behn:
The Comedies

KATE AUGHTERSON

First published 2003 by
PALGRAVE MACMILLAN
Houndmills, Basingstoke, Hampshire RG21 6XS and
175 Fifth Avenue, New York, N.Y. 10010
Companies and representatives throughout the world

PALGRAVE MACMILLAN is the global academic imprint of the Palgrave Macmillan division of St. Martin's Press, LLC and of Palgrave Macmillan Ltd. Macmillan® is a registered trademark in the United States, United Kingdom and other countries. Palgrave is a registered trademark in the European Union and other countries.

ISBN 0–333–96319–9 hardback
ISBN 0–333–96321–0 paperback

This book is printed on paper suitable for recycling and made from fully managed and sustained forest sources.

A catalogue record for this book is available from the British Library.

Library of Congress Cataloging-in-Publication Data
Aughterson, Kate, 1961–
    Aphra Behn : the comedies / Kate Aughterson.
       p. cm. — (Analysing texts)
    Includes bibliographical references and index.
    ISBN 0-333–96319–9 — ISBN 0-333–96321–0 (pbk.)
       1. Behn, Aphra, 1640–1689—Comedies. 2. Women and
literature—England—London—History—17th century. 3. Comedy.
I. Title. II. Analysing texts (Palgrave Macmillan (Firm))

PR3317.Z5A94 2003
822'.4—dc21   2002193072

10 9 8 7 6 5 4 3 2 1
12 11 10 09 08 07 06 05 04 03

Printed in China

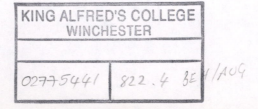

For Jacob William

Contents

General Editor's Preface

This series is dedicated to one clear belief: that we can all enjoy, understand and analyse literature for ourselves, provided we know how to do it. How can we build on close understanding of a short passage, and develop our insight into the whole work? What features do we expect to find in a text? Why do we study style in so much detail? In demystifying the study of literature, these are only some of the questions the *Analysing Texts* series addresses and answers.

The books in this series will not do all the work for you, but will provide you with the tools, and show you how to use them. Here, you will find samples of close, detailed analysis, with an explanation of the analytical techniques utilised. At the end of each chapter there are useful suggestions for further work you can do to practise, develop and hone the skills demonstrated and build confidence in your own analytical ability.

An author's individuality shows in the way they write: every work they produce bears the hallmark of that writer's personal 'style'. In the main part of each book we concentrate therefore on analysing the particular flavour and concerns of one author's work, and explain the features of their writing in connection with major themes. In Part 2 there are chapters about the author's life and work, assessing their contribution to developments in literature; and a sample of critics' views are summarised and discussed in comparison with each other. Some suggestions for further reading provide a bridge towards further critical research.

Analysing Texts is designed to stimulate and encourage your critical and analytic faculty, to develop your personal insight into the author's work and individual style, and to provide you with the skills and techniques to enjoy at first hand the excitement of discovering the richness of the text.

NICHOLAS MARSH

A Note on Editions

References to act, scene and line numbers and extracts from the three comedies studied in this volume are from *Aphra Behn: 'The Rover' and Other Plays*, edited by Jane Spencer, Oxford University Press World's Classics edition, 1995.

Introduction

Analysing Behn's Plays

This book aims to enable students to approach and understand
Behn's plays without being hindered by a surplus of technical and
theoretical terminology. Nevertheless, when we read an old play its
literary and social conventions are necessarily alien. It is useful to
outline some of the analytical terms used in the analyses in this
book. These may be divided into three areas: linguistic form;
imagery; and dramatic form and performance.

Language

Verse, metre, rhythm and rhyme

Behn's plays use a combination of verse and prose. The former is
sometimes what is called **blank verse**. Blank verse is unrhymed and
consists of a ten-beat (or ten-syllable) line, in which there are five
stressed syllables, and five syllables which are not stressed (de **dum**,
de **dum**, de **dum**, de **dum**, de **dum**). Each 'de dum', the combined
stressed and unstressed syllable, is called a **foot**. A ten-beat line with
five stresses is called a **pentameter** (from the Greek, meaning 'five
feet'). Where those stresses fall regularly in an alternating beat, the
line is called an **iambic pentameter**, which is often said to be the
'natural' rhythm of the English language. 'Hello' stresses the second
syllable, and not the first. Where Behn uses blank verse it rarely conforms precisely to a regular iambic pentameter, but there are key
occasions where it does so, and we draw attention to these in our
analysis. Her songs often use an eight-beat line.

Behn frequently makes two adjacent lines rhyme. These pairs of
lines are referred to as **rhyming couplets**. This occurs at key points
in scenes: for example, at the end, or at the exit of a major character.

1

Behn occasionally uses them to make emphatic points. The couplet often sounds like a summative statement.

Behn's plays, however, are mainly in prose. It is important to note the places where she uses both prose and verse, because these are a good indicator of a change of pace, tone and emotion. Behn's prose is usually an indicator of natural speech, and she adapts her rhythms within prose to signal changes in gender, class and character. The landlady's prose in *The Lucky Chance* is a good example.

Imagery

Throughout this book, we analyse the imagery in particular extracts. Imagery is a word, or group of words, which self-consciously creates an image or picture for the purposes of comparison to something else.

There are several different kinds of imagery noted in this book. The first is **metaphor**. A metaphor is an image which claims identity, rather than just comparison, with the idea, thing or concept to which it is referring. The two parts of a metaphor are called the **vehicle** (the actual image of the metaphor) and **tenor** (the meaning of the metaphor), respectively.

The second kind of image is a **simile**. A simile is an image which explicitly compares itself to something else, using 'like' or 'as' to signal the comparison. In a simile, both vehicle and tenor are present: in a metaphor the vehicle is what we see, and we have to intuit the tenor from the surrounding contexts.

The third type of image is **metonymy**. A metonymy is a particular kind of metaphor, where the vehicle is linked by sense to the tenor. One example is the use of 'sail' to refer to a whole ship.

The fourth type of image is a **synecdoche**, where something adjacent to or connected to the tenor becomes the vehicle.

Drama and Performance

You will notice as you read through this book that we talk about the play text both as a dramatic structure and as a performance, trying to envisage it in three dimensions on the stage. There are a few analytical and technical terms we have used, which are defined below.

Blocking is the arrangement of characters on and about the stage during a scene.

Deus ex machina is a term used by drama critics, originating from Greek drama where the god (the *deus*) literally descended from a machine (*ex machina*) in order to produce the dramatic resolution and end the play. It is therefore a term applied by critics to any unexpected arrival who magically brings about a resolution of conflict or problems in a play.

Discovery is used to mean the revealing of events, characters, scenes or action either behind one scene, or as a result of the plot's action. We shall discuss this further in Chapter 3.

In medias res is a latin term meaning 'in the midst of the action'.

Intertextuality is the self-conscious use by one text of themes, language, actions or ideas from another text.

Meta-theatrical literally means 'above' or 'beyond' the theatre, and is used to refer to plays which incorporate a sense of their own theatrical or fictional status within the action, dialogue or structure of the play.

Theatricality is used to denote Behn's self-conscious usage of the devices and machinery of the theatre as an integral part of the play.

PART 1

ANALYSING BEHN'S COMEDIES

1

Openings

Plays tend to open in the middle of a conversation, or piece of action (in classical dramatic theory referred to as *in medias res*, literally, in the middle of things). There are good reasons for this, all of them signalling how distinct drama is from other literary forms, such as the traditional novel. Drama is predicated on action: for the plot to move forward, for characters to clash, to conflict and to come together during the short space of the performance time, the narrative and dramatic structure must foreground action and conflict. The audience needs to be involved and engaged from the beginning. The best way of doing this is to plunge into the middle of a situation encapsulating the themes and conflicts of the whole play. We are then ready to recognise such themes as they develop, and often encouraged, from this very early stage, to take sides.

In studying a play, we should remember that it is a performance, a three-dimensional production, not just a flat text on the page. To help think in this way, it is important that you always ask yourself how the words work in a theatrical context. How are the actors moving around the stage (if at all)? How do costume, setting and lighting affect meaning? Are these explicit in the stage directions, or implicit in the dialogue? What is the relationship between audience and characters, and how does this affect our interpretation of the scene? What is the significance of the scenic structure?

Let us now move on to consider the openings of three of Behn's comedies. How, why and to what extent does she engage our allegiances and opinions in these opening scenes?

*   *   *

The Rover opens thus:

[Act 1, scene i]

> *A chamber*
>
> *Enter Florinda and Hellena.*
>
> *Florinda.*   What an impertinent thing is a young girl bred in a
> nunnery! How full of questions! Prithee, no more, Hellena, I have
> told thee more than thou understand'st already.
>
> *Hellena.*   The more's my grief; I would fain know as much as you,
> which makes me so inquisitive; nor is't enough I know you're a   5
> lover, unless you tell me too who 'tis you sigh for.
>
> *Florinda.*   When you're a lover, I'll think you fit for a secret of that
> nature.
>
> *Hellena.*   'Tis true, I never was a lover yet; but I begin to have a
> shrewd guess what 'tis to be so, and fancy it very pretty to sigh,   10
> and sing, and blush, and wish, and dream and wish, and long and
> wish to see the man, and when I do, look pale and tremble, just as
> you did when my brother brought home the fine English colonel
> to see you – what do you call him? Don Belvile.
>
> *Florinda.*   Fie, Hellena.   15
>
> *Hellena.*   That blush betrays you. I am sure 'tis so; or is it Don
> Antonio, the viceroy's son? Or perhaps the rich old Don Vincentio,
> whom my father designs you for a husband? Why do you blush
> again?
>
> *Florinda.*   With indignation; and how near soever my father thinks   20
> I am to marrying that hated object, I shall let him see I understand
> better what's due to my beauty, birth and fortune, and more to my
> soul, than to obey those unjust commands.
>
> *Hellena.*   Now hang me, if I don't love thee for that dear disobedience.
> I love mischief strangely, as most of our sex do, who are   25
> come to love nothing else. But tell me, dear Florinda, don't you
> love that fine *Inglese*? For I vow, next to loving him myself, 'twill
> please me most that you do so, for he is so gay and so handsome.
>
> *Florinda.*   Hellena, a maid designed for a nun ought not to be so
> curious in a discourse of love.   30
>
> *Hellena.*   And dost thou think that ever I'll be a nun? Or at least till
> I'm so old, I'm fit for nothing else: faith, no, sister; and that which

makes me long to know whether you love Belvile, is because I hope
he has some mad companion or other that will spoil my devotion.
Nay, I'm resolved to provide myself this Carnival, if there be e'er   35
a handsome proper fellow of my humour above ground, though I
ask first.

Florinda.   Prithee be not so wild.

Hellena.   Now you have provided yourself of a man, you take no
care for poor me. Prithee tell me, what dost thou see about me that   40
is unfit for love? Have I not a world of youth? A humour gay? A
beauty passable? A vigour desirable? Well-shaped? Clean-limbed?
Sweet-breathed? And sense enough to know how all these ought
to be employed to the best advantage? Yes, I do, and will; therefore
lay aside your hopes of my fortune by my being a devotee, and   45
tell me how you came acquainted with this Belvile; for I perceive
you knew him before he came to Naples.

Florinda.   Yes, I knew him at the siege of Pamplona: he was then
a colonel of French horse, who, when the town was ransacked,
nobly treated my brother and myself, preserving us from all   50
insolences; and I must own, besides great obligations, I have I
know not what that pleads kindly for him about my heart, and will
suffer no other to enter. But see, my brother.

    Enter Don Pedro, Stephano with a masking habit, and Callis.

Pedro.   Good morrow, sister. Pray when saw you your lover Don
Vincentio?   55

Florinda.   I know not, sir – Callis, when was he here? – for I
consider it so little, I know not when it was.

Pedro.   I have a command from my father here to tell you you ought
not to despise him, a man of so vast a fortune, and such a passion
for you. – Stephano, my things.   60

    [Don Pedro] puts on his masking habit.

Florinda.   A passion for me? 'Tis more than e'er I saw, or he had a
desire should be known. I hate Vincentio, sir, and I would not have
a man so dear to me as my brother follow the ill customs of our
country, and make a slave of his sister; and, sir, my father's will
I'm sure you may divert.   65

Pedro.   I know not how dear I am to you, but I wish only to be
ranked in your esteem equal with the English colonel Belvile. Why
do you frown and blush? Is there any guilt belongs to the name of
that cavalier?

Florinda.   I'll not deny I value Belvile. When I was exposed to such   70

> dangers as the licensed lust of common soldiers threatened, when
> rage and conquest flew through the city, then Belvile, this criminal
> for my sake, threw himself into all dangers to save my honour:
> and will you not allow him my esteem?
>
> *Pedro.*   Yes, pay him what you will in honour; but you must consider   75
> Don Vincentio's fortune, and the jointure he'll make you.
>
> *Florinda.*   Let him consider my youth, beauty and fortune, which
> ought not to be thrown away on his age and jointure.
>
> *Pedro.*   'Tis true, he's not so young and fine a gentleman as that
> Belvile; but what jewels will that cavalier present you with? Those   80
> of his eyes and heart?
>
> *Hellena.*   And are those not better than any Don Vincentio has
> brought from the Indies?
>
> *Pedro.*   Why how now! Has your nunnery breeding taught you to
> understand the value of hearts and eyes?   85
>
> *Hellena.*   Better than to believe Vincentio's deserve value from any
> woman: he may perhaps increase her bags, but not her family.
>
> *Pedro.*   This is fine! Go, up to your devotion: you are not designed
> for the conversation of lovers.
>
> *Hellena. (Aside)*   Nor saints, yet awhile, I hope. – Is't not enough you   90
> make a nun of me, but you must cast my sister away too, exposing
> her to a worse confinement than a religious life?
>
> *Pedro.*   The girl's mad!
>
> (The Rover, 1, i, 1–93)

By the play's opening in the middle of a conversation (signalled
clearly by the exclamatory and exasperated opening line) we are
involved immediately in the disputes and lives of the characters.
What do these opening lines tell us about the play and characters?

Let us first consider setting, costume and structure. The opening
setting is intimate (the stage direction indicates 'a chamber'), replicated in the first 53 lines by the nature and tone of the two women's
conversation. We gain a sense of an easy, friendly and open relationship between Hellena and Florinda over which we have a privileged
view. The first 53 lines stand in marked contrast to the next 40,
when their brother arrives in the chamber, bursting in with his own
agenda, claiming to dominate both the stage and their lives. It is
unusual in this period, even in Behn's work, to find two female characters opening the play. What is its effect? The audience observes

women's points of view from the opening, a perception confirmed as the scene progresses, when we credit Hellena's critique of arranged marriages to older men, not just because it is so witty, but because we have known her and her perspective intimately first.

The scenic division (between women alone, and men invading) mirrors both themes and events which occur later in the play, and establishes a point of view on those themes and events for the audience. By contrasting young, intelligent and likeable young women, with older, rapacious men, Behn utilises a conventional comic device (the young versus the old), and then genders it. This comic device is a serious theme the whole play examines. Their brother's entry, in the process of masking himself, provides a visual contrast to the women. His masked visage suggests a lack of openness, perhaps a hidden agenda, and a gap between public and private persona, particularly in contrast to the women's open and frank speech. Women of their class are not supposed to wander the streets during Carnival (although they break this stricture), whilst the men are free to 'ramble' (1, i, 178) and adventure at will. Pedro's habit and dress, therefore, further signal his privileged gendered position in contrast to the women, who are expected to be both obedient and at home.

How does the content and tone reinforce or alter these opening, more generalised perceptions? The conversation between Hellena and Florinda addresses the intimate and emotional subject of love and lovers, and is conducted in a tone which is both loving and humorous. Neither woman interrupts the other, but the pace of dialogue is fast, and mutually responsive. We gain a good sense of each woman's character, and the differences between them. Hellena teases Florinda, who acts as an older sister from the opening exclamatory and half-exasperated 'What an impertinent thing is a young girl bred in a nunnery!' to the later 'be not so wild' (l. 38). Florinda's initial reluctance to confide her love breaks down in the face of Hellena's persistence: character traits (of reticence and outspokenness, respectively) which are repeated later in the play for both women.

Yet this summary belies Florinda's strength of character, which is clear from her determined defence of Belvile. Hellena's outspoken and frank views on love initially look more radical than those of her sister, who appears to conform to a more conventional model of femininity: modest and restrained ('Fie, Hellena', l, 15). Yet even Florinda speaks her mind on the subject of patriarchal control of marriage: 'how near soever my father thinks I am to marrying that hated object' (ll. 20–1). Both women use a language of justice, rights and self-determination to defend their views and choices. Applying this discourse to women's rights was unusual at the time, and is particularly striking coming at the play's opening. Thus, Florinda talks about what is 'due' to her, and her refusal to obey her father's 'unjust' commands (ll. 22–3), exposing a division between a world arranged by fathers and brothers, and the desires and agency of daughters and sisters. Florinda's language echoes the scenic, comic and visual contrasts we noted earlier. Hellena takes this language further in her delineation of her intended actions ('I'm resolved to provide myself', l. 35, and 'Yes, I do, and will', l. 44), using active declarative verbs, suggesting a woman who intends to be openly in control of her own destiny. Florinda's response to this ('Prithee be not so wild') suggests that the play may offer two divergent methods of resisting patriarchal authority. Both sisters express rational resistance to paternal orders (one against an arranged marriage, the other against confinement in a nunnery): but we will watch divergent approaches to such resistance. This opening scene initiates the question of which method will be best: a question answered by the play's events.

The intimate tone is emphasised by grammatical and syntactical forms: repeated rhetorical questions, where we assume agreement between the sisters; relatively lengthy sentences interspersed with far shorter ones, which engender a sense of informality; and cumulative listing (ll. 10–15 and 39–44) creating a sense of both parody and ebullient opinions. Stage directions are incorporated into the dialogue (for example, on Florinda's blush, and Pedro's entrance), which adds a sense of rapid movement to the scene, and enables actors to use dialogue to naturally construct and direct their physical actions and intimacy.

The tone and language of the second half of the extract differ in various and significant ways from those of the first half. Pedro speaks most frequently, although in the latter part of the extract, Hellena dominates in terms of volume of words. The women's language here is far more formal: they call their brother 'sir' or 'my brother', whereas they called each other by their first names. In the first part, Hellena is silent, and the elder sister alone speaks with her brother. This conforms to convention. Florinda's sentence construction also is much more formal ('I'll not deny I value Belvile', l. 70) than when she was alone with her sister. Nevertheless, despite this formal and linguistic acquiescence to the authority and superior position of her brother, Florinda continues to defy her father's wishes: 'I would not have a man so dear to me as my brother follow the ill customs of our country, and make a slave of his sister' (ll. 62–4). Her continued insistence on self-determination establishes the nature of the subsequent comic conflict. She also refers to Belvile's salvation of her 'honour', a key word and concept for both men and women in the play.

Hellena's approach to her brother is in some contrast to that of Florinda. Although the effect is of a direct attack, she uses various indirect methods to signal her views. The first is an ironic question (ll. 82–3), maligning Vincentio's sources of wealth; the second a witty comment on his likely impotence due to old age (ll. 86–7); the third, an aside to the audience (l. 90), which prefaces a move into a direct appeal (ll. 91–2). This irritates Pedro the most and clearly such a direct attack on the authority of the male establishment is seen to be completely aberrant ('The girl's mad!'). The following exchange (if it can be called that) verbally illustrates Hellena's irritation, and Pedro's inability to impose his views and authority. His interjections to her satiric portrait of life in an arranged marriage are ineffectual and short. The energy of her account (which is both witty and horrific) dominates the scene and her brother, inverting the norm of hierarchical gendered relations. Pedro's character thus appears rigid, devious and inflexible from the opening.

Although Florinda modifies her linguistic register in the more public environment of conversation with her brother, Hellena does not. Her frank account of the probable nature of sexual relations with an elderly husband is explicit, and consequently funny. Hellena represents herself not as a potential nun (as her father designs), but as someone equal in language and attitude to the libertine men of Restoration England. This ambition and self-characterisation is tested in the play.

The play's key themes are signalled clearly in this opening through characterisation, staging, scenic structure and verbal content. The scene configures the conflict between a patriarchal ordering of the world and the needs and desires of an individual woman, in an inversion of conventional openings. Women characters are allowed both implicit and explicit defiance of the patriarchal imperatives: Florinda attacks the 'ill customs' which make women 'slaves', whilst Hellena parallels marriage to 'confinement'. This explicit view on the patriarchal trade in women is made by characters with whom the audience is asked to sympathise. In this extract, Hellena is the only character who speaks directly to the audience (l. 90). The play's opening therefore explicitly signals a radical attack on contemporary conventions. In addition, the opening raises questions about identity and social convention, through disguise; about forced and arranged marriage; and about the economic freedom of women.

* * *

This is the start of *The Feigned Courtesans*:

[Act 1, scene i]

   [*A street*]

   *Enter Laura Lucretia and Silvio, richly dressed; Antonio attending,
   coming all in in haste.*

Silvio.   Madam, you need not make such haste away; the stranger
   that followed us from St Peter's church pursues us no longer, and
   we have now lost sight of him. Lord, who would have thought the
   approach of a handsome cavalier should have possessed Donna
   Laura Lucretia with fear?   5
Laura Lucretia.   I do not fear, my Silvio, but I would have this new
   habitation, which I've designed for love, known to none but him
   to whom I've destined my heart. (*Aside*) Ah, would he know the
   conquest he has made! – Nor went I this evening to church with
   any other devotion, but that which warms my heart for my young   10
   English cavalier, whom I hoped to have seen there; and I must find
   some way to let him know my passion, which is too high for souls
   like mine to hide.

Silvio.   Madam, the cavalier's in view again, and hot in the pursuit.

Laura Lucretia.   Let's haste away then; and Silvio, do you lag 15
  behind; 'twill give him an opportunity of enquiring, whilst I get
  out of sight. Be sure you conceal my name and quality, and tell
  him – anything but truth – tell him I am La Silvianetta, the young
  Roman courtesan, or what you please, to hide me from his
  knowledge. 20

> *Exeunt Laura Lucretia [and Antonio]. Enter Julio and page, in*
> *pursuit.*

Julio.   Boy, fall you into discourse with that page, and learn his lady's •
  name, whilst I pursue her farther.

> *Exit Julio. Page salutes Silvio, who returns it; they go out as talking*
> *to each other. Enter Sir Harry Fillamour and Galliard.*

Fillamour.   He follows her close, whoe'er they be: I see this trade
  of love goes forward still.

Galliard.   And will whilst there's difference in sexes. But Harry, the 25
  women, the delicate women I was speaking of?

Fillamour.   Prithee tell me no more of thy fine women, Frank; thou
  hast not been in Rome above a month, and thou'st been a dozen
  times in love, as thou call'st it. To me there is no pleasure like
  constancy. 30

Galliard.   Constancy! And wouldst thou have me one of those dull
  lovers who believe it their duty to love a woman till her hair and
  eyes change colour, for fear of the scandalous name of an
  inconstant! No, my passion, like great victors, hates the lazy stay,
  but having vanquished, prepares for new conquests. 35

Fillamour.   Which you gain as they do towns by fire, lose 'em even
  in the taking; thou wilt grow penitent, and weary of these
  dangerous follies.

Galliard.   But I am yet too young for both. Let old age and infirmity
  bring repentance, there's her feeble province; and even then, too, 40
  we find no plague like being deprived of dear womankind.

Fillamour.   I hate playing about a flame that will consume me.

Galliard.   Away with your antiquated notions, and let's once hear
  sense from thee. Examine but the whole world, Harry, and thou
  wilt find a beautiful woman the desire of the noblest, and the 45
  reward of the bravest.

Fillamour.   And the common prize of coxcombs: times are altered
  now, Frank; why else should the virtuous be cornuted, the coward
  be caressed, the villain roll with six, and the fool lie with her
  ladyship? 50

Galliard.   Mere accident, sir, and the kindness of fortune; but
a pretty witty young creature, such as this Silvianetta, and
Euphemia, is certainly the greatest blessing this wicked world can
afford us.

Fillamour.   I believe the lawful enjoyment of such a woman, and   55
honest too, would be a blessing.

Galliard.   Lawful enjoyment! Prithee what's lawful enjoyment, but
to enjoy 'em according to the generous indulgent law of nature;
enjoy 'em as we do meat, drink, air and light, and all the rest of
her common blessings? Therefore, prithee, dear knight, let me   60
govern thee but for a day, and I will show thee such a signora,
such a beauty; another manner of piece than your so admired
Viterboan, Donna Marcella, of whom you boast so much.

(*The Feigned Courtesans*, 1, i, 1–63)

This play's opening differs markedly from that of *The Rover*, with its
confident display of female autonomy. Here, by contrast, the first
speaker is a boy page, reassuring his mistress of her safety. Once
again, the play opens *in medias res*, but here the action is dramatic:
Laura Lucretia is being physically and unwillingly pursued by a cavalier. The street setting, in contrast to the domestic interior, suggests a
woman displaced. The opening therefore signals a play in which
women are physically vulnerable, rather than wittily self-contained,
as they seem in *The Rover*.

The extract falls into two parts: the first focuses briefly on the
pursuit of Laura by Julio, and the second on the relationship and
conversation between the two gallants Fillamour and Galliard. The
two parts are thematically related, since the topic of conversation in
both cases is the pursuit of love and eros, but explicitly contrasted.
In the first part we watch a woman's point of view, and in the
second, two points of view from men. Let us concentrate briefly on
the signals the play wants us to pick up from the structural contrast
made between these two parts.

The first part visually displays a woman who is reluctant to be
present on stage in two ways: she is fleeing from the action, and she
is in disguise. This establishes female identity as something under
threat and as absent or invisible from public view and public places,
an impression reinforced by her evident fear of discovery. However,

this is partly counterweighed by her view that her disguise enables her to pursue her own desires, and her attempt to direct the action (ll. 17–19). Like Shakespearean comic heroines, she is in disguise in order to secretly find her beloved. Unlike them, however, she remains in flight and unsuccessful for the whole play. Thus Behn uses a comic convention (the woman in disguise to pursue her beloved), but refuses to allow it to work conventionally. Her disguised woman, rather than being empowered by feigning, is disempowered, and in flight. The opening thus signals a discordant note in comparison with the rest of the scene, which is determinedly in the comic vein. The feigning of the play's title is associated with women rather than with men, and in this first case, is seen as something adopted as a hasty expedient (to get rid of Julio), which later backfires (as we shall see).

This first part additionally contrasts with the second part in the nature of the relationship presented. In the second part we meet two gallants, who treat each other equally. In the first part, despite the fact that Laura is the mistress, Silvio takes the lead. Here the page's gender provides more authority than the aristocratic class status of the mistress, and femininity is literally demonstrated as something weak, powerless, and dependent on a man for credit and authority. Thus the physical arrangement of the whole scene and the action itself contradict Laura's self-perception as liberated by her disguise and intended actions. Stagecraft thus works both to undermine characters' self-presentation, and to display the inequity of gender hierarchies. Stage directions explicitly delineate the hasty movements and entrances and exits, echoing both action and dialogue.

By contrast, the second part of the extract is slower in pace and action. The two men observe the chase of Laura by Julio, but as if from a distance. They are likely to be at the front of the stage, and both their stage position and their commentary on the action ally them with the audience's view of the opening. This double vision of the action (first by ourselves, and then by the gallants) re-emphasises the fact of the pursuit, but this time from an explicitly male viewpoint. Fillamour's first words, 'this **trade** of love goes forward still' (ll. 23–4), suggest both that a woman on the streets is seen as easy prey, and that erotic encounters are figured as commercial enterprises, making explicit what is suggested by Laura's fear: the commodification of women's bodies.

The dialogue between the two gallants sets up a key debate within the play's action, initiated by Galliard's offer 'let me govern thee but for a day' (l. 60), which becomes the basis for the plot's intrigue. That debate is between libertinism and an older chivalric view of love. By making each of the two main male characters symbolise one side of this debate, Behn could be accused of crude allegory, with even their names signifying a representative function ('Fillamour' meaning the son of love, and 'Galliard' a lively dance). Yet, as we shall see, the plot allows this black-and-white model to be compli-cated through temptation and love.

At this point, however, their positions are opposed: Galliard mocks the idea and practice of constancy, and is given the wittiest lines in which to do so. Drawing on the *carpe diem* tradition, a con-vention of erotic love poetry, he argues that continual new conquests and experiences are the only antidote to boredom. The use of mili-tary and geographical metaphors (ll. 34–5, and 40) is conventional in seventeenth-century love imagery. Fillamour opposes this view rationally by pushing at the literal meanings of those metaphors, which are consequently exposed as both violent and exploitative. Thus, Galliard's talk of vanquishing women by conquest is demol-ished by Fillamour's 'Which you gain as they do towns by fire, lose 'em even in the taking' (ll. 36–7). The conventional libertine metaphors are rendered visible and explicit in the dialogue, as they had been by the opening action of the pursuit of Laura. Fillamour's oppositional views (dismissed by Galliard as 'antiquated notions', l. 43) are not only evident in his attack on Galliard's metaphors, but are explicitly expressed: 'the lawful enjoyment of [an honest] woman . . . would be a blessing' (ll. 55–6). The dramatic testing and conflict of these two opposing views of erotic behaviour and erotic codes are thus clearly delineated as both plot and character conflicts, and in the spectacle of the fleeing woman.

Despite the rhetorical eloquence of the libertine stance, it is radi-cally questioned by self-conscious dramaturgy: first by the confu-sion and fear of the opening lines, and secondly by the emphatic literalising and questioning of the supposedly given erotic language.

In contrast to *The Rover*, this latter questioning is performed by a man.

There remains, however, a strong libertine and *carpe diem* argument which is not counteracted at this stage: that based on the 'law of nature' (l. 58). Galliard argues that men should enjoy women 'as we do meat, drink, air and light'. This premise of using natural resources appears to engender Fillamour's tacit agreement to be governed for a day, to test which philosophy will win. Nevertheless, despite his argument's apparent logic, the audience retains a sense of caution about his approach: partly because the debate is so obviously a comic device (it is so black-and-white), and partly because of the phrasing of the offer he makes to Fillamour. His words, 'let me govern thee but for a day', have self-conscious echoes of the devil's pact with Faustus, and therefore of transgressive action ending in tragedy or containment and reform. Given we know this is a comedy, we suspect Galliard's transgression may be answered by reform and marriage. The stage is set, then, for the development and complication of these tensions.

* * *

Before moving on to consider additional ways in which you might look at the opening scene, let us turn now to our last extract, from *The Lucky Chance*.

[Act 1, scene i]

The street at break of day

Enter Belmour, disguised in a travelling habit.

Belmour. Sure, 'tis the day that gleams in yonder east;
         The day that all but lovers blest by shade
         Pay cheerful homage to –
         Lovers, and those pursued, like guilty me,
         By rigid laws, which put no difference   5
         'Twixt fairly killing in my own defence,
         And murders bred by drunken arguments,
         Whores, or the mean revenges of a coward.

(*Looking about*) This is Leticia's father's house,
And that the dear balcony   10
That has so oft been conscious of our loves;
From whence she's sent me down a thousand sighs,
A thousand looks of love, a thousand vows!
O thou dear witness of those charming hours,
How do I bless thee, how am I pleased to view thee   15
After a tedious age of six months' banishment.
            Enter [Mr Jingle and] several with music.
Fiddler.   But hark'ee, Mr Jingle, is it proper to play before the wedding?
Jingle.   Ever while you live; for many a time, in playing after the first
    night, the bride's sleepy, the bridegroom tired, and both so out of
    humour that perhaps they hate anything that puts 'em in mind   20
    they are married.
            [The musicians] play and sing

SONG

Rise, Cloris, charming maid, arise
    And baffle breaking day,
Show the adoring world thy eyes
    Are more surprising gay;   25
The gods of love are smiling round,
    And lead the bridegroom on,
And Hymen has the altar crowned;
    While all thy sighing lovers are undone.

To see thee pass they throng the plain;   30
    The groves with flowers are strown,
And every young and envying swain
    Wishes the hour his own.
Rise then, and let the god of day,
    When thou dost to the lover yield,   35
Behold more treasure given away
    Than he in his vast circle e'er beheld.

        Enter Phillis in the balcony, and throws them money.
Belmour.   Ha, Phyllis, Leticia's woman!
Jingle.   Fie, Mrs Phillis, do ye take us for fiddlers that play for hire?
    I came to compliment Mrs Leticia on her wedding morning   40
    because she is my scholar.
Phillis.   She sends it only to drink her health.
Jingle.   Come, lads, let's to the tavern then.

Exit music.

Belmore.   Ha, said he Leticia?

Sure I shall turn to marble at this news: 45

I harden, and cold damps pass through my senseless pores.

– Ha, who's here?

Enter Gayman wrapped in his cloak.

Gayman.   'Tis yet too early, but my soul's impatient,

And I must see Leticia.

[*Gayman*] *goes to the door.*

Belmour.   Death and the devil, the bridegroom! – Stay, sir; by   50

heaven, you pass not this way.

[*Belmour*] *goes to the door as* [*Gayman*] *is knocking, pushes him*
away, and draws.

Gayman.   Ha, what art thou, that durst forbid me entrance? Stand off.

[*Belmour and Gayman*] *fight a little, and closing, view each other.*

Belmour.   Gayman!

Gayman.   My dearest Belmour!

Belmour.   Oh, thou false friend, thou treacherous base deceiver!   55

Gayman.   Ha, this to me, dear Harry?

Belmour.   Whither is honour, truth and friendship fled?

Gayman.   Why, there ne'er was such a virtue. 'Tis all a poet's
dream.

Belmour.   I thank you, sir.   60

Gayman.   I am sorry for't, or that ever I did anything that could
deserve it. Put up your sword: an honest man would say how he's
offended, before he rashly draws.

Belmour.   Are not you going to be married, sir?

Gayman.   No, sir, as long as any man in London is so, that has but   65
a handsome wife, sir.

Belmour.   Are not you in love, sir?

Gayman.   Most damnably, and would fain lie with the dear jilting
gypsy.

Belmour.   Ha, who would you lie with, sir?   70

Gayman.   You catechize me roundly: 'tis not fair to name, but I am
no starter, Harry; just as you left me, you find me; I am for the
faithless Julia still, the old alderman's wife. 'Twas high time the
city should lose their charter, when their wives turn honest. But
pray, sir, answer me a question or two.   75

Belmour.   Answer me first: what make you here this morning?

Gayman.   Faith, to do you service. Your damned little jade of a

mistress has learned of her neighbours the art of swearing and
lying in abundance, and is –
Belmour. (*Sighing*)   To be married!   80
Gayman.   Even so, God save the mark; and she'll be a fair one for
many an arrow besides her husband's, though he's an old
Finsbury hero this threescore years.
Belmour.   Who mean you?
Gayman.   Why, thy cuckold that shall be, if thou be'st wise.   85
Belmour.   Away, who is this man? Thou dalliest with me.
Gayman.   Why, an old knight, and alderman here o'th' city, Sir
Feeble Fainwould: a jolly old fellow, whose activity is all got into
his tongue; a very excellent teaser, but neither youth nor beauty
can grind his dudgeon to an edge.   90

(*The Lucky Chance*, 1, i, 1–90)

This extract teems with a succession of activity, divided into three
distinct parts. The first is Belmour's arrival in disguise and soliloquy
in front of the balcony; the second, the wedding song episode; and
the third the encounter between Belmour and Gayman. Let us look
at each in turn.

Belmour's opening speech self-consciously echoes the balcony
scene in Shakespeare's *Romeo and Juliet* (2, ii, 3), in actual words,
setting and time. It thus immediately introduces both explicitly and
intertextually the theme of thwarted and potentially tragic love. This
is important because it casts a shadow over the play, and posits a
darker ending than that suggested by either of the two openings we
have just analysed. It forces the audience to ask questions about the
forthcoming events. Are we to expect a tragic conclusion? Do
Belmour's references to his killing of a man in self-defence presage
further violence and conflict, as they do in Shakespeare's play? Thus,
although his speech at the balcony is ostensibly about recollected
love ('From whence she's sent me down a thousand sighs'), and the
joy of his return, we suspect all will not be well. In addition, his presence in cloaked disguise, in the dark of pre-dawn, suggests his mar-
ginal status, as well as more broadly the theme of hidden identity.

The opening of this scene narrates some past history, often a sure-
fire way to bore an audience. The narrative content here, however, is
counteracted by the dramatic nature of the situation. As we learn

that this man's beloved is about to be married, but that he has returned to claim her, our interest is aroused in the potential for conflict and tragedy. Situation thus quickly overcomes lengthy narrative background.

Here Belmour's language distinguishes his character and point of view from others by its poetic content and form. The first sixteen lines are in blank verse, with a few exceptions and irregularities. Thus lines 3 and 10 only contain six beats, indicating by both content and rhythm a pause for recollection of past events. The two final lines each contain six feet, an alexandrine rather than a pentameter. What does the use of verse signify here? As we have already noted, the play deliberately echoes *Romeo and Juliet*, and the use of verse intensifies a poetic representation of doomed love. Nevertheless, it would sound old-fashioned to a Restoration audience, and also now to us, suggesting a nostalgic, archaic view of love. The self-conscious reference to a renowned Shakespearean play, in combination with the archaic verse, asks the audience to think further about genre: is this is a comedy or tragedy? Such a question destabilises our response to what is ostensibly a comic opening, focusing on lovers' intrigues. By wrong-footing the audience's expectations, Behn forces us to pay attention and to ask questions.

The time of the opening is also critical: dawn was paradoxically a time of hope and of doom. Belmour's language plays with both the literal physical setting (the half-light of dawn) and the metaphorical meanings implicit in the lightness/darkness opposition. The conceptual and physical actions of the whole play continue and deepen this opposition, as we shall see.

Having opened in this ambiguous manner, Belmour must retreat to one side of the stage as the musicians enter beneath the balcony. The musicians, using the language of the 'mechanicals', offer a musical tribute to the bride. At one level, this is simply a dramatic device to tell both Belmour and the audience that his beloved is about to be married. At another, it signals Behn's more complex plotting in this play, the integration of ordinary people with the life of the gallants. Through short juxtaposed parts of scenes like this, Behn manages to convey a fluid representation of London street life. One of non-satiric comedy's functions is to suggest a festive world in which all classes co-exist without conflict and all conflicts are resolved. The presence of ordinary Londoners as musicians, therefore, signals a coherent and cohesive world: but in juxtaposition to the *Romeo and Juliet* opening, this is registered by the audience as an ironic self-deception. Thus, in the case of both first sections, the intertextual links to genre create a dissonant atmosphere which is deliberately at odds with the ostensibly happy content (of lovers and weddings).

The song performed by the musicians is in a conventional metric form: alternately rhymed lines, in alternate eight-, six-, eight-, six-beat lines. However, there are significant irregularities in the rhythms: lines 29, 35 and 37 are too long, and break up the elegance and eloquence of the song. Such irregularity indicates the amateurism of these local musicians, rather than the ineptitude of the playwright. The retreat of the musicians to the tavern further suggests their citizen status. Thus poetic metre is used in both of the first two opening parts to force the audience to dissociate form from content and recognise dissonant meanings.

Belmour's disguise enables him to stand at the edge of the stage, hidden and unrecognised by those on stage, and thus to act as an interpreter for the audience. He speaks directly to us about the events on stage: his response to the news of Leticia's forthcoming marriage uses apparently archaic language straight from a tragedy: 'Sure, I shall turn to marble at this news: / I harden, and cold damps pass through my senseless pores' (ll. 45–6). Once again, the linguistic register suggests potential tragedy to the audience.

The third part of this opening extract juxtaposes Belmour's previously liminal status, with his involvement in action. Gayman arrives, also wrapped in a cloak, to enter Leticia's house, and appears to be the bridegroom (l. 50). Belmour's readiness to engage in sword-fight with an unknown man marks his character as fiery, and potentially unstable, and throughout the subsequent conversation he jumps to conclusions before asking for the facts. His characterisation here, therefore, reinforces his opening lines: that he has killed a man in a fight. Intemperance and impetuous decisions dominate his actions. The dialogue between the two men is alternately intimate and formal. Belmour uses the 'sir' to preface a possible insult or response to an insult, while Gayman uses the intimate 'Harry'. Once again, Belmour comes across as quick-tempered, whilst Gayman, both in his address and in his account of his intentions (that he has come to plead Belmour's cause), as more equable. Gayman's linguistic register is clearly that of a gallant: witty, somewhat laid back, and explicitly sexualised. He uses phallic puns to denigrate Sir Feeble Fainwould ('activity is all got into his tongue . . . neither youth nor beauty can grind his dudgeon to an edge'). This contrasts with the much more old-fashioned poetic register of unrequited romantic love, of both Belmour's opening and the musicians' song. Finally, the portrait of Fainwould (from his name onwards) posits a satirical representation of city men, deliberately contrasted with the views and life of the gallants, and to the gentler representation of the citizen musicians.

Thus this opening is a succession of short, contrasting episodes. Each furthers the action, but in juxtaposition they all add slightly conflicting messages. Is this a tragedy or comedy? Is Belmour's or Gayman's approach to love to dominate? Are the citizens to be mocked or celebrated? These questions are posed by the staging and scene itself, and in order to involve and tease the audience. We need to watch further to answer them.

Conclusions

The initial openings of plays tell us a surprising number of things about the action to come, and about how we might begin to think about it. It is therefore always rewarding to study just the first 100 or so lines, to begin to ask the kinds of questions we have asked in this chapter. What kinds of overall conclusions can we come to at this point?

1. Behn uses a variety of comic openings: each differs in its presentation of events, although in each case she engages the audience in active criticism. Thus in *The Rover*, she opens unusually with two young women plotting their love affairs, rather than focusing either on men or on pairs of lovers, as do more conventional comedies. In *The Feigned Courtesans* she moves to a street setting,

showing a woman fleeing an interested man's pursuit, usually a subject for a discovery scene, or a potential tragic episode (as we see later in *The Rover*, for example). In *The Lucky Chance* she deliberately juxtaposes different linguistic and dramatic registers to engage her audience in thinking critically about characters, genre, outcome, and the masculine discourses of love. In each play, therefore, we are presented either with women's views first, or with critical dramatic views on male behaviour. By incorporating such perspectives into the comic genre Behn reinvents comedy as a critical tool.

2. Behn typically parallels characters: Hellena and Florinda in *The Rover*, Fillamour and Galliard in *The Feigned Courtesans* and Gayman and Belmour in *The Lucky Chance*. In each case such doubling is used to set up dramatic contrasts between two views or two approaches to the same subject: Is female chastity or libertinism the best course of action for women (*The Rover*)? Can libertinism provide greater happiness than constancy (*The Feigned Courtesans*)? Do the modes and practices of chivalric love fit into modern city life (*The Lucky Chance*)? In each case, the two sets of views are tested by the action of the play, and we ask ourselves whether the play comes to any conclusions about such views and debates. This is a question we shall return to throughout this book.

3. Behn also uses sets of characters to contrast other sets of characters: for example, young women versus old men; or young women versus brothers or/and fathers; young gallants versus old men; gallants versus old city aldermen. In each play's opening we are immediately introduced to such a set of contrasts, all of which are used to signal future dramatic conflict and the play's potential action. By using such contrasts, Behn can signal political and sexual themes and views. If we sympathise with the young women, who are clearly opposed to brothers and fathers (for example, in *The Rover*), then Behn asks us to engage in a gendered debate about self-determination, arranged marriages and patriarchal imperatives. In sympathising with young gallants as opposed to old city gentlemen (as in *The Lucky Chance*), we are encouraged to take up political views, against city mercan-

tilism and for the aristocratic status quo. Additionally, such character contrasts help produce a dynamic plot, doubling intrigues and conflicts, and giving the audience different perspectives on such conflict.

4. Themes of sexual and marital politics, views on arranged marriages, and gendered language and behaviour are foregrounded from the plays' very first lines and action. Such themes are common in comedies, of course; however, it is also clear that in Behn's plays such themes are presented in non-conventional ways: either from a woman's viewpoint on stage, or by making the audience critical of conventional masculine language, views or behaviour.

5. Behn's methods of characterisation place characters in the middle of situations which are potentially troublesome, about to be resolved in a way they do not like or approve of, or in the middle of some conflict. Again, this is a typical dramatic convention, but it enables the most extreme characteristics to be viably represented. It also enables the audience to judge very quickly the potential and nature of central characters through their responses to the situation. Characterisation is therefore signalled mainly through debate and conflict, rather than soliloquy (although Belmour's sole entrance in *The Lucky Chance* is a minor exception).

6. The dialogue is fast-paced and usually in prose (we have discussed the exceptions to this in our analysis of *The Lucky Chance*). This creates a contemporary and unaffected atmosphere. Characters use frank, sexual, racy and colloquial language. Although the situations and conflicts she represents are common to many Restoration comedies, Behn enables us to believe they are true to life in London in the late seventeenth century. Despite the fiction, the language helps construct our belief and involvement in the validity of that fiction.

7. Finally, despite the conventional comic subject matter (marriage, and intrigue to that end), Behn manages to re-examine and question that convention in a more radical context. We begin these plays by being forced to think about marriage as something arranged by men, in which women are objects or pawns. This

feminisation of the audience's response is achieved through staging, manipulation of linguistic and generic registers, character point of view on stage, and explicit demonising of the patriarchal models for marriage. We shall return to this subject as we proceed through the book.

Methods of Analysis

The following analytical approaches have been used to think about the extracts in this chapter, and are a useful starting point when you begin to analyse a play:

1. **The text as drama**. When you first read or view a play, imagine how it plays on stage. What effect will it, or does it, have on an audience? Where are the characters placed on stage and why? How does their position or clothing give a clue to their relationship to the audience? Do they move around the stage? If so, when and why? Is there music and song, and what effect do these have in relation to the conventional dialogue?

2. **Visuals**. What does the stage look like? Where are the characters placed on stage, and how does their visual relationship help construct meaning?

3. **Language**. Are there any key words and phrases? Do specific responses stand out in any way, or is the dialogue evenly balanced? Do different characters speak in different ways? Why? Why is poetry used instead of prose (or vice versa)?

4. **Imagery**. Who uses imagery and why? Is its meaning clear to you? Is it meant to be clear? Do the images have anything in common; are there recurrent key images or key words? What is the significance of these?

5. **Poetry**. Behn uses poetry rarely in her comedies. Where she does, think about the kind of forms she uses, the different metres and variations on them. What is the effect and purpose in each case?

6. **Rhythm**. Look at rhythm in the poetry, but also consider the way in which prose has its own patterns of imagery, balance and contrast.

7. **Scenic structure**. Look at the way the scene is divided up into parts, both thematically and between characters and events. What is the effect of the division and juxtapositions?

8. **Sentences**. Look closely at sentences for meaning and delivery. Are they long or short, broken up, exclamatory or declamatory? How does close analysis illuminate characterisation?

9. **Subject matter**. What do the characters actually say? What happens in this scene? We can often concentrate on smaller matters, such as imagery, poetry and character, and forget the bigger picture of how the scene as a whole fits into the plot.

10. We introduced some new terms, most noticeably, '*in medias res*' and 'intertextuality'. These are useful terms with which to analyse Behn's work, and will crop up later in the book. You may wish to refer to the introduction to refresh your memory of their meaning.

You should add to this list yourself as you analyse the plays: try to use as many of these approaches as possible in the following suggested work.

Suggested Work

The Rover
Look at the remainder of Act 1, scene i. How does the scene end? What is the significance of ending the scene as it began, with the two women? What is the significance of their views on Carnival and their plans? Consider the ways Act 1, scene ii is an explicit contrast to Act 1, scene i (such as setting, characters, language, themes). What are the effect and importance of the relationship between these two opening scenes?

The Feigned Courtesans
How does the rest of Act 1, scene i reinforce or contrast with our conclusions about the first part? We are introduced to additional characters: does this change or extend our views of the gallants? You should consider the ways in which Behn uses the second scene to

contrast or interrogate the first scene. How do the themes interrelate? What kind of audience perspective is created and why? Are there any characters appearing in both scenes? Why?

The Lucky Chance

This play has the most complex opening act, and requires the most attention to analyse its disparate parts. We have already seen how, even within 100 lines, Behn packs in three divergent and contrasting scenic events. This continues in the rest of Act 1, scene i. Comment on the divisions in the rest of the scene, and their interrelationship. How are the themes developed?

Act 1 is divided into three scenes: comment on their overall relationship to each other. For example, scene ii may be seen as a pivot scene between scene i and scene iii. What else does it do (look at content, setting and theme)?

Act 1, scene iii is a key scene in the play. It is the first time we really meet many of the characters we have glanced at in scene i. Comment on the characterisation of Leticia and her relationship to the audience. How does the setting and framing of the scene (a marriage celebration) contribute to the scene's overall meaning?

Your analyses of these scenes will further illuminate and extend our conclusions on the immediate openings of the plays. You should now be finding it easier to visualise the scene as if it were on stage, although you may feel that you need to read it aloud with friends, to help you gain this three-dimensional sense of drama.

2

Endings

Endings of comedies tell us a lot about how the dramatist wants us to understand the play's events, conflicts and debates. If all loose ends are tied up, all characters happy participants in a celebratory closure, and all discord resolved, the ending produces a feeling of completion and inclusion. We are presented with an image of a cohesive, festive society. If, on the other hand, loose ends are left unexplained, characters are left outside the social festivity, or discordant notes are sounded, the audience is left critical of the festive and inclusive images. Comedies employing the former method tend to be labelled 'romantic', and those the latter, 'satiric'. We shall consider Behn's endings in the light of these comments, starting with *The Rover*.

* * *

[Act 5, scene i]

Hellena.   The very same. Ha, my brother! Now, captain, show your love and courage; stand to your arms, and defend me bravely, or I am lost forever.

Pedro.   What's this I hear? False girl, how came you hither, and   495
what's your business? Speak.

   [*Pedro*] *goes roughly to* [*Hellena*]. [*Willmore*] *puts himself between*
   [*them*].

Willmore.   Hold off, sir, you have leave to parley only.

Hellena.   I had e'en as good tell it, as you guess it. Faith, brother,

my business is the same with all living creatures of my age: to love,
and be beloved; and here's the man.   500

Pedro.   Perfidious maid, hast thou deceived me too, deceived thyself
and heaven?

Hellena.   'Tis time enough to make my peace with that;
Be you but kind, let me alone with heaven.

Pedro.   Belvile, I did not expect this false play from you. Was't not   505
enough you'd gain Florinda (which I pardoned) but your lewd
friends too must be enriched with the spoils of a noble family?

Belvile.   Faith, sir, I am as much surprised at this as you can be. Yet,
sir, my friends are gentlemen, and ought to be esteemed for their
misfortunes, since they have the glory to suffer with the best of   510
men and kings: 'tis true, he's a rover of fortune,
Yet a prince, aboard his little wooden world.

Pedro.   What's this to the maintenance of a woman of her birth and
quality?

Willmore.   Faith, sir, I can boast of nothing but a sword which does   515
me right where'er I come, and has defended a worse cause than a
woman's; and since I loved her before I either knew her birth or
name, I must pursue my resolution, and marry her.

Pedro.   And is all your holy intent of becoming a nun, debauched
into a desire of man?   520

Hellena.   Why, I have considered the matter, brother, and find, the
three hundred thousand crowns my uncle left me, and you cannot
keep from me, will be better laid out in love than in religion, and
turn to as good an account. [*To the others*] Let most voices carry
it: for heaven or the captain?   525

All. (*Cry*)   A captain! A captain!

Hellena.   Look ye sir, 'tis a clear case.

Pedro.   Oh, I am mad! (*Aside*) If I refuse, my life's in danger. [*To
Willmore*] Come, there's one motive induces me.
[*Don Pedro*] *gives* [*Hellena*] *to* [*Willmore*].
Take her: I shall now be free from fears of her honour; guard it   530
you now, if you can; I have been a slave to't long enough.

Willmore.   Faith, sir, I am of a nation that are of opinion a woman's
honour is not worth guarding when she has a mind to part with it.

Hellena.   Well said, captain.

Pedro. (*To Valeria*)   This was your plot, mistress, but I hope you have 535
married one that will revenge my quarrel to you.

Valeria.   There's no altering destiny, sir.

Pedro.   Sooner than a woman's will: therefore I forgive you all, and
   wish you may get my father's pardon as easily, which I fear.
>   *Enter Blunt dressed in a Spanish habit, looking very ridiculously;*
>   *his man adjusting his band.*
Man.   'Tis very well, sir.   540
Blunt.   Well, sir? 'Adsheartlikins, I tell you 'tis damnable ill, sir. A
   Spanish habit, good Lord! Could the devil and my tailor devise no
   other punishment for me, but the mode of a nation I abominate?
Belvile.   What's the matter, Ned?
Blunt. (*Turns round*)   Pray view me round, and judge.   545
Belvile.   I must confess thou art a kind of an odd figure.
Blunt.   In a Spanish habit with a vengeance! I had rather be in the
   Inquisition for Judaism, than in this doublet and breeches; a
   pillory were an easy collar to this, three handfuls high; and these
   shoes too, are worse than the stocks, with the sole an inch shorter   550
   than my foot. In fine, gentlemen, methinks I look altogether like a
   bag of bays stuffed full of fool's flesh.
Belvile.   Methinks 'tis well, and makes thee look *en cavalier*. Come, sir,
   settle your face, and salute our friends. [*Turns to Hellena*] Lady –
Blunt.   Ha! (*To Hellena*) Say'st thou so, my little rover? Lady, if   555
   you be one, give me leave to kiss your hand, and tell you,
   'adsheartlikins, for all I look so, I am your humble servant. [*Aside*]
   A pox of my Spanish habit.
>   *Music is heard to play.*
Willmore.   Hark, what's this?
>   *Enter page.*
Page.   Sir, as the custom is, the gay people in masquerade, who make   560
   every man's house their own, are coming up.
>   *Enter several men and women in masking habits, with music;*
>   *they put themselves in order and dance.*
Blunt.   'Adsheartlikins, would 'twere lawful to pull off their false
   faces, that I might see if my doxy were not amongst 'em.
Belvile. (*To the maskers*)   Ladies and gentlemen, since you are come
   so apropos, you must take a small collation with us.   565
Willmore. (*To Hellena*)   Whilst we'll to the good man within, who
   stays to give us a cast of his office. Have you no trembling at the
   near approach?
Hellena.   No more than you have in an engagement or a tempest.
Willmore.   Egad, thou'rt a brave girl, and I admire thy love and   570
   courage.

> Lead on, no other dangers they can dread,
> Who venture in the storms o'th' marriage bed.

Exeunt

(*The Rover*, 5, i, 492–573)

What is significant about this extract? Much of the action only makes sense when read as the culmination of the intrigues and action of the whole of Act 5, which opened with Blunt's imprisonment of Florinda, and the competition between the male characters to possess her. Angellica has threatened the comic and festive possibilities by threatening to kill Willmore for falsity, in the process unmasking Willmore's character and sexual history to Hellena, disguised as a boy. This extract opens just after Hellena, still disguised as a boy, has subsequently successfully negotiated her own marriage with Willmore. Florinda and Belvile have been married, and Pedro has forgiven them.

The final part of the Act falls into three sections here: the first focusing on the encounter between Pedro and Hellena and Willmore (ll. 497–539); the second on Blunt (ll. 540–58); and the third the finale of promised wedding and feast (ll. 559–73). Let us examine each part in turn, before commenting on the choreography of the relationship between the parts.

The main party have just entered before this extract begins, and with Hellena cross-dressed, her physical separation from the others in the previous scenes of Act 5, as well as her distinctive dress, continue to signify her transgressive and independent agenda.

The opening altercation here is an important visual and narrative paradigm of many of the themes of the play. Hellena introduces the metaphor which runs throughout this extract both verbally and visually: that of love as war (ll. 492–4). We can read this in two ways (and much will depend on the actor who delivers the lines). The first is that she is acquiescing to, even condoning, the patriarchal arrangement whereby women are pawns in a strategic game between men, and passed between fathers (or brothers) and husbands. The second way to read it is in the context of her situation (she is cross-dressed, has pursued her man and arranged the marriage herself), and that she herself directs the men's actions. Her use of conventional language draws our attention both to her understanding and to her simultaneous manipulation of the conventions which govern her life and others' views of her behaviour, a Hellena we recognise from the rest of the play.

The language of war and violent acquisition is then replicated in Pedro's first action, emphasised by the stage direction: he '*goes roughly to*' Hellena, a violence echoing violence against women earlier in the play. This significantly tells the audience that Pedro has not been changed or moved by the play's action. Pedro refers to Hellena as 'the spoils of a noble family' (l. 507), suggesting she is a trophy to be won in battle. Willmore also naturally uses the language of war in describing his actions: his 'sword' which 'does him right' is defending the 'cause' of a woman. So, whilst Hellena appears to use such language self-consciously, Pedro and Willmore reduce sex and women to battlefield actions. This draws attention to a gender divide both in linguistic usage and in attitudes to sex and marriage, and to potential future conflict between Hellena and Willmore.

In this first section, Pedro's character is further demonised by his continued assertion of his role as representative of his father and of paternal rule and order. For example, he interrogates the others, asking a set of five questions, the first two and last one to Hellena, and the other two addressed to Belvile, his newly acquired brother and Willmore's friend. His questions to Hellena accuse her of falsity (l. 495), perfidy, deception (l. 501) and debauchery (ll. 519–20), and are all delivered in a patronising tone and manner (for example his rough handling and calling her 'girl'). His refusal to see Hellena as an equal can be seen in his assumption that he should speak to the men about the larger issues than her moral behaviour, in his linguistic construction of her as a chattel, and in his tonal delivery. His questions to Belvile are equally revealing. The first laments the loss of family wealth to an adventurer, suggesting a mutual responsibility amongst the men for the wealth and assets of the family, including the women. The second question ('What's this to the maintenance of a woman of her birth and quality?' l. 514) suggests Hellena's economic and social position is his main responsibility and concern. Status, business arrangements between men, questions of male honour and the maintenance of wealth dominate his language and attitude to marriage.

Pedro's language continues to cause the audience some discomfort: his two further statements betray a disturbing misogyny. His first is to Valeria, whom he also blames, and he hopes that her husband 'will revenge my quarrel to you', albeit said in a joking tone. His final statement both echoes this misogyny and reminds us of his role as surrogate patriarch: 'Sooner than a woman's will: therefore I forgive you all, and wish you may get my father's pardon as easily, which I fear' (ll. 538–9). He acquiesces in the marriage only because it is impossible to change a woman's will (overt misogyny), and then reminds us that the father is absent, and is unlikely to approve. This signals further discord to come, which remains unresolved by the end of the play.

Hellena's language indicates her refusal to accept her brother's view of the world and her position in it, showing her as both proactive and able to manipulate situations. Her self-confidence and autonomy are clearly signalled in her three responses to her brother. Her first defence of herself ('my business is the same with all living creatures of my age', l. 499) utilises the language of natural equality in an appeal to the audience's view of equity. She alone refers to 'love' as a determining factor in marriage, in contrast to her brother's and Willmore's military language. Her second, shorter defence argues that religious conviction is her own business, positing a private space for belief and moral accounting. Her third defence shows an escalation of her outspoken autonomy (ll. 521–5), and an explicit articulation of an understanding of the economics of marriage: 'the three hundred thousand crowns my uncle left me, and you cannot keep from me, will be better laid out in love than in religion'. She thus opens a gap between paternal approval and economic self-determination in marriage arrangements. This suggests to the audience that women of independent means (and sufficient strength of character) alone have the means for self-determination in marriage (and other matters). Hellena is thus freed: but indirectly she acknowledges that women without money will be dependent upon the men in their family. The message here is therefore simultaneously optimistic (for Hellena) and bleak (for most other women).

This section of the extract closes on Pedro's ominous statement that he does not believe his father's approval will be forthcoming, and is interrupted by what at first sight appears to be a comic episode: Blunt's entrance extravagantly dressed in Spanish clothes. Sandwiched as it is between the confrontation we have just observed, and the final call to music, marriage and feast, this interlude looks simply like a device to bring Blunt onto the stage for a few final laughs. Yet if we examine the content of these twenty lines, we can gauge a different purpose.

Blunt enters still in the process of being dressed (as the stage direction makes clear). We recall that he lost all his clothes in Act 4, and has appeared at the beginning of Act 5 dressed only in underwear. To cap these previous ritual humiliations, he is now dressed in the fashionable gear of a Spaniard, a nation he proclaims to hate, but who are the conquerors of the occupied Naples in the play. Blunt, the near-rapist, is thus emblematically dressed in the outfit of invaders. Blunt's anglophilia is a marked aspect of his character at earlier points in the play, and represented as a narrow, puritanical and hypocritical nationalism, in contrast to the cosmopolitan and European identities of all the other main characters. Blunt is therefore visually ridiculed and shamed, as well as condemned, by this change of dress. Furthermore, it is clear that the other men wear their clothes comfortably, and change them as the need arises (disguise in the Carnival being one such example). By contrast, Blunt (as his name suggests) is neither subtle nor flexible, and the disguises and shifting identities which are so much a part of Willmore's character, and a defining feature of the cavalier, are the precise opposite of Blunt.

His entry now in this guise has several effects. It reminds us of both the parallels and contrasts between Blunt, and Willmore and Belvile: Blunt's blind folly, in taking the blandishments of a prostitute for the' love of a wealthy woman, was the dupe's version of Wilmore's and Belvile's own pursuit of women during Carnival, his fury at the duping quickly converting to a universal and violent misogyny, the culmination of which is the imprisonment and threatened rape of Florinda at the end of Act 4. Yet, as we see at the beginning of Act 5, this misogyny is shared by all the men in the play, for all jostle to possess the woman Blunt has captured, believing her to be a woman of the streets. Blunt's character is therefore used by Behn to hint at the dark and violent side of the apparently civilised face of masculine courtship.

Such shadowing is clear in what Blunt says and does in this short episode, when his words to Hellena appear to be overly familiar. He uses the report of her as a gypsy ('my little rover') to imply she might also be interested in him sexually ('a pox on my Spanish habit'). Blunt, it seems, has been changed by his Carnival experiences: but only to the extent that he now appears to see all women as fair sexual game. This does not mesh comfortably with the posited happy ending of comedy in which all couples are matched in love, and the future is represented as unthreatening.

It is in this context, of two episodes suggesting problems for the future, that the swift finale of the comedy is acted out. Although a wedding, music and feast are proposed, we do not watch them, only a masked dance as a prelude to further celebrations. Blunt remains outside these lawful celebrations, giving voice to his dislocation by wondering whether the 'doxy' who conned him might be behind one of the masks. Hellena and Willmore still remain unmarried during the action of the play. As the characters move to go inside, Hellena and Willmore's final conversation ends the play, suitably enough, by re-invoking the military metaphors of the first part of this extract. Once again, it is Hellena who introduces this metaphor (l. 569), by comparing her feelings prior to marriage to his before a battle or tempest. This then feeds into Willmore's rhyming couplet which closes the play. The last word of the play is 'bed', an explicit acknowledgement of the play's sexual frankness. Yet that word, which should connote celebration, warmth and domesticity, is complicated by the metaphors Willmore uses: '. . . no other dangers they can **dread**, / Who venture in the storms o'th' marriage bed', where the echoing 'bed / dread' resounds as a counterpoint to the plot's apparent happy closures. The final metaphoric image is of marriage as perilous, storm driven and beset with danger ('ventures'). An ostensibly happy and conventional comic ending is shadowed by Willmore's metaphors, echoing the other loose ends and discomfort in the first two parts of this extract.

Let us now move on to *The Feigned Courtesans*, and see whether
such complexity is typical of Behn's other comic endings.

* * *

[Act 5, scene iv]

Marcella. In this disguise we parted from Viterbo, attended only
by Petro and Philippa; at Rome we took the title and habit of two
courtesans; both to shelter us from knowledge, and to oblige   130
Fillamour to visit us, which we believed he would in curiosity, and
yesterday it so fell out as we desired.

Fillamour. Howe'er my eyes might be imposed upon, you see my
heart was firm to its first object; can you forget and pardon the
mistake?   135

Julio. She shall; and with Octavio's, and my uncle's, leave, thus
make your title good.
    [*Julio*] *gives* [*Marcella*] *to Fillamour.*

Octavio. 'Tis vain to strive with destiny!
    [*Octavio*] *gives* [*Marcella to Fillamour*].

Morosini. With all my heart; but where's Cornelia all this while?

Galliard. Here's the fair straggler, sir.   140
    [*Galliard*] *leads* [*Cornelia*] *to Morosini,* [*who*] *holds his cane*
    up at her.

Morosini. Why, thou baggage, thou wicked contriver of mischief,
what excuse hadst thou for running away? Thou hadst no lover.

Cornelia. 'Twas therefore, sir, I went, to find one; and if I am not
mistaken in the mark, 'tis this cavalier I pitch upon for that use
and purpose.   145

Galliard. Gad, I thank ye for that; I hope you'll ask my leave first;
I'm finely drawn in, i'faith! Have I been dreaming all this night of
the possession of a new-gotten mistress, to wake and find myself
noosed to a dull wife in the morning?

Fillamour. Thou talk'st like a man that never knew the pleasures   150
thou despisest; faith, try it Frank, and thou wilt hate thy past loose
way of living.

Cornelia. And to encourage a young setter-up, I do here promise to
be the most mistress-like wife. You know, signor, I have learnt the
trade, thou I had not stock to practise, and will be as expensive,   155
insolent, vain, extravagant, and inconstant, as if you only had the

keeping part, and another the amorous assignations; what think ye,
sir?

Fillamour.   Faith, she pleads well, and ought to carry the cause.

Galliard.   She speaks reason, and I'm resolved to trust good   160
nature. – Give me thy dear hand.

     They all join to give [Galliard Cornelia's] hand; he kisses it.

Morosini.   And now you are both sped, pray give me leave to ask ye
a civil question: are you sure you have been honest? If you have,
I know not by what miracle you have lived.

Petro.   Oh, sir, as for that, I had a small stock of cash, in the hands   165
of a couple of English bankers, one Sir Signal Buffoon –

Sir Signal. (*Peeping*)   Sir Signal Buffoon! What a pox, does he mean
me, trow?

Petro.   And one Mr Tickletext.

Tickletext.   How, was that – *certo*, my name!   170

     [Tickletext] peeps out and [he and Sir Signal] see each other,
     their faces being close together, one at one side of the curtain,
     and the other at the other.

Galliard and Fillamour.   Ha, ha, ha!

Sir Signal.   And have I caught you, i'faith, Mr Governor? Nay,
ne'er put in your head for the matter, here's none but friends,
mun.

Galliard.   How now, what have we here?   175

Sir Signal.   Speak of the devil, and he appears.

     [Sir Signal] pulls his governor forward.

Tickletext.   I am undone; but, good Sir Signal, do not cry whore
first, as the old proverb says.

Sir Signal.   And good Mr Governor, as another old proverb says, do
not let the kettle call the pot black-arse.   180

Fillamour.   How came you hither, gentlemen?

Sir Signal.   Why, faith, sir, divining of a wedding or two forward, I
brought Mr Chaplain to give you a cast of his office, as the saying
is.

Fillamour.   What, without book, Mr Tickletext?   185

Cornelia.   How now, sure you mistake; these are two lovers of mine.

Sir Signal.   How, sir, your lovers? We are none of those, sir, we are
Englishmen!

Galliard.   You mistake, Sir Signal; this is Silvianetta.

Sir Signal and Tickletext. (*Aside*)   How!   190

Galliard.   Here's another spark of your acquaintance; do you know
him?

Tickletext. How, Barberacho? Nay, then all will out.

Galliard. Yes, and your fencing and civility-master.

Sir Signal. Aye? [*To Petro*] Why, what was it you that picked our   195
pockets then, and cheated us?

Galliard. Most damnably; but since 'twas for the supply of two fair
ladies, all shall be restored again.

Tickletext. Some comfort that.

Fillamour. Come, let's in, and forgive all; 'twas but one night's   200
intrigue, in which all were a little faulty.

Sir Signal. And, governor, pray let me have no more domineering
and usurpation; but as we have hitherto been honest brothers in
iniquity, so let's wink hereafter at each other's frailties:
Since love and women easily betray man,   205
From the grave gownman to the busy layman.

(*The Feigned Courtesans*, 5, iv, 128–206)

The final act is intricately plotted, the denouement postponed again
and again as improbable action follows improbable action, and different men believe that they will spend, or have spent, the night with
'La Silvianetta'. What actually happens in this final scene, before we
encounter the conclusions of this extract?

The scene opens with Tickletext and Sir Signal creeping into
Laura's chamber, unbeknownst to each other, and believing her to be
'La Silvianetta' (one of the 'feigned' courtesans of the play's title). At
the close of the previous scene (Act 5, scene iii), Petro, Fillamour,
and Octavio and Julio in pursuit of them, had also entered this
house, and as they enter the chamber, Tickletext and Sir Signal hide
behind curtains to evade discovery. In the ensuing confusion, Laura's
moral status is maligned by her brother but defended by Galliard,
and Julio realises that the woman he has been pursuing is in fact
Laura, to whom he is already pre-contracted. Sir Signal and
Tickletext act as commentators on the action by peeping out from
the curtains. Galliard believes that Laura-as-La Silvianetta is the
same as Cornelia-as-La Silvianetta, and defends her honour. Laura is
forced to yield to Julio, despite her own desire for Galliard, by her
pre-contract and by her brother. At this point Cornelia and Marcella
emerge, both dressed as boys, and Marcella confesses her love for
Fillamour, rejecting her brother's choice of husband for her.

Meanwhile Cornelia taunts Galliard for the loss of his lover, but he eventually recognises her and they retreat to the back of the stage to confer. It is at this point that this extract opens. The setting, a bedroom, is an unusually intimate one for the end of a play, but suitably risqué for a play which examines the elision between prostitute and wife, explicit sexual desire and conventional marriage.

What do we notice in these final 79 lines of the play? As we have already seen, many of the play's intrigues are resolved in the first half of the scene: Julio and Laura are paired off, Octavio gives up his claim on Marcella, and Morosini acquiesces in his decision. This earlier resolution enables the audience to focus on two other groups of characters: Cornelia and Galliard, and Tickletext and Sir Signal, ostensibly an odd focus for the finale, because the latter two characters always seemed to belong to a minor sub-plot. The comic resolutions are tinged with darkness: Marcella's and Fillamour's union is at the expense of the exclusion of Octavio from the new social order; whilst Laura makes it clear that she feels forced into marriage. Thus the scene as a whole divides into two: the first half brings about compromised resolutions, whilst the second half (represented here) acts as a counterpoint. To what degree is that counterpoint successful?

At one level, it is very successful, because, as with many of Behn's most independent female characters and her male rakes, the audience are invited to be most intimate with Cornelia and Galliard, and we have much of our emotional energy involved in and desirous of their union. The resolution of that union (to which we shall turn in a moment) therefore marks an emotionally satisfactory closure to the play's sexual intrigue. However, that structural resolution belies much of the complexity of the content. Indeed, as we found with *The Rover*, the play's closing focus on that union is dispersed, both by the darker union that preceded it, and by the appearance of Tickletext and Sir Signal. This makes us question whether Cornelia's hopes are justified: but it equally puts into perspective the debate about arranged marriages and marriages for love, asking us to abhor the former and celebrate the latter. Laura is forced to marry according to her brother's will; Cornelia has the freedom to choose. Dramatic scenic structure (with two parts acting in counterpoint) thereby enacts a contemporary sexual debate and asks the audience to choose the more radical view. We shall discuss this method and theme in greater detail in subsequent chapters.

As this extract shows, however, Cornelia's success is represented only within the framework of conventional marriages. The re-instatement of Julio's and Laura's arranged marriage acts as a prelude to paternal (via her brother) approval of Marcella's independent choice. This section of the scene illustrates visually the patriarchal convention of the men literally handing over Marcella to Fillamour: both Julio (her brother) and Octavio (her former fiancé), in succes-sive ritualised actions, physically give her over to Fillamour. The doubling of the action of 'giving away the bride' (clearly stated in the stage directions, ll. 137–8) draws the audience's attention specifically to the patriarchal system which passes daughters and sisters from the legal care of a father to that of a husband. By emphasising this as visual stage business, Behn comments on a convention which treats women as chattels. It is at this point that Cornelia enters, providing a potential contrast to representations of women as passive or as chattels.

Cornelia holds centre stage for a mere twenty lines, a much shorter resolution than the Laura plot before the opening of this extract. There are two themes discussed in these twenty lines: the question of her uncle's approval and views, and the question of her identity within marriage. Her uncle Morosini is surprisingly muted in their exchange. Although he calls her a 'baggage' and a 'wicked contriver of mischief' (l. 141), such views do not inform his actions. He acquiesces in the common approval of her choice of partner (l. 162), and thus neutralises paternalistic disapproval of autonomous sexual behaviour in women. This is more benign than the hinted paternal disapproval we noted in *The Rover*.

The second theme is that of sexual conduct within marriage. Both Galliard and Cornelia maintain that marriage is dull and con-straining, and lacks sexual excitement, echoing Galliard's views in the opening scene, which we analysed in the last chapter. Galliard re-expresses this view here (ll. 146–9) with anticipatory horror. Interestingly, his horror is met by two responses. Fillamour con-tinues to moralise: marital pleasures must outweigh those of 'loose living' (ll. 151–2), although such moralising has failed to change

Galliard's behaviour during the play. By contrast, Cornelia uses a different argument: she will be both mistress and wife. She wittily uses her 'experience' as a feigned courtesan to suggest sexual knowledge, and suggests that men desire both the 'keeping' of women (their wives), and access to other women (mistresses), by suggesting that Galliard mirrors her own doubling as mistress and wife in a doubling as husband and amorous adventurer. So, whilst her radical solution redefines marriage as sexual pleasure rather than property transfer, it has two additional, more troubling effects. The first is that it also enables Galliard to save face and accept marriage, in a conventional comic closure. The second, that she suggests the only way for marriage to be viable is to lead a split existence: sex and the public persona must be kept separate, echoing the troubling divide with which the play has experimented, between men's simultaneous desire for sexy prostitutes and for chaste wives. She is thus simultaneously radical and conservative, a stance shared by Hellena in *The Rover*. Both characters appropriate the sobriquet 'inconstant' (here l. 156; *The Rover*, 5, i, 489), in an attempt to characterise themselves as female libertines.

What is significant about the way in which the betrothal is represented? First, it is Cornelia, rather than the man, who initiates the discussion about marriage and the radical solution. Secondly, Galliard proposes directly to her, and not through either her brother or uncle. Thirdly, unlike previous betrothals represented on stage, all the characters together present Cornelia's hand to Galliard. Thus the stage directions tell actors and directors to visually display the difference between this betrothal and the two previous ones. Cornelia's views and intentions are given social sanction by a fictional community represented by all the characters on stage. Finally, patriarchal authority is diluted by the replacement of brothers/uncles with community. This is radical both in its visual dramatic contrast with the first two betrothals, and in its expressed content. Words and physical action combine to show an alternative model of sexual politics.

Yet once this has happened, why does the play not end here? We are presented with another 40 lines of near-buffoonery. What is the purpose of the appearance of the sub-plot here? The first and most immediate effect is humour: the appearance of the two characters' heads through the curtains, laughed at by both gallants and audience, reinforces our connection to the gallants and distances us from the follies of Tickletext and Sir Signal. We are thereby linked to a cosmopolitan Europeanism against what is represented as a reductive, stupid, and hypocritical puritanism. This creates a feel-good factor in the audience (we are as sophisticated and witty as these gallants), and simultaneously satirises English puritanism.

Yet despite this distancing of these two characters through laughter, Behn ensures that parallels are made between their behaviour and attitudes and those of the gallants. Throughout the play, scenes with these two buffoons are interleaved with those of Galliard, Fillamour and Julio, and both sets of men follow explicitly parallel paths of desire and seduction in their pursuit of 'La Silvianetta'. Tickletext and Sir Signal are not successful, but their conduct and values replicate at an absurd level the more sophisticated language of all the gallants. Their presence here therefore reminds us that beneath and behind the civility of the three betrothals lies a subtext of sex and male sexuality as rapacious and amoral. This reminder serves to shadow the up-beat celebratory presentation of Cornelia to Galliard at line 162.

Despite Galliard's conventional comic articulation and plea for 'forgiveness' for all, and the reminder that the night's action is over (l. 200), the play actually ends on a misogynistic couplet by Sir Signal. The last ten lines of the play thus replicate and echo the structure of the last 70 lines: we are proffered a model of forgiveness and the promise of a new social order through a re-modelling of marriage, and this is starkly contrasted with evidence that misogyny prevails. By ending on a couplet here, Behn helps ensure that Sir Signal's words will stay in our minds as we leave the theatre ('Since love and women easily betray man, / From the grave gownman to the busy layman'). Comic closure is foreshadowed by gloomy predictions of a replication of the original Fall, and by evidence that Englishmen still view women both as a threat to masculinity and as the source of all betrayal. This is a gloomy ending to a play that has raised so many other possibilities for women's identity, and an echo of the darkness of the opening. Nevertheless, we still see the speaker as a buffoon, and it is in direct contrast to the new agreement forged

between Cornelia and Galliard. In effect, the audience is given a
choice. Which version of masculinity and femininity do you prefer,
the new one proposed by Cornelia, or the older one paraded by Sir
Signal?

*   *   *

Let us now turn to *The Lucky Chance*.

[Act 5, scene vii]

> *Lady Fulbank.*   What bleeding wound? Heavens, are you frantic,
>   sir?
> *Sir Feeble.* (*Weeps*)   No; but for want of rest, I shall ere morning.
>   She's gone, she's gone, she's gone. (*He weeps*)
> *Sir Cautious.*   Aye, aye, she's gone, she's gone indeed.   110
>   *Sir Cautious weeps.*
> *Sir Feeble.*   But let her go, so I may never see that dreadful vision.
>   Hark'ee sir, a word in your ear: have a care of marrying a young wife.
> *Sir Cautious.* (*weeping*)   Aye, but I have married one already.
> *Sir Feeble.*   Hast thou? Divorce her, fly her; quick, depart, be gone:
>   she'll cuckold thee, and still she'll cuckold thee.   115
> *Sir Cautious.*   Aye, brother, but whose fault was that? Why, are not
>   you married?
> *Sir Feeble.*   Mum, no words on't, unless you'll have the ghost about
>   your ears; part with your wife, I say, or else the devil will part ye.
> *Lady Fulbank.*   Pray, go to bed, sir.   120
> *Sir Feeble*   Yes, for I shall sleep now, I shall lie alone. (*Weeps*)
>   Ah, fool, old dull besotted fool, to think she'd love me; 'twas by
>   base means I gained her: cozened an honest gentleman of fame
>   and life.
> *Lady Fulbank.*   You did so, sir, but 'tis not past redress: you may   125
>   make that honest gentleman amends.
> *Sir Feeble.*   Oh, would I could, so I gave half my estate.
> *Lady Fulbank.*   That penitence atones with him and heaven. –
>   Come forth, Leticia, and your injured ghost.
>   [*Enter Leticia, Belmour, and Phillis.*]
> *Sir Feeble.*   Ha, ghost; another sight would make me mad indeed.   130
> *Belmour.*   Behold me, sir, I have no terror now.

Sir Feeble.   Ha, who's that, Francis? My nephew Francis?

Belmour.   Belmour, or Francis; choose you which you like, and I am either.

Sir Feeble.   Ha, Belmour! And no ghost? 135

Belmour.   Belmour, and not your nephew, sir.

Sir Feeble.   But art alive? Od's bobs, I'm glad on't, sirrah. But are you real, Belmour?

Belmour.   As sure as I'm no ghost.

Gayman.   We all can witness for him, sir. 140

Sir Feeble.   Where be the minstrels? We'll have a dance, adod we will. [*To Leticia*] Ah, art thou there, thou cozening little chits-face? A vengeance on thee, thou madest me an old doting loving coxcomb; but I forgive thee, and give thee all thy jewels, – [*to* [*Belmour*] and you your pardon, sir, so you'll give me mine; for I 145 find you young knaves will be too hard for us.

Belmour.   You are so generous, sir, that 'tis almost with grief I receive the blessing of Leticia.

Sir Feeble.   No, no, thou deserv'st her; she would have made an old fond blockhead of me, and one way or other you would have had 150 her, od's bobs you would.

      Enter Bearjest, Diana, Pert, Bredwell, and Noisy.

Bearjest.   Justice, sir, justice: I have been cheated, abused, assassinated and ravished!

Sir Cautious.   How, my nephew ravished!

Pert.   No, sir, I am his wife. 155

Sir Cautious.   Hum, my heir marry a chamber-maid!

Bearjest.   Sir, you must know I stole away Mrs Di, and brought her to Ned's chamber here, to marry her.

Sir Feeble.   My daughter Di stolen!

Bearjest.   But I being to go to the devil a little, sir, whip – what does 160 he, but marries her himself, sir; and fobbed me off here with my lady's cast petticoat.

Nosiy.   Sir, she's a gentlewoman, and my sister, sir.

Pert.   Madam, 'twas a pious fraud, if it were one, for I was contracted to him before. See, here it is. 165

      [*Pert*] *gives* [*a paper to*] *them.*

All.   A plain case, a plain case.

Sir Feeble. (*To Bredwell, who with Diana kneels*)   Hark'ee sir, have you had the impudence to marry my daughter, sir?

Bredwell.   Yes, sir, and humbly ask your pardon, and your blessing. 170

Sir Feeble.   You will ha't whether I will or not. Rise, you are still
     too hard for us. – Come, sir, forgive your nephew.
Sir Cautious.   Well, sir, I will; but all this while you little think the
     tribulation I am in: my lady has forsworn my bed.
Sir Feeble.   Indeed sir, the wiser she.   175
Sir Cautious.   For only performing my promise to this gentle-
     man.
Sir Feeble.   Aye, you showed her the difference, sir; you're a wise
     man. Come, dry your eyes, and rest yourself contented; we are a
     couple of old coxcombs, d'ye hear, sir, coxcombs.   180
Sir Cautious.   I grant it, sir, – (*to Gayman*) and if I die, sir, I
     bequeath my lady to you, with my whole estate: my nephew has
     too much already for a fool.
Gayman.   I thank you, sir. – Do you consent, my Julia?
Lady Fulbank.   No, sir: you do not like me. 'A canvas bag of   185
     wooden ladles were a better bed-fellow.'
Gayman.   Cruel tormentor! Oh, I could kill myself with shame and
     anger!
Lady Fulbank.   Come hither, Bredwell: witness, for my honour,
     that I had no design upon his person, but that of trying of his   190
     constancy.
Bredwell.   Believe me sir, 'tis true. I feigned a danger near, just as
     you got to bed; and I was the kind devil, sir, that brought the gold
     to you.
Bearjest.   And you were one of the devils that beat me and the   195
     captain here, sir?
Gayman.   No, truly, sir, those were some I hired, to beat you for
     abusing me today.
Noisy.   To make you 'mends sir, I bring you the certain news of the
     death of Sir Thomas Gayman, your uncle, who has left you two   200
     thousand pounds a year.
Gayman.   I thank you, sir; I heard the news before.
Sir Cautious.   How's this: Mr Gayman, my lady's first lover? I find,
     Sir Feeble, we were a couple of old fools indeed, to think at our
     age to cozen two lusty young fellows of their mistresses; 'tis no   205
     wonder that both the men and the women have been too hard for
     us; we are not fit matches for either, that's the truth on't.
               That warrior needs must to his rival yield,
               Who comes with blunted weapons to the field.
                                        (*The Lucky Chance*, 5, viii, 106–209)

Let us first consider how the structure of this extract informs an audience's response. It takes place in an antechamber: a semi-public place in which all the characters meet in a semi-intimate manner.

This part divides clearly into five sections: the conversation between the old men (ll. 108–29); the revelation to Feeble and Cautious that Belmour is alive (ll. 130–51); the arrival and marriages of Bearjest and Diana, Pert and Bredwell (ll. 152–73); the conversation between Sir Feeble, Lady Fulbank, Sir Cautious her husband, and Gayman (ll. 173–203); and the final seven lines spoken by Sir Cautious, which act as a kind of epilogue and moral commentary on the action of the whole play (ll. 204–9). This structure is a microcosm of the action of the play: the greed and excessive desire of the old men for young, rich and aristocratic women triggers the unhappiness of Leticia and Lady Fulbank, the banishment of Belmour, the secret marriages of Diana and Pert, and the final humiliation, Sir Cautious's loss of his wife in a wager. These final 100 lines replicate an acknowledgement of that responsibility: we see the old men bewailing their losses, blaming their misfortune on having young wives; and then we watch while each of their mistakes is rectified by the actions and rebellion of wives, niece, daughter, and masculine opponent. Each successive part is a further blow to their authority and pride: we watch them progressively decline as the 100 lines draw on. There is some comedy in this: their weeping (possibly holding onto each other), bewailing the perfidy of young women and their tendency to cuckold old men, exactly mirrors their self-centred, misogynistic and greedy view of the world. The audience are amused, not sympathetic. Nevertheless, Sir Cautious is allowed to speak the moralised conclusion, giving him the status of a purveyor of wisdom, and (as with the other plays) leaving a sense that old men's views of women are not changed by their experience, or by the action of the play. The structure of this part of the scene thus illustrates the narrative pattern of the whole play in microcosm, and suggests that some characters and their views may be irredeemable. This is a sobering message for a comedy.

The moralised, epilogue-like last seven lines summarise the message of the play: old fools should not try to cozen lusty young men out of their lovers, and the old should give way to the young. Sir

Cautious also acknowledges that 'both the men and the women have been too hard for us' (l. 206), invoking and recognising an equality between men and women which his past behaviour has belied.

Behn doubles and parallels her characters again here, placing them in similar or diverse situations in order to examine alternative modes of living and identity. Sir Feeble and Sir Cautious, often appearing in successive scenes in parallel situations, have both lost their wives here, although for different immediate reasons. Their age and greed and lechery have led them to this loss, and all illustrate their function as the 'blocking figures' of conventional comic form. This term is used to signify those characters (usually fathers, uncles, or old husbands) who block, dispute or prevent the satisfactory resolution of the love interests of the young heroes and heroines. By making these two men so similar, in economic status, in their marriage to young wives who love another, and in their blind and selfish characters, Behn intensifies her warning message. By making them comic (their repeated refrain, 'she's gone, she's gone, she's gone'), she ensures we are distanced from their plight: they are caricatures of rich, greedy city types, not three-dimensional characters. This throws our sympathies onto the lovers and their desires, despite the fact that we thereby approve of divorce.

Belmour and Gayman, also paralleled throughout the play, move on twin tracks here, although the outcomes of their declared love and intrigues differ slightly. We are not sure of Gayman's marital future, although his financial standing is given a boost by the *deus ex machina* announcement of his uncle's fortuitous death. The grouping of two sets of characters (Cautious and Feeble vs. Gayman and Belmour) acts as a physical reminder of one of the play's main themes, that of youth versus age.

Finally, women characters are also doubled: Leticia and Lady Fulbank make an interesting contrast. Although they are both in unhappy, arranged marriages, and in love with a younger man, their responses to their situations have been very different in the play, and remain so here. The former remains a virgin at the close of the play, the latter is an experienced married woman. Leticia does not speak at all here, while Lady Fulbank admonishes, arranges, rebukes, and states her own views and wishes clearly.

Diana and Pert have plotted together to arrange marriages to the men of their choice, and to avoid the orders of employers and fathers, but they are of different social status. Here Behn shows that women have interests in common across classes, and can act in concert to empower themselves. By paralleling her characters, she illustrates this point neatly.

This is an appropriate point to consider the question of how women's choices are represented here. What is remarkable about this play is the extent to which women's choices in marriage dominate the resolution. This is less clear in Leticia's case: she remains silent here, although she has renounced her marriage. But all the others have been active in pursuit of love and an autonomous identity. Pert deceives Bearjest in order to force him to honour a pre-contract, and Diana has been instrumental in achieving her marriage. Lady Fulbank refuses to agree to her husband's arrangement of her life, repeating her objections to him having treated her as a gambling chit.

This leads us to the question of the play's resolution. We view a conventional ending in the marriages of Bearjest and Pert, Diana and Bredwell, and Belmour and Leticia, and those who have sinned are forgiven by the older men. But the love between Lady Fulbank and Gayman remains unrequited to a point sometime in the future when Sir Cautious should die ('I bequeath my lady to you', ll. 181–2), and indeed, as sanctioned by her husband, rouses our suspicions. This leaves a sense of unfinished business and a set of questions. We need to remember that at the beginning of this scene Lady Fulbank had vowed a permanent separation from her husband, in anger at his disposal of her as piece of property. She remains separated from her husband, but unattached to Gayman at the end. This enables Behn to avoid accusations of immorality: she has not sanctioned divorce and remarriage, but simultaneously suggests a radical perspective on unhappy marriages. Lady Fulbank asserts her own separate identity from her husband, and disputes the idea that women are the property of men. By their remaining separated at the end, this radical message stays in the audience's mind.

Finally, let us comment on the imagery. The closing couplet is particularly remarkable, invoking both martial and phallic imagery

('That warrior needs must to his rival yield, / Who comes with blunted weapons to the field'). Erotic pursuit and military enterprise are frequently linked by Behn's characters, although, as we saw in *The Rover*, women usually use such metaphors with some irony. Here the assertion of a model of competitive enterprise between men as a suitable description of social and erotic behaviour seems to indicate again that Sir Cautious still views marriage and love on a business and military model, a model we are left with as the play ends.

Wagers, betting and gaming are an important part of the play's action and themes, as indicated in the title itself, and frequently occur in metaphors and similes. Here such metaphors reappear in Sir Feeble's attack on Leticia ('thou cozening little chits-face', l. 142), and in the several references to games and matches. Play and disguise are reiterated here in Sir Feeble's confusion about Belmour's identities as ghost, Francis and Belmour (ll. 130–5). This sets up two, possibly paradoxical, interpretations. At one level, disguise and play are seen to bring about social success, particularly for the young lovers and the married women. However, conversely, gaming has been shown to treat women as explicit pawns in a game between men, both young and old, both gallants and wealthy business men. Thus play and gaming are exposed as both tantalisingly attractive and simultaneously disastrous for women.

The final metonym to note here is one which recurs in Behn's plays, that of women as property: Sir Cautious, as we have noted, says 'I bequeath my lady to you' (ll. 181–2). In his usage this is not a metaphor (he means it literally), but we recognise it as one because the play has made us conscious of the human problems caused by treating women as chattels. By making an audience conscious of the real meanings of what seemed dead metaphors, Behn makes a political point about the status of women in the early modern period.

Conclusions

1. All these plays end as conventional comedies, in which most of the major conflicts are resolved, various marriages concluded, young lovers made happy, older generations reconciled to

younger, feast and song celebrated. All these narrative closures metaphorically represent an image of a new social order of social cohesion, forgiveness and new ideas. However, in Behn's comedies such endings are supplemented or queried in several ways. One way is through the use of commentator characters (such as in *The Feigned Courtesans*, or Sir Cautious' moralised commentary at the end of *The Lucky Chance*), who remind us that the old order will continue. Another way of supplementing or querying the optimism of the comic message is through the use of characters who are incongruously excluded or who fail to change their character at the end of the play (such as Willmore himself, or Blunt in *The Rover*). Their continued misogyny, greed, self-regard or self-interest jar significantly with the other images of conciliation and re-birth. The final way in which Behn manipulates dramatic convention to query the political status quo is through structural contrasts with non-conventional aspects of comedy. For example, in *The Lucky Chance* one of the couples remains unmarried and one is divorced. In *The Feigned Courtesans* the characters of the sub-plot dominate the ending, rather than the main characters. In both cases the juxtaposition of convention with transgression allows Behn to write popular comedies which remain critical of the sexual and marital topics that all her plays address.

2. In each case there are key characters who remain outside or unsatisfied by the resolution: Angellica in *The Rover*, Laura and Octavio in *The Feigned Courtesans*, and the two old men in *The Lucky Chance*. This establishes a critical viewpoint for the audience on both the structure and content of the play. Crucially, this critical viewpoint coincides with views expressed by these very characters about double sexual standards, and about the autonomy of female identity. Their absence or silence remains a presence in the more general happy conclusion, and the questions raised by their non-incorporation or absence are left for the audience to consider.

3. *The Lucky Chance* differs from the other two comedies, particularly in its ending, for two reasons. First, one of the central female characters stands apart from marriage and erotic fulfilment in defence of her own autonomy. Secondly, the excluded

characters are not women, but men, suggesting a social model in which an old-fashioned patriarchal masculinity really is out-moded.

4. Tragedy remains a potential future outcome in these plays: because of partial resolutions, because key characters are seen not to have changed, or because elements of potential conflict have been postponed.

5. Self-conscious disguise, intrigue, revelation and playful gaming are revealed finally as being successful modes of action, by the play's resolution. Both young women and young men engage in disguise, trickery and deception, only to achieve their desires and help resolve the obduracy of the blocking figures. This posits a model of successful social identity as performance.

6. Characters are doubled, paralleled and contrasted as a key dramatic method to illustrate different solutions and outcomes to social or political problems. This enables drama to stage debates and offer potential outcomes.

7. Behn's use of caricatures and allegorical names enables her to make satirical points about the contemporary social and sexual order.

Methods of Analysis

1. We have used some of the methods of analysis discussed in the first chapter, including thinking about how the final moments are played out upon the stage and how this is integrated with character, action and language.

2. We have explicitly examined the ways in which the conventional comic openings are resolved or left open by the endings, and considered in what ways questions asked by the openings are left answered or unanswered by the endings. This is both a methodological approach and a more general analytical one. By the latter I mean that where the endings leave open questions confronted during the action of the play, we know that the dramatist is asking us to debate those questions. By doing this, the viewer can get a good handle on some of a play's key debates and ideas. For

example, in *The Rover*, the opening asks questions about the validity of fraternal and paternal control of women's lives and destinies. The closure shows us that although the women's brother is forced to acquiesce in a *fait accompli*, he threatens that his father may not be so easily persuaded. We are thus left with questions about how far entrenched social and political views and power can really be changed.

3. We have seen how comedy can enable debate about social issues, usually those concerning marriage, sexuality and identity. By using genre (comedy), structural repetition, caricature, and the juxtaposition of comic closure with non-conventional closures, dramatic method forces us to ask questions about these issues, and to refuse to accept either the status quo, or that problems are easily resolvable.

4. We have introduced some new terms in our analysis of comedy, these include: 'comic conventions', '*deus ex machina*', 'blocking characters', and 'resolution'. By seeing these terms as expressing **integral methods** of comic writing (rather than as critical terms) we can use them to actively consider the ways in which authors manipulate comic form to their own dramatic and thematic ends.

Suggested Work

All the plays' final Acts are complexly plotted: in *The Rover* the action occurs within one single long scene, whilst the other two plays divide the action clearly into scenic units (four in *The Feigned Courtesans* and seven in *The Lucky Chance*). It is easiest to understand the denouement and its dramatic and thematic meanings, if we fully understand how that denouement has happened. Comment on the relationship between scenes and between different parts of the action.

Comment on the significance of change of set and venue within the last acts. What are the differences between the beginnings and ends of the Acts? Are there common images or metaphors dominating the Act? Do different scenes act as juxtapositional contrasts or complements? What is the effect on the audience's interpretation?

How is the sub-plot integrated into the main plot in the fifth Act? Why does Behn change narrative direction at various points, as well as changing the scene in the swift final Act? Do our sympathies change our views of the overall resolution? Consider, for example, the case of Angellica in Act 5 of *The Rover*.

Do not be put off by the apparently complicated and convoluted plot-lines, which Behn fuses in complex denouements. By concentrating first on what happens on a small scale within these scenes, and then moving on to consider the larger questions, you will have developed your own sophisticated repertoire of analytical tools. We are beginning to see how she uses comic form, character manipulation, caricature, and scenic structure to manipulate and produce a visual and intellectual narrative which raises and addresses social and sexual issues.

3

Discovery Scenes

Discovery scenes are ones in which the machinery and mechanisms of stage business (for example, the revealing of an interior room, or garden or closet behind the set) coincide with the revelation of key new information to characters or audience, and usually, the consequent turning of the play's action towards resolution. The new theatres of Restoration London were constructed with a proscenium arch, and side shutters to enable the swift changing of scenes, and most dramatists were eager to incorporate the theatrical possibilities offered by these technical improvements. Most, but not all, discovery scenes occur in the latter part of the play's action. Revelation through unveiling one set behind another thus acts as a spatial metaphor for plot and character revelations. In cases where such stage mechanisms are used earlier in the plot, we need to pay attention to why the dramatist chooses to stage an early scene in this way. Of the extracts that follow, two are from Act 5 (*The Rover* and *The Lucky Chance*), whilst one, from *The Feigned Courtesans*, occurs at the opening of the second scene. By relating the stage mechanisms to the meanings invoked by a scene and its positioning, we can discuss Behn's stagecraft, plotting, and ability to use contemporary theatrical conventions to her own dramatic ends. We shall therefore consider how the key themes and issues of the play are effectively coalesced by her stagecraft.

*   *   *

In an early scene we can observe some of the key dramaturgical
mechanisms and methods simply as theatrical devices, before pro-
ceeding to consider what happens when these converge with plot
crises. Let us then read through this early scene from *The Feigned
Courtesans*.

[Act 1, scene ii]

> *Draws off [to Tickletext's room] and discovers Mr Tickletext a-trim-*
> *ming, his hair under a cap, [and] a cloth before him. Petro snaps*
> *his fingers, takes away the basin, and [begins] wiping [Tickletext's] face.*

Petro.   Ah *che bella*! *bella*! I swear by these sparkling eyes, and these
soft plump dimpled cheeks, there's not a signora in all Rome,
could she behold 'em, were able to stand their temptations; and for
la Silvianetta, my life on't, she's your own.

Tickletext.   *Teze, teze,* speak softly! But, honest Barberacho, do   5
I, do I indeed look plump, and young, and fresh and – ha?

Petro.   Aye, sir, as the rosy morn, young as old time in his infancy,
and plump as the pale-faced moon.

Tickletext.   Hee; why, this travelling must needs improve a man.
(*Aside*) Why, how admirably spoken your very barbers are here! –   10
But, Barberacho, did the young gentlewoman say she liked me?
Did she, rogue? Did she?

Petro.   'A doted on you, signor, doted on you.

Tickletext (aside)   Why, and that's strange now, in the autumn of
my age too, when nature began to be impertinent, as a man may   15
say, that a young lady should fall in love with me. – Why,
Barberacho, I do not conceive any great matter of sin only in
visiting a lady that loves a man, ha?

Petro.   Sin, sir! 'Tis a frequent thing nowadays in persons of your
complexion.   20

Tickletext.   Especially here at Rome, too, where 'tis no scandal.

Petro.   Aye signor, where the ladies are privileged, and fornication
licensed.

Tickletext.   Right: and when 'tis licensed 'tis lawful, and when 'tis
lawful it can be no sin. Besides, Barberacho, I may chance to turn   25
her, who knows?

Petro.   Turn her, signor? Alas, any way, which way you please.

Tickletext.   Hee, hee, hee! There thou wert knavish, I doubt; but I
mean convert her; nothing else, I profess, Barberacho.

Petro.   True, signor, true, she's a lady of an easy nature, and an   30
   indifferent argument well handled will do't. Ha, (*combing out*
   [*Tickletext's*] *hair*) here's your head of hair, here's your natural
   frizz! And such an air it gives the face! So, signor; now you have
   the utmost my art can do.
       [*Petro*] *takes away the cloth, and bows.*
Tickletext.   Well, signor, and where's your looking-glass?   35
Petro.   My looking-glass?
Tickletext.   Yes, signor, your looking-glass! An English barber
   would as soon have forgotten to have snapped his fingers, made his
   leg, or taken his money, as have neglected his looking-glass.
Petro.   Aye, signor, in your country the laity have so little honesty,   40
   they are not to be trusted with the taking off your beard unless you
   see't done; but here's a glass, sir.
       Gives him the glass. Tickletext sets himself and smirks in the glass,
       Petro standing behind him, making horns and grimaces which
       Tickletext sees in the glass. [*Tickletext*] *gravely rises* [*and*] *turns*
       towards Petro.
Tickletext.   Why how now, Barberacho, what monstrous faces are
   you making there?
Petro.   Ah, my belly, my belly, signor: ah, this wind-colic, this   45
   hypocondriac does so torment me! Ah!
                              (*The Feigned Courtesans*, 1, ii, 1–46)

The opening scene of this play takes place in the street, presumably
in front of various houses. As this second scene opens, we observe
the set '*draw off*', revealing an interior of one of the houses. The
stage directions in this scene are very exact. In the opening direction
the set revelation '**discovers Mr Tickletext**', a self-conscious stage
direction giving a technical description of the act of drawing off one
painted set to reveal one behind it. Behn's use of this term shows
that she has a working dramatist's understanding of the technical
mechanisms of stage business. It also shows us that to call such
scenes 'discovery' scenes is not simply a critical imposition, but the
application of a technical production term: something is literally discovered behind a painted shutter. Behn illustrates a sophisticated
convergence of technical dramaturgy with plotting.

Other stage directions here illustrate an intricate setting of scene,
situation and character. We already know from scene i that Petro is

disguised as a barber in order to gull the English buffoons, Tickletext and Sir Signal. When the scene draws off, we immediately recognise Petro in disguise, helped by the explicit stage directions showing him in the midst of shaving, and we anticipate subsequent trickery. Shaving by a trickster figure was a common motif in Renaissance plays, to indicate the beginning or completion of some elaborate confidence trick.

The audience's positioning is another key feature of a discovery scene: we are usually complicit with at least one of the characters on stage, and this raises an expectant tension (whether for comedy or conflict depends on the place in the plot). In this scene complicity against Tickletext and Sir Signal, created by the conjunction of the mechanism of scene discovery with our knowledge of an up-coming con, is established from their first appearance in the play. A discovery scene thus ensures audience alliances, and the butts of some of the play's satiric thrust. The stage directions throughout this short extract are aimed at reinforcing our views. Petro exaggeratedly acts out his part of barber in the gestures and movements described (for example at lines 31 and 34). These choreographed gestures mesh with his self-characterisation as a servile, flattering, but well-connected barber.

The presence of trickery and disguise or pretence are also commonly found in discovery scenes, and the threat of their revelation maintains tension in the scene: thus content is complicit with stage business. The exaggerated delineation and self-presentation of Petro invites and plays with discovery of his true intents and identity. Here some of the motifs and mechanisms of a discovery scene are used to farcical purpose. The threat of revelation is briefly realised in the mirror episode, but unlike the next two discovery scenes we look at, does not at any point threaten tragedy for any character. Petro flaunts his disguise by making faces and horns in the mirror behind Tickletext, and is required to act out another part in order to protect his disguise: he pretends to have the colic. The need to improvise a new explanation, identity or disguise is typical of discovery scenes: usually in an attempt to ward off tragedy or complete discovery. Here such improvisation merely fuels the humour and the audience's delight in Petro's trickery.

There is a self-conscious theatricality about the characters aligned with the audience in these scenes: we know and they know most of the truth, but other characters on stage are kept necessarily in the dark. In order to maintain the fiction they have created, and the audience's allegiance, such characters are required to display a self-consciousness about their own roles. This is often signalled by the explicit and directed asides spoken by them, rather than by those in the dark. Here, however, it is only Tickletext who speaks asides. This is a bold move by Behn, because it depends on us recognising completely Petro's deception, seeing Tickletext as the gullible and foolish mark, and allying ourselves with Petro. This is achieved through several means: first, by our recognition of Petro from the previous scene; secondly, by the actor's ability to carry off the characterisation of Barberacho in a sufficiently exaggerated fashion that it is both amusing in itself, and incredible that Tickletext does not realise he is being gulled; thirdly, by Tickletext's own characterisation being equally exaggerated: the greedy, self-regarding, lecherous, hypocritical parson and Englishman abroad, fitting a stereotype recognisable even today. By drawing on such stereotypes, Behn encourages the audience to see Tickletext as the butt of jokes and satire. This neutralises his asides to the audience, which are then read as further illustrations of his own self-importance and self-deception. Deception is thus a dual theme in this extract: the trickster figure plays out a deception on Tickletext, and Tickletext is displayed as self-deceiving. The audience are placed as knowing observers through the agency of Petro, in conjunction with the revelation of the opening 'discovery' of a scene behind a painted set. We literally meet, as well as observe in our judgements of characters, a world of false appearances, shifting identities and deceit.

The drawing off of one set to display another behind thus aids our sense of a society with layers of disguise, deception, identity and meaning to be discovered. Scenic changes can therefore be used spatially and metaphorically to suggest hidden meanings, hidden identities, and shifting understandings of situations. The use of such techniques enables different perspectives to be played to the audience in successive scenes or moments.

* * *

Let us now consider the extract from *The Rover*.

[Act 5, scene i]

Blunt.   . . . I have got into my possession
   a female, who had better have fallen under any curse, than the ruin   70
   I design her. 'Adsheartlikins, she assaulted me here in my own
   lodgings, and had doubtless committed a rape upon me, had not
   the sword defended me.
Frederick.   I know not that, but o' my conscience thou hadst
   ravished her, had she not redeemed herself with a ring; let's see it,   75
   Blunt.
         Blunt shows the ring.
Belvile. [*Aside*]   Ha, the ring I gave Florinda, when we exchanged
   our vows. – Hark'ee, Blunt –
         [*Belvile*] *goes to whisper to* [*Blunt*].
Willmore.   No whispering, good colonel, there's a woman in the
   case; no whispering.   80
Belvile [*aside to Blunt*]   Hark'ee, fool, be advised, and conceal both
   the ring and the story for your reputation's sake; do not let people
   know what despised cullies we English are: to be cheated and
   abused by one whore, and another rather bribe thee than be kind
   to thee, is an infamy to our nation.   85
Willmore.   Come, come, where's the wench? We'll see her; let her
   be what she will, we'll see her.
Pedro.   Aye, aye, let us see her; I can soon discover whether she be
   of quality, or for your diversion.
Blunt.   She's in Fred's custody.   90
Willmore (*to Frederick*)   Come, come, the key.
         [*Frederick*] *gives* [*Willmore*] *the key;* [*Willmore, Frederick, Blunt
         and Don Pedro*] *are going.*
Belvile. (*Aside*)   Death, what shall I do? – Stay, gentlemen. – [*Aside*]
   Yet if I hinder 'em I shall discover all. – Hold, let's go one at
   once; give me the key.
Willmore.   Nay, hold there, colonel; I'll go first.   95
Frederick.   Nay, no dispute; Ned and I have the propriety of her.
Willmore.   Damn propriety; then we'll draw cuts.
         Belvile goes to whisper [*to*] *Willmore.*

– Nay, no corruption, good colonel; come, the longest sword
carries her.

> *They all draw, forgetting Don Pedro, being as a Spaniard, had the
> longest.*

Blunt.   I yield up my interest to you, gentlemen, and that will be   100
revenge sufficient.

Willmore. (*To Pedro*)   The wench is yours. [*Aside*] Pox of his toledo,
I had forgot that.

Frederick.   Come, sir, I'll conduct you to the lady.

> *Exeunt Frederick and Pedro.*

Belvile. (*Aside*)   To hinder him will certainly discover her. (*To*   105
Willmore), [*who is*] *walking up and down out of humour*) Dost know,
dull beast, what mischief thou hast done?

Willmore.   Aye, aye; to trust our fortune to lots! A devil on't, 'twas
madness, that's the truth on't.

Belvile.   Oh, intolerable sot!   110

> *Enter Florinda, running, masked, Pedro after her: Willmore
> gazing round her.*

Florinda. (*Aside*)   Good heaven, defend me from discovery.

Pedro.   'Tis but in vain to fly me; you're fallen to my lot.

Belvile. (*Aside*)   Sure she's undiscovered yet, but now I fear there is
no way to bring her off.

Willmore.   Why, what a pox, is not this my woman, the same I   115
followed but now?

Pedro. (*Talking to Florinda, who walks up and down*)   As if I did not
know ye, and your business here.

Florinda. (*Aside*)   Good heaven, I fear he does indeed.

Pedro.   Come, pray be kind; I know you meant to be so when you   120
entered here, for these are proper gentlemen.

Willmore.   But, sir, perhaps the lady will not be imposed upon;
she'll choose her man.

Pedro.   I am better bred, than not to leave her choice free.

> *Enter Valeria, and is surprised at sight of Don Pedro.*

Valeria. (*Aside*)   Don Pedro here! There's no avoiding him.   125

Florinda. (*Aside*)   Valeria! then I'm undone.

Valeria. (*To Pedro, running to him*)   Oh, have I found you, sir? The
strangest accident – if I had breath – to tell it.

Pedro.   Speak: is Florinda safe? Hellena well?

Valeria.   Aye, aye, sir; Florinda – is safe – [*aside*] from any fears of   130
you.

Pedro.   Why, where's Florinda? Speak.

Valeria.   Aye, where indeed sir, I wish I could inform you; but to
    hold you no longer in doubt –

Florinda (*aside*)   Oh, what will she say?   135

Valeria.   – She's fled away in the habit – of one of her pages, sir; but
    Callis thinks you may retrieve her yet; if you make haste away,
    she'll tell you, sir, the rest – (*aside*) if you can find her out.

Pedro.   Dishonourable girl, she has undone my aim. [*To Belvile*] Sir,
    you see my necessity of leaving you, and hope you'll pardon it; my   140
    sister, I know, will make her flight to you; and if she do, I shall
    expect she should be rendered back.

Belvile.   I shall consult my love and honour, sir.
      Exit Pedro.

                                                (*The Rover*, 5, i, 66–143)

This discovery scene teeters on the brink of total exposure (not only
of Blunt's imprisonment of Florinda, but of Florinda's and Belvile's
elopement) for most of its action, and the consequent dramatic
tension is crucial to our responses and the characters' actions
throughout. The action is set in Blunt's chamber, into which Belvile,
Willmore, Frederick and Pedro break. A door to the back or side of
the stage leads back to the chamber where he has sequestered
Florinda, and from which she emerges in this extract after Pedro has
won the wager. The staging of this discovery scene is different from
that in *The Feigned Courtesans*, in which the backdrop is drawn aside
to reveal a room or scene behind it. Here the setting of Blunt's
chamber remains on stage from the end of Act 4 into Act 5. We are
continually threatened with a discovery that does not in fact take
place: Florinda's rape, or exposure of her identity. The set is a buffer
between the streets and the chamber where Florinda is held. The
potential unveiling of that inner chamber, both literally and in terms
of the plot, makes this a discovery scene. Its staging holds back from
complete revelation of what is behind the scenes and of Florinda's
body, as the plot eventually also holds back from revealing all to
Pedro.

    The situation is also key to a successful discovery scene. Here our
fears have been raised both by the violence at the end of Act 4 as
Blunt manhandles Florinda, and in his assumptions, echoing those

of Willmore, that a woman out alone must be a prostitute. Potential violence hangs over the scene: Blunt's language and actions threaten rape. The other men's arrival means discovery of Blunt's actions, but may also mean discovery of Belvile's and Florinda's intentions to elope. It might also trigger a potential gang-rape. Various secrets, developed with the audience's knowledge through the play's action, here risk being exposed to characters not in the know. The anxieties engendered by the situation are typical of a good discovery scene.

The stage directions are again complex and explicit, delineating careful blocking and choreography of characters. Thus, for example, the showing of the ring, the handing over of the key, and the competition for the longest sword are all carefully drawn out matters of stage business which symbolically signal Florinda's absent fragility in the face of masculine views of ownership, competition and sexual rights. Each stage prop, in combination with the stage business surrounding it, triggers heightened dramatic tension. Belvile recognises Florinda's ring, but with Pedro present he cannot say this, increasing tension on the stage and for us. This is the point at which the audience's knowledge coincides exactly with Belvile's, and he becomes the key character on stage, for whom discovery of the truth will be most damaging. The audience are therefore placed in a position where, although we want to know all the details, we do not want those details disclosed to Pedro. The tension created by this (wanting a resolution, but one postponed until the lovers can escape) is key to the management of plot-lines in a discovery scene. The dramatist allows the characters to repeatedly teeter on the edge of complete discovery as the action progresses.

Stage properties are used symbolically. The handling and passing over of the key between the men, combined with the dialogue about their 'rights' to see the 'wench', visually underlines the symbolic and actual power men hold over women in the society we see represented on stage. The handling of the key suggests how women can be handed between and handled by men, owned and subordinated as though it were natural. The men talk about who has 'propriety' over her (ll. 96, 97), in other words, rights of ownership: visual stage props echo and reinforce the linguistic representation of women by men. There is no one on stage who queries this order of things.

Throughout the play, the audience, however, have been encouraged both to see Florinda as a victim of circumstances and irrational male violence, and to question the masculine equation between women on the streets and sexual availability. The appearance and handling of the key therefore reminds the audience of our positioning as sceptical and critical of masculine patriarchal views and behaviour. The stage prop distances the audience from all the characters on stage, asking us to sympathise with Florinda against all the men: we want to prevent any further discovery.

Willmore's proposed wager for Florinda introduces another symbolic stage prop: the longest sword can win her. The five men on stage all draw out their swords at the same moment: a spectacular but ridiculous display. This must occur roughly centre-stage for there to be room for both the drawing and raising of swords, producing an image of male display and unity, despite the fact that they are competing against each other. The central forceful image of a body of men holding swords aloft is both powerfully threatening and comically phallic, and Behn is conscious of this dual theatrical effect in scripting this action here. For at one and the same time, we literally see the potential violence linked to all men in this play, and we see this display as an effort to assert the greatest sexual prowess. The comic effect of this is lessened, of course, by the fact that the winner may then rape Florinda. Visual props again can act to distance the audience from the actors on stage: we both fear a tragic discovery, and wish for a failure of discovery.

The third stage prop here is the ring: symbolic of true love and Belvile's constancy, but here interpreted by Blunt and Fred as meaningless. To Belvile, it signals that it is Florinda in the chamber, thereby raising tension about potential discovery by Pedro. It also acts as a fragile symbol of romantic love against the violence we see on stage.

Finally, the stage directions linked to Florinda are important features of this extract. Those after line 110, where she runs onto the stage pursued by her brother, are crucial for a couple of reasons: at first we fear this means her brother has recognised her or is about to, and that her desires will be quashed. But when we see that she is still masked, we are simultaneously relieved and anxious, as it becomes clear that he and others still believe her to be a prostitute. Stage directions insist that the visual appearance of Florinda conveys this to the audience prior to any dialogue. Visual cues are crucial symbols of meaning and mark the relief and raising of tension in discovery scenes. The speaking of asides can be a means of manipulation of audience sympathy. Here the asides are spoken by Belvile, then Florinda, then Valeria. Each of these characters has an interest in postponing discovery, and their asides here strengthen the sympathies the audience has for them. Asides also reinforce the appearance of a division between those characters in the know and those in the dark, a crucial division for maintaining tension in a discovery scene.

What about the internal structure of this extract? The situation begins with characters at various cross-purposes. Blunt wants to keep his woman secret, the others want to share her. Once Belvile realises who she is, he needs to keep her identity secret because of Pedro's presence; the others (and Willmore most forcefully) want to see her immediately. There are four possible outcomes to the situation at this point: Blunt rapes Florinda; Pedro possesses her and discovers she is his sister; Willmore carries her off (as he threatened in Act 4); Belvile wins her and carries her off. The presence of diverse potential outcomes to a discovery scene is crucial for its success: we, the audience, have to want one outcome more than the others, and fear several of the others. In this case, and comically, none of these occur: instead Behn utilises a *deus ex machina* function through Valeria's entrance. Because Valeria knows what is going on, and sympathises with Florinda, she can manipulate the situation in the interests of the resolution that the audience want. She alone can produce a fifth outcome, the marriage of Florinda and Belvile, both because Pedro trusts what she says and because she successfully improvises a solution. As we saw in the first extract, improvisation is a key characteristic of the character who manages the outcome of a discovery scene.

Another feature we find here is the coalescence of some of the play's central themes. From Blunt's opening story (ll. 66–73), in which he gives a version of events that we know to be wrong (having witnessed the events in the preceding scene), men's stories are opposed to women's stories, men's words to women's words. We know Blunt's words are fiction: but the other men accept his account at face value. Frederick amends the story slightly, and Belvile knows from the ring that Blunt must be lying, but the fundamental danger posed by this discovery scene is caused by the fact that most of the men who are present believe Blunt's account and Blunt's word. By contrast, the words (in the form of her actions) of Florinda are disbelieved, or rather, taken to mean something else. Pedro claims she meant to be 'kind' (have sex) when she came into the building off the streets (l. 120). Florinda herself does not speak directly to any character, other than asides to the audience, and the final thank you to Valeria. Linguistically and physically she is isolated: to us, her actions denote fear, but to the men, proof of dishonour. The gap between the audience's perception of reality, and that of most of the male characters, is central to the way Behn asks us to think about masculinity as a dangerous force. Here it is women's actions, not their words, that are seen to display their honour. The opposition between masculine power, dependent on their word of honour (being believed), and women's lack of power because their words are not as important as the appearance of virtue, is a crucial issue examined by the play's action, narrative and characters. That fundamental conflict is central to the tension of the discovery scene, as is the audience's positioning against the dominant action on stage.

Finally, Behn self-consciously draws our attention to this scene's status as a discovery scene. In these eighty or so lines the word 'discover' is used three times (ll. 88, 93, 105), 'discovery' once (l. 111), and 'undiscovered' once (l. 113). With the exception of one 'discover' (l. 88), all are used by Belvile and Florinda, in fearful anticipation of what they see as inevitable unveiling and ruin. The mechanism of discovery is thereby explicitly exposed as dangerous to the characters with whom we sympathise most, by those very characters. These characters, in addition to acting their parts within the plot, also act as authorial markers of interpretation for the audience. By manipulating some of the conventions of discovery, and linking it to violence rather than comic closure, as was the usual Restoration convention, Behn suggests that disguise, trickery and secrecy may be necessary to female survival in the society she represents.

* * *

We now look at four scenes from *The Lucky Chance.*

[Act 5, scene iv]

> *Exeunt* [*Sir Cautious, Lady Fulbank, and the men,*] *severally.*
> *Gayman peeps out of the chest, and looks round him wondering.*
> Gayman.   Ha, where am I? By heaven, my last night's vision! 'Tis
> that enchanted room, and yonder the alcove! Sure,'twas indeed   75
> some witch, who knowing of my infidelity, has by enchantment
> brought me hither. 'Tis so, I am betrayed. (*Pauses*) Ha! or was it
> Julia, that last night gave me that lone opportunity? But hark, I
> hear some coming.
> > [*Gayman*] *shuts himself in* [*the chest*]. *Enter Sir Cautious.*
> Sir Cautious. (*lifting up the chest lid*)   So, you are come, I see.   80
> > [*Sir Cautious*] *goes and locks the door.*
> Gayman. (*Aside*)   Ha, he here! Nay, then I was deceived, and it was
> Julia that last night gave me the dear assignation.
> > *Sir Cautious peeps into the bedchamber.*
> Lady Fulbank. (*Within*)   Come, Sir Cautious; I shall fall asleep, and
> then you'll waken me.
> Sir Cautious.   Aye, my dear, I'm coming. [*To Gayman*] She's in   85
> bed; I'll go put out the candle, and then –
> Gayman.   Aye, I'll warrant you for my part.
> Sir Cautious.   Aye, but you may over-act your part, and spoil all;
> but, sir, I hope you'll use a Christian conscience in this business.
> Gayman.   Oh, doubt not, sir, but I shall do you reason.   90
> Sir Cautious.   Aye, sir, but –
> Gayman.   Good sir, no more cautions; you, unlike a fair gamester,
> will rook me out of half my night. I am impatient.
> Sir Cautious.   Good lord, are you so hasty? If I please, you shan't
> go at all.   95
> Gayman.   With all my soul, sir; pay me three hundred pound, sir.
> Sir Cautious.   Lord, sir, you mistake my candid meaning still. I am
> content to be a cuckold, sir; but I would have things done decently,
> d'ye mind me?
> Gayman.   As decently as a cuckold can be made, sir. But no more   100
> disputes, I pray, sir.
> Sir Cautious.   I'm gone, I'm gone –

[Sir Cautious] going out, returns.
but hark'ee, sir, you'll rise before day?
Gayman. Yet again!
Sir Cautious. I vanish, sir; but hark'ee: you'll not speak a word, but 105
let her think 'tis I?
Gayman. Be gone, I say, sir.
  [Sir Cautious] runs out.
   I am convinced last night I was with Julia.
   Oh, sot, insensible and dull!
  Enter softly Sir Cautious.
Sir Cautious. So, the candle's out; give me your hand.   110
  [Sir Cautious] leads [Gayman] softly in.

[Act 5, scene v]

  A bed-chamber

  Lady Fulbank supposed in bed. Enter Sir Cautious and Gayman
  by dark.
Sir Cautious. Where are you, my dear?
  [Sir Cautious] leads [Gayman] to the bed.
Lady Fulbank. Where should I be? In bed. What, are you by dark?
Sir Cautious. Aye, the candle went out by chance.
  Gayman signs to him to be gone; he makes grimaces as loth to go,
  and exit.

[Act 5, scene vi]

  Scene draws over, and represents another room in the same house.

  Enter parson, Diana, and Pert dressed in Diana's clothes.
Diana. I'll swear, Mrs Pert, you look very prettily in my clothes; –
and since you, sir, have convinced me that this innocent deceit is
not unlawful, I am glad to be the instrument of advancing Mrs
Pert to a husband she already has so just a claim to.
Parson. Since she has so firm a contract, I pronounce it a lawful 5
marriage. But hark, they are coming, sure.
Diana. Pull your hoods down, and keep your face from the light.
  Diana runs out. Enter Bearjest and Noisy, disordered.

Bearjest.   Madam, I beg your pardon: I met with a most devilish
   adventure. – Your pardon, too, Mr Doctor, for making you wait;
   but the business is this, sir: I have a great mind to lie with this   10
   young gentlewoman tonight, but she swears if I do, the parson of
   the parish shall know it.
Parson.   If I do, sir, I shall keep counsel.
Bearjest.   And that's civil, sir; come, lead the way –
           With such a guide, the devil's in't if we can go astray.
       Exeunt.

[Act 5, scene vii]

       Scene changes to the antechamber.

       Enter Sir Cautious.

Sir Cautious.   Now cannot I sleep, but am as restless as a merchant
   in stormy weather, that has ventured all his wealth in one bottom.
   Woman is a leaky vessel: if she should like the young rogue now,
   and they should come to a right understanding, why then am I
   a – wittol, that's all, and shall be put in print at Snow-Hill with   5
   my effigies o'th' top, like the sign of cuckold's haven. Hum,
   they're damnable silent; pray heaven he have not murdered her,
   and robbed her. Hum: hark, what's that? A noise: he has broke his
   covenant with me, and shall forfeit the money. How loud they are!
   Aye, aye, the plot's discovered; what shall I do? Why, the devil is   10
   not in her, sure, to be refractory now, and peevish; if she be I must
   pay my money yet, and that would be a damned thing. Sure,
   they're coming out: I'll retire and harken how 'tis with them.
       [*Sir Cautious*] *retires* [*a little distance*]. *Enter Lady Fulbank,*
       undressed; Gayman, half undressed, upon his knees, following
       her, holding her gown.
Lady Fulbank.   Oh! you unkind – what have you made me do?
               Unhand me, false deceiver, let me loose.   15
Sir Cautious. (*Aside, peeping*)   Made her do? So, so, 'tis done; I'm
   glad of that.
Gayman.   Can you be angry, Julia?
               Because I only seized my right of love.
Lady Fulbank.   And must my honour be the price of it?   20
               Could nothing but my fame reward your passion?
               What, make me a base prostitute, a foul adulteress?
               Oh, be gone, be gone, dear robber of my quiet. (*Weeping*)

Sir Cautious. [*Aside*]   Oh, fearful!

Gayman.   Oh! Calm your rage, and hear me: if you are so,   25
                    You are an innocent adulteress.
                    It was the feeble husband you enjoyed
                    In cold imagination, and no more;
                    Shyly you turned away, faintly resigned.

Sir Cautious. (*Aside*)   Hum, did she so?   30

Gayman.   Till my excess of love betrayed the cheat.

(*The Lucky Chance*, 5, iv, 74 to 5, vii, 31)

These four scenes are remarkably short, interlinked by plot and setting, but elegantly juxtaposed one to another to raise tension in the audience's response. The first scene is set in the outer chamber to the bedroom of Sir Cautious and Lady Fulbank, and although we can hear her and envisage the events in the room beyond, we never see into that room in full light on stage. The following scene (Act 5, scene v) occurs in the dark – we only hear the voices of the characters as they take their places. This scene, and the subsequent ones, tease the audience with the prospect of that scenic discovery (the full revealing of the bedroom and the conclusion of the wager), but that discovery is never fully actualised. There are three quick changes of scene here: from antechamber to bedroom, which is 'discovered' behind the chamber; from there to another room in the house, where Diana, Pert and Bearjest are preparing their plans for secret marriages; and back to the antechamber to the bedroom. This rapid change of setting, still within one house, provides a snapshot view of the secrets behind its different walls, and helps create, therefore, a sense of a world in which private plotting in private rooms is necessary to establish personal freedom. Equally, it provides a visual and spatial model of a society in which intrigue and secrecy are endemic. Staging and dramaturgy are used to render Behn's ideas in a three-dimensional, physical manner.

The successively revealed places in the house, where successive aspects of both plot and sub-plot play out, provide the audience with increasing insights into the internal workings of a house and a marriage. We feel more intimate with the characters, seeing them in their night clothes, their bedchamber, and with the anticipation of an erotic encounter. Here, as with the two previous extracts we examined, stage directions, as well as the choreography of scenic change and characters' positioning on stage, aid the intimate atmosphere (describing Lady Fullbank as '*undressed*' and Gayman as '*half undressed*', 5, vii, 13). Thus, for example, the actions and movements of Sir Cautious across the stage clearly illustrate his fears, his voyeurism, his jealousy of his wife, and his concern to see that the literal letter of his wager is redeemed. The dialogue here is almost incidental to the blocking of this character across, behind, and in front of the stage: and most of this is indicated by authorial stage directions. Behn's consciousness of how the scenes will work on stage, how they intersect with each other, and when the plot should change direction (by the changing of a scene) to both titillate and raise tension, is clear from stage directions, descriptions of characters, and the points at which scenes change.

Let us illustrate this point. Scene iv ends when Sir Cautious extinguishes the candle and leads Gayman towards the bedroom. Thus the demands of the plot (that Gayman go in darkness) coincide with the discovery of the bedroom behind the antechamber. However, unusually, this 'discovery' takes place in the near dark. The audience are able to distinguish enough shadows to believe we might see a bed ('*Lady Fulbank supposed in bed*'), and Sir Cautious's expressions as he departs the room ('*makes grimaces as loth to go*'). The usual enlightenment that should accompany a discovery is here deliberately shadowed by the lighting, echoing the nature of the situation, which calls for secrecy on the part of both Sir Cautious and Gayman. For Cautious cannot tell his wife he has lost her in a wager and Gayman cannot tell Cautious that he is the man with whom his wife has been in love. Although the audience understand all this, the discovery scene merely threatens the revelation of these secrets. As we noted in the scene from *The Rover*, audience anticipation of a variety of possible outcomes from a discovery scene defines its tensions. Here, again, our knowledge of this coincides with the knowledge of only one character (Gayman), making his point of view dominant.

This is true, however, only until the secrets are brought into the open in the last of the scenes here (Act 5, scene vii), to which we shall return. Let us first turn to a consideration of the relationship between the individual scenes. The short scene in the bedroom (a mere three spoken lines, although there is some stage business to take up time) ends as Gayman approaches the bed, leaving the audience to speculate on the outcome of this encounter. The tension created by closing the scene *in medias res* is cleverly judged. The characters (and actors) are not sexually compromised on stage, more is left to our imagination, and we are left anxiously wondering what effect the revelation will have on Lady Fulbank. Behn's structural dramatic intelligence is clear – and is enhanced by moving at this point to the sub-plot, rather than back to Sir Cautious.

The opening of Act 5, scene vi, in another part of the house, reminds us of parallel plots to undermine Sir Cautious's authority, acting as an intensified juxtapositional theme to the main threat to his authority via Gayman, and indirectly, his wife. In terms of the strict chronology of events, there is no need to place this scene at this point. Therefore, its only function is to postpone the revelations we await, raising tension, and simultaneously making the thematic point. The mechanism by which the scene opens ('*Scene draws over*') makes the audience anticipate that this will be the lighted bedroom, or the bed revealed behind curtains: the revelation of a room in another part of the house is bathetic. Here Behn plays with our desire for resolution, and deliberately denies our expectations of how subsequent discovery scenes should work. Yet she denies us the pleasure for a mere 15 lines, before changing scenes again back to the antechamber, and not the bedroom. This is clever plotting, because whilst it is amusing to watch Sir Cautious's anxiety, we really want to know what has happened in the bedroom. This part of the scene coalesces the possible outcomes once again into one which the audience may not have expected. Discovery takes place off stage in the bedroom: Lady Fulbank marches onto the stage in the middle of a verbal attack on both men. This produces the feeling that we have participated in some of the events of the discovery, but that some remain still hidden. Once again, a staging device (a character arriving in the middle of a speech) has the effect of simultaneously (and paradoxically) revealing and concealing information.

This is the moment of full revelation, of Cautious's perfidy and Gayman's own plot to get into Julia's bed. It is at this point that our allegiance with Gayman alters: he is the verbal and visual supplicant to Lady Fulbank (he is half dressed and on his knees), whose anger at both men's manipulation of her body and bed is clearly articulated. Her righteous anger, expressed rationally and logically, gains the audience's support in contrast to the now humbled men. Final discovery in this play, however delayed by staging devices, shifts the audience's allegiances clearly to Lady Fulbank. Mechanical discovery then is made to coincide with her own self-revelation (she now decides to separate completely from her husband and Gayman), and with the clearest revelation to the audience of the human costs of the power and financial games undertaken by the men. Personal self-discovery coincides with staging (including changing scenes, lighting, and setting), and this precipitates the resolution of the play.

Finally, it is worth noting that these scenes share similar metaphoric fields: the language and images of cheating, gaming, chance, playing and disguise are repeated at various points, for example, scene iv, lines 82, 87–9, 92–3; scene v, line 3; scene vi, line 2; scene vii, lines 2, 8–10. These intersect with metaphors and staging playing with lightness and dark, which suggest paradoxical interpretations: darkness both contains and hides truth. Such language denotes an ideology of adventuring and gaining, in which erotic encounters are placed within a theory of social behaviour based on games and competition, in a system of relative values. This view is contrasted strongly with the language used by Lady Fulbank when she attacks both men. Gayman's defence ('I only **seized** my right of love', 5, vii, 19) is opposed by her 'And must my honour be the price of it?' She claims two things: her rights to an independent identity by effectively pointing out the human costs of such an ideology, and a belief in a concept of absolute honour. The play's title (*The Lucky Chance*) is here exposed as a masculine gaming, competitive ideology in which women become both conceptual and literal pawns. This is a key message the play delivers to the audience, and it is therefore crucial that both this ideology and the language and behaviour associated with it are exposed during the discovery scene. The refutation of these metaphors through a discourse signalling women's autonomy coincides with Behn's manipulation of the discovery scene, ensuring Lady Fulbank's views and language dominate the resolution and our view of the play's deceptions. Discovery scenes are thus used here to reinforce or change an audience's perspective on ideological and social behaviour.

Conclusions

1. Behn uses discovery scenes to intensify, bring to a head and reveal key themes and conflicts of her plots. They are therefore both an essential, structural dramatic device, and a visual one: we witness, experience, see and understand in a comprehensive theatrical mode.

2. Discovery scenes were often used by Behn's male contemporaries as ways of revealing women's bodies (in a bedroom or boudoir) in scenes which potentially threatened women's safety or chastity. In two of the plays we have examined here (*The Rover* and *The Lucky Chance*) that potential threat is an explicit thread of the narrative. We anticipate with dread the possible rape of Florinda, and the exposure as unknowing dupe, of Lady Fulbank. Yet, whilst Behn raises this potential outcome for her plot, she deliberately eschews the conventional 'discovery' of the woman's half naked body. Thus the focus on women's bodies as theatrical icons is both admitted and refused by her own plotting and manipulation of discovery scenes. The simultaneous admittance and refusal, in combination with other devices which engender sympathy for the women characters, sets up questions about the validity of manipulating women's bodies for titillating the masculine gaze. In Behn's plots where we do await the revelation of an undressed woman, when we encounter such women we clearly see that any disempowerment is the result of masculine machinations, game playing, and sexual manipulation. We are thus led to criticise masculine commodification of women's bodies through the very mechanisms which other male playwrights used to display female bodies as objects for sexual manipulation, fantasy and pleasure. Behn therefore uses conventional theatrical and dramaturgical devices in an unconventional way for critical effect.

3. We have observed (in discussions of set changes, character blocking, stage directions, scenic juxtapositions, plotting, and

audience manipulation) that Behn's dramatic and theatrical skills are technical and efficient. She blends plot and theme with sophisticated production values.

4. The audience is a key player in all the discovery scenes we have analysed. We are both voyeur and critic, our allegiance courted and then shifted, according to the demands of the scene and the play's overall message. Our greater knowledge of events and plots is played upon to ensure that we feel we are expected to come to some kind of critical judgement, as Behn makes use of and manipulates our position as both voyeur and critic, sometimes playing one off against the other.

5. Discovery scenes usually coincide with the beginning of the dramatic denouement, although Behn uses the same techniques for comic and thematic illustration as well. As such, they tend to coalesce the play's key conflicts.

6. Discovery scenes can often coincide with a main character's self-revelation (as we saw with *The Lucky Chance*). This increases the sense of realism in the play: events are seen to alter characters and produce new knowledge and a change of direction. It also allows Behn to posit a radical view that characters' decisions do not have to be determined by convention: in *The Lucky Chance* she uses the revelations to suggest a rejection of dominant social codes.

7. Such scenes begin with various possible outcomes, they are open-ended and threaten potential tragedy. Comic endings are assured by producing the most benign resolution for the characters about whom we care most.

8. Discovery scenes unite the visual and spectacular with the narrational, intensifying and coalescing dramatic plot-lines to engender crisis and resolution.

9. In certain cases discovery scenes act as juxtapositional visual commentaries on the action of the plot elsewhere.

Methods of Analysis

This chapter has continued to use and build on some of the methods of analysis we used in the first two chapters. In addition, we have introduced and applied some understanding of drama as a structural form and a technical theatrical performance.

1. We have identified key scenes which coalesce the play's central themes. This has involved thinking about the play as a structural whole, and looking for scenes which change the direction of the narrative or plot. In general, such scenes pre-empt the play's denouement.
2. We have also particularly commented upon changes of scene and setting, and related these to more general movements of plot and revelations about characters.
3. We have introduced new terms of theatrical analysis, including: blocking, discovery, scenic juxtaposition, and stage props, and looked at how the dramatist integrates her manipulation of these physical elements of theatrical production with the verbal elements of the playtext itself. Stage directions are a key way in which we can see this fusion.
4. We have deliberately thought about how and where the audience is positioned by the mechanics of stage production as well as the ways in which the plot and sub-plots work together.

Suggested Work

By their nature, discovery scenes usually appear only once in a play: there is only one structural point at which all the plot-lines can meet, clash, and be resolved. This limits further work you can do on *The Rover* and *The Lucky Chance*, where the discovery scene is precursor to the denouement. You could think about how the scenes leading up to the discovery scene help raise or disperse the plot and narrative tensions. Are there continuous patterns of imagery? How are we made to think about the machinations that lead to the discovery scene? How are the heroines placed by these scenes, and why? In *The Rover* the discovery scene is followed by the confrontation between Angellica and Willmore (5, i, 206–357), and subsequently by his encounter with Hellena (5, i, 400–89). The content of these two episodes contains elements shared by the discovery scene. What is the effect of the juxtaposition of the three confrontations of the Act (the Blunt episode, the Angellica episode and the Hellena/Willmore episode)? What are the common themes? What do we learn from our answers to these questions?

In *The Feigned Courtesans*, look at the succession of scenes in Act 5: each builds up tension by changing the setting, and using doubled sets of doors to create and perpetuate confusion amongst the characters about which house and which woman they are going to visit. Once again, the people in the audience are the only ones with all the knowledge. In what ways do the theatrical mechanisms resemble those of other discovery scenes? How and why is deception a central theme in these scenes? How and why is sexual titillation used dramatically? How does the setting aid our interpretation? Comment on the use of stage directions and character blocking. How are we led to interpret the events and themes of the play by the staging?

4

Heroines and Whores

Behn's most compelling characters are women, from the heroines to the marginalised whores: she enlivens their characters with a greater sense of interiority, wit and eloquence than she does the men. She asks us to recognise them as women in a particular society. We shall examine one speech, or participation in dialogue, of each of the main female characters in each play, and consider Behn's modes of characterisation. We have already seen how femininity, gender and sexual identity are flagged up as key issues in the plays' openings, and how the endings leave us asking questions about social and gender inequalities. Let us consider now how Behn furthers these questions through characterisation.

* * *

In this extract from the final Act of *The Rover* Angellica has accosted Willmore, finally convinced that his promises in bed meant nothing. She is holding a pistol to his breast, whilst he claims that his language of love was merely the conventional language of seduction, with no promise of commitment. Willmore's immediately preceding argument was that, as a courtesan kept by a wealthy old lover, Angellica had cuckolded him previously, and that his own rakish behaviour merely matched hers.

[Act 5, scene i]

> *Angellica.*   All this thou'st made me know, for which I hate thee.
> Had I remained in innocent security,
> I should have thought all men were born my slaves,
> And worn my power like lightning in my eyes,   285
> To have destroyed at pleasure when offended:
> But when love held the mirror, the undeceiving glass
> Reflected all the weakness of my soul, and made me know
> My richest treasure being lost, my honour,
> All the remaining spoil could not be worth   290
> The conqueror's care or value.
> Oh, how I fell, like a long worshipped idol,
> Discovering all the cheat.
> Would not the incense and rich sacrifice,
> Which blind devotion offered at my altars,   295
> Have fallen to thee?
> Why wouldst thou then destroy my fancied power?
>
> (*The Rover*, 5, i, 282–97)

Few characters in this play address the audience directly through a monologue or soliloquy, so the audience gains a sense of character through dialogue, action and situation. Angellica's speech to Willmore is one of her lengthiest, and focuses on describing and analysing herself, rather than engaging in debate about proposed or past actions, and thus makes a good introduction to our discussion of characterisation.

The situation is a key interpretative marker we need to consider when discussing how characterisation works. This encounter takes place either just outside or just inside Blunt's building, and the long conversation between Willmore and Angellica (just over 100 lines) takes place with them alone on stage. This solitude, combined with the physical situation – Angellica is holding a pistol to Willmore's breast, and as he retreats across the stage, she follows – produces an atmosphere of intense intimacy and danger at the same time. Through the cumulation of previous scenes where Willmore switches his allegiance between women, using the same promises to each, the audience has been encouraged to view him critically. We have been impressed by Angellica's wit and her eloquent rhetorical defence of the economy of prostitution as a mode of achieving equality with men. The balance of power, poised visually on stage, shifts throughout these hundred lines. The pistol in Angellica's hand forces Willmore across the stage, and deprives him of, or at least matches, his arrogant, powerful self-regard. Yet the audience also perceive the pistol as both a desperate and a temporary assertion of a woman's power against a man: thus it works as a visual stage prop in two ways simultaneously. It represents both an expression of phallic power appropriated by woman, and a visual reminder of the very limits of that power. Equally, the visual and thematic contrast of the two characters, alone on stage and in pursuit and retreat, here symbolises in stark oppositional terms one of the play's central conflicts: between the contrasting freedoms of men and women in the society we view. Situation, visual props, and the physical relationship between characters on stage are essential creators of character. It is in this context, then, that we should turn to look more carefully at Angellica's speech.

Her solitude, her previous experiences, her desperation with the gun and Willmore's previous conduct, put the audience on Angellica's side. The language, style and content of her speech act as a lyrical lament for her lost self-sufficiency. We still witness her eloquence in her metaphors, but the speech is nevertheless an admission of defeat. This is one of the few metrical speeches in the play, although it is by no means conventionally regular. A few lines are standard iambic pentameters (ll. 284, 285, 294, 297), and others carry 11 beats, with the last syllable as a falling beat, or with an elided beat in the middle, delivering an aural feel of an iambic pentameter (ll. 282, 283, 286, 289, 292, 295). This model then allows variations within it, used to express extreme emotion, either anger or anguish. Here there are three very short lines (ll. 291, 293 and 296). In each case the shorter line indicates a pause for emphasis, thought, or weeping. They can also indicate time for stage business, such as the further thrusting of the gun at Willmore, or movement across the stage. Emotion and physical movement are thus caught up in the rhythms of the speech, and appear to be a natural part of the character's emotional expression.

This speech contains a succession of metaphors and similes, producing an intensification of emotion in the scene. There are six separate figures of speech within these 15 lines: that men were born slaves (l. 284); describing her power 'like lightning' (l. 285); love as a mirror of revelation (ll. 287–8); female honour as treasure (l. 289); honour as war-spoil (ll. 290–1); and others' past erotic conduct as pagan idolatry (ll. 292–6). These metaphors share a common subject: Angellica's past power and present powerlessness, which is partly universalised as a conflict between men as active and women as passive possessions. The images thus visually echo the narrative content, which contrasts her former belief in her power with her current perception of women as victims. As such, and combined with the blank verse, this speech is closer to a soliloquy of self-realisation at the end of a tragedy, than it is to the end of a comedy. The speech resonates throughout the rest of the scene, casting a shadow over the comic closure to come.

Finally, the content of the speech is a key indicator of Angellica's strength of character and symbolic function within the play: she has been pleading for men's words to women to be honoured. One of the key themes of the play is the difference between a man's 'word of honour' to a fellow man, and those to women. The former are sacrosanct, the latter subject to a man's personal whim. Additionally, the content acts as an analytic commentary on men's behaviour throughout the play, the manipulation and supposed idolisation of women, followed by their commodification as wives or whores. This speech thus acts as a critical platform for the audience: criticism of masculine practices and ideology comes from within the play through a character with whom, and with whose situation, we sympathise.

* * *

The following extract encapsulates a key dramatic moment: Blunt is sitting reading in the near dark, plotting revenge for his sexual and physical humiliation at the hands of Lucetta. He has lost all his clothes, and is dressed in ragged underwear, but has strapped an old rusty sword to his waist. Florinda, having waited in the garden for Belvile, has been discovered and pursued by a drunken Willmore, and is fleeing from his rapacious pursuit.

[Act 4, scene v]

> [*Blunt*] *sits down again and reads. Enter to him Florinda.*
> *Florinda.*   This house is haunted, sure; 'tis well furnished and no
>   living thing inhabits it. Ha, a man; heavens, how he's attired! Sure   20
>   'tis some rope-dancer, or fencing master. I tremble now for fear,
>   and yet I must venture now to speak to him. – Sir, if I may not
>   interrupt your meditations –
>   [*Blunt*] *starts up and gazes.*
> *Blunt.*   Ha, what's here? Are my wishes granted? And is not that a
>   she creature? 'Adsheartlikins, 'tis! – What wretched thing art thou,
>   ha?   25
> *Florinda.*   Charitable sir, you've told yourself already what I am: a
>   very wretched maid, forced by a strange unlucky accident, to seek
>   a safety here, and must be ruined, if you do not grant it.
> *Blunt.*   Ruined! Is there any ruin so inevitable as that which now   30
>   threatens thee? Dost thou know, miserable woman, into what den
>   of mischiefs thou art fallen, what abyss of confusion, ha? Dost not
>   see something in my looks that frights thy guilty soul, and makes
>   thee wish to change that shape of woman for any humble animal,
>   or devil? For those were safer for thee, and less mischievous.   35
> *Florinda.*   Alas, what mean you, sir? I must confess, your looks have
>   something in 'em makes me fear, but I beseech you, as you seem
>   a gentleman, pity a harmless virgin that takes your house for
>   sanctuary.
>
>   (*The Rover*, 4, v, 19–39)

Florinda rarely speaks at length about herself: the most she speaks in self-reflection is in the opening scene which we looked at in Chapter 1. This is paradigmatic of her characterisation: she is always represented in the middle of a dramatic crisis or piece of action, and her speeches describe or respond to that situation, rather than initiating new situations, or developing an internalised perspective on herself or her situation. This apparently simple fact is crucial to the way the audience are led to see her. We view her repeatedly as a victim of circumstance, rather than an agent of her own destiny. Thus, even though she marries the man she chooses at the end of the play, she is buffeted by crises and near-rapes, which illustrate the vulnerability of both a passive woman and a woman who chooses to move out of the confines of family and domestic space.

Her speeches contain little metaphoric language (often an indicator of self-reflection), and are not as witty as Hellena's. She tends
to speak straightforwardly and literally. Here she describes to the
audience what she sees: first the interior of the house, then her shock
at seeing a man, and a description of his clothing. Her linguistic register is polite, which reflects her class status, but also her lack of
worldliness. She simply does not perceive or anticipate the danger
she may be in. The audience, however, having seen Blunt's intention
for revenge, and been shown the vulnerability of lone women on the
streets through Florinda's encounter with Willmore, are already more
street-wise than she. This lack of awareness makes for a dramatic and
tense situation, and is a crucial means of showing us how the passivity and seclusion of women erodes their intellectual and physical
self-protection.

Florinda's language maintains a ladylike politeness throughout,
even as the potential violence against her becomes clearer. She is
shown to have few additional resources of self-protection: in contrast
to Hellena's improvisational skills. Her linguistic register is used to
suggest her lack of adaptability, and the dangers of a narrow, singular
model of femininity. She appeals to Blunt's status as gentleman, her
own as 'virgin', and chivalric ideals of sanctuary. This language is
ineffective for this situation and she has no other resources to
counter Blunt's perceptions or physical violence. Although his linguistic violence escalates, the nature of her response is merely repeti-
tious. Passive femininity is displayed as completely vulnerable to
men, who view women as commodities. The linguistic register, the
content of the dialogue, and the characters' physical appearance thus
act out what the initial situation suggested. The action confirms our
first presuppositions and this further illustrates how Florinda's character is represented as compliant with, and subject to, the circumstances in which she finds herself. Let us now turn to consider the
ways in which her sister is represented in contrast.

*   *   *

Like Florinda, Hellena is most often characterised through fast-
moving dialogue, although it is usually wittier and more outspoken.

Here we see her at the end of the first scene, just after her brother
has instructed them on their behaviour and on Florinda's marriage,
and then left.

[Act 1, scene i]

> *Hellena.*   But hark you, Callis, you will not be so cruel to lock me
> up indeed, will you?   165
> *Callis.*   I must obey the commands I have; besides, do you consider
> what a life you are going to lead?
> *Hellena.*   Yes, Callis, that of a nun: and till then I'll be indebted a
> world of prayers to you, if you'll let me now see, what I never did,
> the divertisements of a Carnival.   170
> *Callis.*   What, go in masquerade? 'Twill be a fine farewell to the
> world, I take it; pray, what would you do there?
> *Hellena.*   That which all the world does, as I am told: be as mad as
> the rest, and take all innocent freedoms. Sister, you'll go too, will
> you not? Come, prithee be not sad. We'll outwit twenty brothers,   175
> if you'll be ruled by me. Come, put off this dull humour with your
> clothes, and assume one as gay, and as fantastic, as the dress my
> cousin Valeria and I have provided, and let's ramble.
>
> (*The Rover*, 1, i, 164–78)

The rhythms of Hellena's speech are lively – often indicated by the use
of exclamatory phrases, and questions at the end of sentences, which
engage her companions in her ideas (for example, l. 175). This delivery
is typical of her discourse throughout the play. Equally, she makes
forthright declarative statements, something Florinda does only in
quiet asides. Hellena's declarative statements assert her own views,
rather than reflecting or responding to those of others. Other linguistic
strategies create a sense of the independent woman: her request to go
to the Carnival is not phrased as a question or a plea, but as a negotiation: 'if . . . then . . .' (ll. 168–70). Similarly, her language to her sister
is phrased as a series of hortatory, albeit inclusive, questions and orders
('will you not?', 'come', 'let's', 'put off'). Her register, contrasting with
Florinda's, is expansive and exaggerated ('We'll outwit twenty brothers',
l. 175). All these modes of speech create a character who is self-aware,
active, attractive, witty and who can pull the audience to her side.

The speeches' content is also outspoken: she tells us clearly what she thinks of her brother, and how to manipulate his orders to her own ends; she decries her future career as a nun; and she initiates suggestions for action. She alone comes up with the idea of dressing up and going out during Carnival. She is explicit about their intentions to 'outwit' their brother, constructing herself as an equal to the men in her own plotting. She is always inclusive: including her sister and Callis in her plans, using 'we' rather than 'I'. She describes herself, both here and elsewhere in the play, as 'mad', placing herself on the margins of social acceptability and norms. Finally, she appropriates both the language and actions of the masculine world: 'That which all the world does . . . take all innocent freedoms.' 'Let's **ramble**' deliberately uses the verb that the male rakes of Charles I's court used to describe their sexual perambulations in the fashionable St James's Park. Her plea to exchange clothes and identity for the masks and physical freedom of Carnival identify her embracing of danger, non-conformity, fluidity and self-expression as fundamental aspects of her being. She talks about 'assuming' (l. 177) an identity as a way of defining pleasure and freedom for the individual. She goes on to take on a multiplicity of roles, from loving sister to gypsy and boy, in the rest of the play. This theme, and whether such an assumption is as possible for women as it is for men, is one of the play's key debates.

Let us now turn to our next play, *The Feigned Courtesans*.

* * *

In the following extract, the two women tell us about their reasons for being in disguise as courtesans, and the potential pitfalls confronting them. We first view this conversation from afar through the prism of a short interlude where the two women are watched by the men, commodified and judged as objects of the male erotic gaze and potential possession. Thus visual appearance and physical presence are literally seen to determine female identity in the masculine world.

[Act 2, scene i]

Marcella.   But prithee, mad Cornelia, let's be grave and wise, at   40
least enough to think a little.

Cornelia.   On what? Your English cavalier, Fillamour, of whom you
tell so many dull stories of his making love! Oh, how I hate a civil
whining coxcomb!

Marcella.   And so do I, I'll therefore think of him no more.   45

Cornelia.   Good lord! What a damnable wicked thing is a virgin
grown up to woman.

Marcella.   Why, art thou such a fool to think I love this Fillamour?

Cornelia.   It may be not at Rome, but at Viterbo, where men are
scarce, you did; and did you follow him to Rome, to tell him you   50
could love no more?

Marcella.   A too forward maid, Cornelia, hurts her own fame, and
that of all her sex.

Cornelia.   Her sex! A pretty consideration; by my youth (an oath I
shall not violate this dozen year) my sex should excuse me, if, to   55
preserve their fame, they expected I should ruin my own quiet, in
choosing an ill-favoured husband such as Octavio before a young
handsome lover, such as you say Fillamour is.

Marcella.   I would fain persuade myself to be of thy mind; but the
world, Cornelia!   60

Cornelia.   Hang the malicious world.

Marcella.   And there's such charms in wealth and honour, too!

Cornelia.   None half so powerful as love, in my opinion: 'life, sister,
thou art beautiful, and hast a fortune too, which before I would
lay out upon so shameful a purchase, as such a bedfellow for life   65
as Octavio, I would turn arrant keeping courtesan, and buy my
better fortune.

Marcella.   That word, too, startles me.

Cornelia.   What, courtesan! Why, 'tis a noble title, and has more
votaries than religion; there's no merchandise like ours, that of   70
love, my sister; and can you be frighted with the vizor which you
yourself put on?

Marcella.   'Twas the only disguise that could secure us from the
search of my uncle and Octavio. Our brother Julio is by this too
arrived, and I know they'll all be diligent; and some honour I was   75
content to sacrifice to my eternal repose.

Cornelia.   Spoke like my sister: a little impertinent honour we may

chance to lose, 'tis true; but our right-down honesty, I perceive
you are resolved we shall maintain through all the dangers of love
and gallantry; though, to say truth, I find enough to do to defend   80
my heart against some of those members that nightly serenade us,
and daily show themselves before our window, gay as young
bridegrooms, and as full of expectation.
Marcella.   But is't not wondrous, that amongst all these crowds we
should not once see Fillamour? I thought the charms of a fair   85
young courtesan might have obliged him to some curiosity at least.
Cornelia.   Aye; and an English cavalier too, a nation so fond of all
new faces.
Marcella.   Heaven, if I should never see him, and I frequent all
public places to meet him; ot if he be gone from Rome, if he have   90
forgot me, or some other beauty have employed his thoughts!
Cornelia.   Why, if all these ifs and ors come to pass, we have no
more to do than to advance in this same glorious profession, of
which now we only seem to be; in which, to give it its due, there
are a thousand satisfactions to be found, more than in a dull   95
virtuous life! Oh, the world of dark-lantern men we should have;
the serenades, the songs, the sighs, the vows, the presents, the
quarrels; and all for a look or a smile, which you have been hitherto
so covetous of, that Petro swears our lovers begin to suspect us
for some honest jilts, which by some is accounted much the lewder   100
scandal of the two; therefore I think, faith, we must e'en be kind
a little, to redeem our reputations.
Marcella.   However we may rally, certainly there's nothing so hard
to woman, as to expose herself to villainous man.
Cornelia.   Faith, sister, if 'twere but as easy to satisfy the nice   105
scruples of religion and honour, I should find no great difficulty in
the rest. Besides, another argument I have, our money's all gone,
and without a miracle can hold out no longer honestly.

(*The Feigned Courtesans*, 2, i, 40–108)

The scene's opening sets up a situation which makes us anxious to
understand how the expressed and interior feelings of the two
women match or contrast with the assumptions the men make
about their external appearance. Behn satisfies this immediately in
the initial content of their conversation. Situation and dialogue
thereby complement and build upon each other. Visual prompts for

the audience (they are dressed as gaudy courtesans) create a sense of both playfulness and danger in their characterisation. This is then reflected in their dialogue about the nature of their disguise and its possible consequences if play has to become real.

The two characters are contrasted in both delivery and content. The contrast enables us to visualise them as distinct characters. Cornelia is more outspoken, open to new experiences and carefree (apparently prepared to embrace prostitution if the alternatives are too awful), whilst Marcella is more hesitant and single-mindedly fixed on the purpose of her disguise, which is to find Fillamour. Their oppositional but parallel characterisation is similar to that of Florinda and Hellena in *The Rover*. Marcella produces moralised statements about how women are and should be perceived (for example 'A too forward maid . . . hurts her own fame, and that of all her sex', ll. 52–3), with warnings about what 'the world' will think of their conduct. This caution, and replication of the perceptions and language of the men we have just seen on stage, is contrasted with Cornelia's words. She uses exclamations and oaths to ridicule Marcella's views (l. 54 and l. 61). Marcella is also more conventional in her expression of how marriage should work: she points out the desirability of wealth in marriage, and worries about courtesans' reputation and activities. Cornelia emphasises instead their own economic power (ll. 63–4), and the potentially liberating economic and sexual status a courtesan may achieve (ll. 69–72). Even whilst the latter defence is a witty commonplace among Restoration rakes, from a woman it becomes a potential cry for sexual freedom and autonomy.

Their debate embraces an analysis of what female honour means (some external honour may be lost, but 'right-down honesty', l. 78, can be maintained). Cornelia draws our attention to the fact that 'the nice scruples of religion and honour' (ll. 105–6) construct the rules and prohibitions which constrain female behaviour. Her analytical stance contrasts with Marcella's more self-absorbed reflections about the whereabouts of Fillamour, and about her own status. Cornelia's more philosophical outlook establishes her character as open and adventurous, and demonstrates her ability to voice trenchant criticisms of the social and political status quo. For example, she reminds us of the necessity of economic support for women without a father or husband to support them: without the protection of their domestic families, these two women are dependent on Petro and their jewels. Their final discussion (what then . . . ?) is broken off and unresolved. The audience are unclear whether they will turn to prostitution, or return to their family and their arranged fates. This open-ended closure is an effective way of leaving the problem of female economic autonomy deliberately unresolved.

The debate between the two women, aided by their oppositional characterisation, is crucial to the play's whole dialectic, and directly poses a set of questions. Should women conform to patriarchal models of female conduct, in both deed and word? Does sexual liberation bring about equality for men and women? Should we care about appearances? To what extent can prostitution be an act of self-determination? The scenic juxtaposition between the masculine views at the scene's beginning, and the more complex debate here about the situation in which the men see and judge women, uses structural dramatic techniques to visually illustrate and further question the way in which double standards about gender and sexuality operate.

Their language replicates fields of reference elsewhere in the play. Thus, Cornelia talks about marriage and autonomous sexual conduct as an economic transaction (ll. 64–6, and 70–1). However, she refuses to become an object of exchange in a transaction ordered and organised by others. She proposes taking control of their own merchandise: a truly free market. Equally, the language of disguise and masking is used as a metaphor for autonomy and self-realisation, rather than of vulnerability, as it is for Laura.

There are several key words here, which also appear in *The Rover*, illustrating both character and self-realisation. Marcella calls Cornelia 'mad' (l. 40), a description Hellena applied to herself in the previous extract. This epithet allows Behn to distance herself from Cornelia's radical views whilst simultaneously giving her dramatic space to express them. Her outspoken views, exclamations, oaths and attacks can, if necessary, be labelled as mad. The repetition and discussion of questions of 'honour' raises the theme of the differences and double standards between the world's views of masculine and feminine honour. Finally, the word 'kind' (l. 101) is used to signify the giving of sexual favours (as it is, particularly by Willmore, in *The Rover*). Behn's work uses it punningly, drawing attention to both its contextual meaning, and its original derivation. To men, a 'kind' woman is free and generous with her sexual gifts, but she is also behaving according to 'kind', according to her nature. By punning on its misogynistic derivation, Behn reminds us that sexual behaviour, identity and expectations are all set up from a male perspective. Linguistic use therefore echoes plot, scenic construction, and themes. Let us consider a much more ambiguous heroine: Laura Lucretia.

*   *   *

At the end of Act 3 of *The Feigned Courtesans*, Laura, as La Silvianetta, welcomed Julio into her chamber, believing he was Galliard, with whom she had fallen in love. We do not know Laura's fate, nor her response to discovering that the man she had led to her bedchamber was not Galliard, but the one whom she had been fleeing. Finally, Octavio, her brother, had followed Julio into the house, and just before this speech, Julio exits, pursued by Octavio wielding his sword.

[Act 5, scene i]

> *Laura Lucretia.*   He's gone, he's gone, perhaps for ever gone. –
>   Tell me, thou silly manager of love, how got this ruffian in? How
>   was it possible, without thy knowledge, he could get admittance?
> *Sabina.*   Now, as I hope to live and learn, I know not, madam, unless
>   he followed you when you let in the cavalier, which being by dark,   100
>   he easily concealed himself; no doubt some lover of the
>   Silvianetta's, who mistaking you for her, took him, too, for a rival.
> *Laura Lucretia.*   'Tis likely, and my fortune is to blame,
>   My cursèd fortune, who, like misers, deals
>   Her scanty bounties with so slow a hand,   105
>   That or we die before the blessing falls,
>   Or have it snatched ere we can call it ours.
>   (*Raving*) To have him in my house, to have him kind!

> Kind as young lovers when they meet by stealth;
> As fond as age to beauty, and as soft   110
> As love and wit could make impatient youth,
> Preventing even my wishes and desires;
> Oh Gods, and then, even then, to be defeated,
> Then from my o'erjoyed arms to have him snatched,
> Then, when our vows had made our freedom lawful!   115
> What maid could suffer a surprise so cruel?
> – The day begins to break: go, search the streets,
> And bring me news he's safe, or I am lost.
>
> (*The Feigned Courtesans*, 5, i, 96–118)

Laura's language echoes that of a tragic rather than comic heroine. Like Angellica in *The Rover*, Laura is prepared to have sex, whilst the other women only play with the idea. Their tragic self-presentation, and their exclusion from happiness at the play's closure, may be conservative moral punishments, in conventional comic mode, for any behaviour not conforming to the dominant model of how sexual relationships should work. However, there is an alternative way to read and view this. By placing a tragic register within a comic frame, Behn demands that we listen to these women's voices. We see them marginalised not only by their own desires and attempt to enact them, but by the constraints placed upon them by men's attitudes. Additionally, in each play their views are echoed and paralleled by a successful woman (Hellena and Cornelia respectively), intimating that there should be a space for female sexual autonomy, but that social constraints prevent this.

The rhythm of the spoken verse is extremely regular: most lines are a standard iambic pentameter. There are two exceptions in the 15 lines of her main speech. The first (l. 113) is of 12 beats, and the lengthier line in combination with the repetition of 'even then' suggests an excess of emotion at this point. Equally, the second (l. 115), of 11 beats, places an additional, and again repetitive 'Then' at the beginning of the line. Disruptions to metrical regularity are thereby used emphatically to signal disrupted and disturbed thoughts: the repetitions of 'then' recall their sexual encounter, and break the rhythm of her delivery. The metaphors reveal character: her berating of fortune as a miser (ll. 104–8) posits herself as a passive victim of circumstance, a tragic closure to her active efforts to arrange an assignation with the man she pursues. Her use of the sexualised 'kind' indicates her own sexual knowledge and potential transgression as a woman.

Stage directions here place Laura in a more negative light than the other women in the play: at line 108 she is described as '(*Raving*)', and this appearance of madness is more damning than either Cornelia's or Hellena's madness, which are represented as high spirits. Female transgression and madness are displaced onto the near-tragic figure who is partially punished by the play's closure. By appearing to rant and rave, Laura may begin to lose an audience's sympathies.

Finally, the content is also critical in at least two ways. First, we learn that she still does not know the true identity of the man she slept with, and this both raises the tension, and postpones the final denouement and her own personal tragedy. Secondly, Laura makes it clear to the audience that 'vows' made their coupling 'lawful' (l. 115), and this later turns out to be doubly true, when it is revealed it was her betrothed, not Galliard. Let us now move on to consider the final play, *The Lucky Chance*.

*   *   *

This intimate scene takes place in Lady Fulbank's antechamber, and opens six lines earlier than this extract with her sitting at her mirror. Sir Cautious demands his marital rights, which, from their conversation, is evidently unusual. A frank conversation follows about their sexual relationship.

[Act 5, scene iv]

> *Sir Cautious.* . . . But I think 'tis all one to thee, thou car'st not for my compliment; no, thou'dst rather have a young fellow.
> *Lady Fulbank.* I am not used to flatter much; if forty years were taken from your age, 'twould render you something more agreeable   10 to my bed, I must confess.
> *Sir Cautious.* Aye, aye, no doubt on't.
> *Lady Fulbank.* Yet you may take my word without an oath: were you as old as time, and I were young and gay as April flowers,

which all are fond to gather,   15
          My beauties all should wither in the shade,
          Ere I'd be worn in a dishonest bosom.
Sir Cautious.   Aye, but you're wondrous free, methinks, sometimes,
    which gives shrewd suspicions.
Lady Fulbank.   What, because I cannot simper, look demure, and   20
    justify my honour when none questions it?
          Cry 'fie', and 'out upon the naughty women',
          Because they please themselves? – and so would I.
Sir Cautious.   How, would; what, cuckold me?
Lady Fulbank.   Yes, if it pleased me better than virtue, sir.   25
          But I'll not change my freedom and my humour,
          To purchase the dull fame of being honest.
Sir Cautious.   Aye, but the world, the world –
Lady Fulbank.   I value not the censures of the crowd.
Sir Cautious.   But I am old.   30
Lady Fulbank.   That's your fault, sir, not mine.
Sir Cautious.   But being so, if I should be good-natured, and give
    thee leave to love discreetly – ?
Lady Fulbank.   I'd do't without your leave, sir.
Sir Cautious.   Do't: what, cuckold me?   35
Lady Fulbank.   No; love discreetly, sir, love as I ought, love
    honestly.
Sir Cautious.   What, in love with anybody but your own husband?
Lady Fulbank.   Yes.
Sir Cautious.   Yes, quotha: is that your loving as you ought?   40
Lady Fulbank.   We cannot help our inclinations, sir,
          No more than time or light from coming on;
          But I can keep my virtue, sir, entire.
                                        (*The Lucky Chance*, 5, iv, 7–43)

The situation here is doubly ironic: the audience know that Sir
Cautious has already wagered and lost his wife for this night to
Gayman, but he insists on pretending to her that he is going to sleep
with her. Secondly, despite his own betrayal he is quick to read
betrayal in his wife's words. His double standards are blatantly displayed through both situation and dialogue. Thus, he presents his
wife with several tests of her fidelity: first suggesting she would
rather have a younger husband (ll. 7–8); secondly, that her behav-

iour is 'wondrous free', resulting in suspicions (ll. 18–19); thirdly, a direct question as to whether she would cuckold him (l. 24); and fourthly, a suggestion that he might allow her to 'love discreetly' (l. 36), that is, to have an affair to which he turned a blind eye. In each case Lady Fulbank's answer is both unconventional and illustrative of her character. Her responses also raise tension in the audience about the forthcoming discovery. Let us then look at Julia's responses and the way in which her character is revealed by this extract.

One of the main characteristics evident here is her honesty: rather than flattering her husband about his age and sexual performance, she acknowledges that a younger man would be 'more agreeable' (l. 10). Such honesty and self-knowledge (she claims she cannot flatter) is welcome and unusual in this play, where game-playing, disguise and deceit dominate action and character. Yet Julia goes on to swear that despite her theoretical preference, she is not going to compromise her sexual honesty ('My beauties all should wither in the shade, / Ere I'd be worn in a dishonest bosom,' ll. 16–17). Verbal and sexual honesty mark her character.

She links honesty with a refusal to play social games or conform to behavioural models imposed by the world ('I cannot simper, look demure', l. 20; and 'I value not the censures of the crowd', l. 29). This argument confuses her husband, who believes she means she would have an affair after all. His misapprehensions about her meaning run through this extract. For example, when she says she would please herself, he stutters, 'How, would; what, cuckold me?' But by pleasing, she means she would have freedom of choice according to her own sense of what is right: and at the moment she chooses virtue (l. 25). When she claims she can love whomsoever she wants, he again assumes this means sexual betrayal, whilst she claims she can love at a distance, and remain virtuous. Here Behn gives her characters oppositional understanding of the same situation, suggesting incommensurable masculine and feminine interpretations of both language and the world. Lady Fulbank's assertion of an independent will and desires, albeit ones of virtue, confuses her husband, and later Gayman, but makes her autonomy and maturity attractive to the audience. It contrasts with Leticia's greater passivity and lesser self-knowledge, and with conduct strictures of the period which expected wives to be obedient and subservient to their husband and to social convention.

Self-knowledge marks her character, descriptive expressions about herself abound: she does not flatter, she won't be worn by a dishonest bosom (owned by another man), she wishes to please herself, she will not change her 'freedom and . . . humour' (l. 26) to suit other people or for appearances' sake, and she will love whom she pleases if her husband is unloveable, but will 'keep my virtue . . . entire' (l. 43). Despite her husband's apparently tempting offer that she can love 'discreetly', she does not compromise this set of ethical values. She knows her own mind, and it does not change under pressure or force of circumstances.

Despite the questions posed by Sir Cautious, and the fact that she is seated at the mirror and '*undressed*', with her husband moving around the stage and standing above her, she dominates both linguistically and physically. Her responses catch him unawares (his stuttering replies), as do her arguments about pleasure and virtue. The stage prop of the mirror helps the audience see both her face and her back or side, and acts as a metaphor for the self-knowledge which marks her character, and not one of vanity, as is more conventional.

The metaphors she uses to describe herself and her values all come from the natural world ('young and gay as April flowers', l. 14; and 'we cannot help our inclinations . . . / No more than time or light from coming on,' ll. 41–2), whilst figurative language applied to social conventions uses images from the market-place ('**purchase** the dull fame of being honest, l. 27). The language of natural imagery to describe and denote conduct was typical of Restoration rakes and libertines: but Julia applies the same language slightly differently. She defends freedom of choice, but allies it with the path of virtue. Thus she both appropriates and transforms libertine ideology to an ideology of female virtuous independence and free-thinking. She acts as a convincing critique of two types of masculinity: the libertine, and the married husband whose double standards are explicitly laid bare here. Finally, she often delivers her words in blank verse: intimating an elevated social position in comparison with her husband.

* * *

Let us now turn to our other heroine. This scene opens on the margins of the wedding celebrations of Sir Feeble and Leticia. From this small 'melancholy' (l. 2) room to which Leticia has retreated, we can hear music, dance and feasting from the garden.

[Act 2, scene ii]

> *Sir Feeble's house*
>
> *Enter Leticia, pursued by Phillis . . .*
> Leticia.   Tell him I wish him luck in everything,
>   But in his love to me.
>   Go, tell him I am viewing of the garden.   10
>   *Exit Phillis. Enter Belmour at a distance behind* [*Leticia*].
>   Blessed be this kind retreat, this 'lone occasion
>   That lends a short cessation to my torments,
>   And gives me leave to vent my sighs and tears! (*Weeps.*)
> Belmour. [*Aside*]   And doubly blessed be all the power of love,
>   That gives me this dear opportunity.   15
> Leticia.   Where were you, all ye pitying gods of love,
>   That once seemed pleased at Belmour's flame and mine,
>   And smiling joined our hearts, our sacred vows,
>   And spread your wings and held your torches high?
> Belmour.   Oh!   20
>   [*Leticia*] *starts* [*and*] *pauses.*
> Leticia.   Where were you now, when this unequal marriage,
>   Gave me from all my joys, gave me from Belmour?
>   Your wings were flagged, your torches bent to earth,
>   And all your little bonnets veiled your eyes.
>   You saw not, or were deaf and pitiless.   25
>   (*The Lucky Chance*, 2, ii, 8–25)

This is one of the few scenes where Leticia speaks her feelings and views: and she does so because she believes she is alone. The device of Belmour eavesdropping enables her solitary distress to be incorporated into the plot's action. Both characters speak in iambic verse, most of which contains standard 10-beat lines. This elevates their courtship and emotions to a poetic plane uninhabited by the play's other characters, and makes it appear to be one belonging to a chivalric lost past, partially distancing their love from the audience. The tragic potential in their situation is also enhanced by the poetic delivery.

The content is equally poetic: she addresses the gods of love, in an extended personification in conventional lyrical terms (ll. 16–19), as so many cupids (they have wings), whose torches first celebrated her betrothal to Belmour, but failed to defend her against 'this unequal marriage' (l. 21). Such conventional imagery gives us little intimate insight into her character, although it suggests her unhappiness, youth, powerlessness, and love for Belmour. Despite a conventional use of love imagery, and her apparently passive unhappiness (l. 13), she explicitly opposes Sir Feeble in the message sent back with Phillis: 'Tell him I wish him luck in everything, / But in his love to me' (ll. 8–9). Through this message we gain a sense of a core strength which explains her loyalty to Belmour.

The staging of Leticia's retreat from the party deepens our understanding of her character. We can hear what she is escaping from (we can still hear the noise), and anticipate Belmour's intervention both in this scene and in the wider plot. The extract literally stages, from a side room in the house, a critical viewpoint on the festive wedding and strengthens the potentially tragic thread in the plot. This play typically uses spaces which are not part of the main house or the main action to suggest women's perspectives on that main action, from which their desires are often excluded. Later in the play such spaces enable women to rebel by using the very liminality of their position: the short scene where Diana and Pert exchange clothes amidst the discoveries of Act 5, is a good example. Space and place are used symbolically by Behn to intimate both entrapment and potential freedom.

These 15 lines are perhaps the only point in the play where, when Leticia speaks, it is as a soliloquy rather than dialogue, albeit interrupted by Belmour's asides to the audience. Nevertheless, her overall character is still seen to be defined by and dependent on Belmour, and against Sir Feeble. Her weeping, whilst understandable in the circumstances, further emphasises her powerlessness. Belmour's presence on stage underlines the fact that only a man can rescue her. Thus the poetic quality of her delivery, language and metaphors come across as an ineffective response to a forced marriage. We can contrast Lady Fulbank's actions and language in response to her own forced marriage, both in the extract examined above, and in some of the suggested work at the end of this chapter.

Conclusions

1. Behn constructs a variety of female characters, for contrast and comparison and to enable the audience to make judgements about possible courses of action from similar scenarios. In each play there are three main female characters (although Diana in *The Lucky Chance* plays a far more minor part than the third characters in the other two plays). Each of these three characters, and their actions in the plot, set up slightly different questions about, and answers to, gender, sexuality, identity and marriage. The audience must decide which responses are viable.

2. Behn often uses a courtesan, or a feigned courtesan, to crystallise and focus debates about female sexuality. Through their characterisation and function within the narrative, she asks key questions about sexuality and economics, sexuality and self-determination, and the relationship between sexuality and freedom. There are no easy answers to these questions in her plays: her heroines all get married at the end, thereby conforming to both comic and social convention. But the presence of the courtesan figures, and their parallel with one of the soon-to-be-married women, force the audience to consider their arguments and situation as universal rather than particular. The courtesan is a useful dramatic device for Behn, because she is clearly outside the play's final social norms and conventions, yet the disruptive ideas represented by her views still resonate at the end.

3. Characterisation is established through action, dialogue, opposition and paralleling with other characters, and the use of conventional situations and language contrasted to unconventional ones (for example, the two different scenes we have just analysed from

The Lucky Chance). Soliloquies are rarely used to display a character's inner life and thoughts.

4. Comic action is often as dependent upon female action and decisions, as upon male action: for example, the extracts from *The Rover* and *The Feigned Courtesans*. Female passivity is often seen to be the victim of male aggression, or masculine assumptions.

5. Sexual identity is discussed with a great deal of frankness by the women characters. It is displayed as a social and political construction: both Hellena in *The Rover* and Cornelia in *The Lucky Chance* discuss alternative sexual identities than those of virgin (as nuns) or wife. Additionally, they both argue explicitly that social and religious convention determines views about femininity, and that such views can, and should, be challenged. Virtue and whoredom are shown to be constructed and mis-constructed by men's views of outward appearances. By displaying male views of virtue as simply a set of beliefs dependent on circumstances (for example, through the Florinda episode), Behn asks questions about both the value of such views and their eventual power.

6. Sexual desire is both expressed and determined by women characters: they pursue men and give voice to their desires in words and action. Such desire informs the direction of the plot. However, in the cases of Angellica and Laura their ability to choose their own destiny is mocked by the lack of comic closure for their desires.

7. By making identity and character so explicitly political, verbal and social, Behn emphatically places her comedies within the social world. She does not engage in intrigue or fantastical comedy: not only do her characters refuse to retreat from the world, but her audiences are not allowed to either. She sets up debates and questions which have validity for her audience.

8. Identity is seen to be constructed and therefore also something which can be 'assumed' as a role.

9. Spaces in which women speak are often domestic or liminal: rooms inside, bedchambers, retreats, balconies. Where women do act and speak outdoors, they are threatened by men, or seen as prostitutes. Behn uses space and place to signal how social codes

of behaviour work, how women are expected to respond to them, and what happens to women who do not acknowledge them. Some women use the secrecy of domestic space as a means for self-liberation.

Methods of Analysis

We have combined contextual with linguistic and dramatic analysis. When examining a speech or dialogue for character you should remember:

1. Look first at the internal rhythms and shifts of meaning, and then at how these may contrast with those of other speakers in the dialogue. Are there any pauses in rhythm? Why?
2. Always contextualise speech: Why is this being spoken here and now? Is it a rational or irrational response? Where is it happening? Where is the character on stage? How are the audience positioned by the speech and by the characters on stage? What is the significance of this when we judge the character?
3. Does this particular speech change our views of this particular character? Does it conform to or differ from previous and subsequent appearances? In what ways does it develop our insights? Does it make links to other speeches or key words spoken by this character, or other characters? What is the effect of such links?
4. What lies behind the character's words? Do we understand and empathise with them, or are we asked to retain a critical distance?

Suggested Work

Using the above ways of looking at speeches, choose speeches by some of the main characters, and consider how these reinforce or contradict the conclusions about the main characters. Some good passages to look at are:

• Laura's opening speech at 1, i, 5–20 in *The Feigned Courtesans*;

- Marcella's disguised assignation as a courtesan with Fillamour in *The Feigned Courtesans* (4, i, 1–130), and Cornelia's as La Silvianetta with Galliard in the subsequent scene (4, ii, 47–213);
- Angellica's first private dialogue with Willmore (2, ii, 52–155) and her fears on his departure (4, ii, 396–411) in *The Rover*;
- Florinda, Hellena and Valeria's conversation at 3, i, 1–70 in *The Rover*, under Angellica's balcony;
- Hellena's and Willmore's negotiation of the terms of their relationship and sexual congress (5, i, 400–89);
- The function and language of Leticia's asides in Act 1, scene iii of *The Lucky Chance*, and Lady Fulbank's contributions to the debate from 2, ii, 110–38;
- Lady Fulbank's divorce from her husband (5, vii, 56–76).

- How many scenes do each of the main women characters appear in? To what extent is the action of those scenes, and subsequent actions, determined by them?
- Look at the heroines dressing as boys: Hellena in *The Rover* (Act 4, scene ii) and Laura, Cornelia and Marcella in *The Feigned Courtesans* (Act 3, scene i; Act 5, scenes i and vii). Does cross-dressing reveal more about their characters? Does it enable their desires to be resolved? Does it affect our views about female sexuality?
- The third female character in *The Lucky Chance*, Diana, has a minor role, but it is still instructive to consider her. Look at 4, i, 245–66 and how her characterisation complements the other women.
- The landlady character in *The Lucky Chance* (particularly in Act 2, scene i) is a bawdy and lower-class contrast to the other women. What effect does she have on our judgement about gender and sexuality? Why is she made to be so comically repulsive? Lucetta has a key role in *The Rover* (Act 3, scenes ii and iii). Why is she characterised as a rapacious prostitute? What redeeming characteristics and function does she have? With whom and why is she contrasted in the play?

5

Rakes and Gallants

One of the best-known characters in Restoration theatre is the rake hero, and Behn's heroes share many typical rake characteristics. They are self-conscious libertines, self-interested, witty and sexy. Nevertheless, Behn uses this hero in a distinctive manner that sets her apart from many of her contemporaries: she objectifies these men through plotting, characterisation, the success of the heroine-tricksters, and the strategic employment of the courtesans' characterisation.

* * *

Our first example is from *The Rover*.

[Act 4, scene i]

A fine room

> *Discovers Belvile as by dark, alone.*

Belvile. When shall I be weary of railing on fortune, who is resolved never to turn with smiles upon me? Two such defeats in one night none but the devil, and that mad rogue, could have contrived to have plagued me with. I am here a prisoner, but where, heaven knows; and if there be murder done, I can soon decide the fate of   5
a stranger in a nation without mercy; yet this is nothing to the torture my soul bows with, when I think of losing my fair, my dear Florinda. Hark, my door opens: a light; a man, and seems of quality; armed, too! Now shall I die like a dog, without defence.

> *Enter Antonio in a night-gown, with a light; his arm in a scarf,*
> *and a sword under his arm. He sets the candle on the table.*

Antonio.   Sir, I come to know what injuries I have done you, that   10
could provoke you to so mean an action as to attack me basely,
without allowing time for my defence.

Belvile.   Sir, for a man in my circumstances to plead innocence,
would look like fear: but view me well, and you will find no marks
of coward on me, nor anything that betrays that brutality you   15
accuse me with.

Antonio.   In vain, sir, you impose upon my sense. You are not only
he who drew on me last night, but yesterday before the same
house, that of Angellica.

> Yet there is something in your face and mien   20
> That makes me wish I were mistaken.

Belvile.   I own I fought today, in the defence of a friend of mine, with
whom you (if you're the same) and your party were first engaged.

> Perhaps you think this crime enough to kill me,
> But if you do, I cannot fear you'll do it basely.   25

Antonio.   No, sir, I'll make you fit for a defence with this.
   [*Antonio*] *gives* [*Belvile*] *the sword.*

Belvile.   This gallantry surprises me; nor know I how to use this
present, sir, against a man so brave.

Antonio.   You shall not need; for know, I come to snatch you from
a danger that is decreed against you: perhaps your life, or long   30
imprisonment; and 'twas with so much courage you offended, I
cannot see you punished.

Belvile.   How shall I pay this generosity?

Antonio.   It had been safer to have killed another, than have
attempted me. To show your danger, sir, I'll let you know my   35
quality: and 'tis the viceroy's son, whom you have wounded.

Belvile.   The viceroy's son!

> (*Aside*) Death and confusion! was this plague reserved
> To complete all the rest? Obliged by him!
> The man of all the world I would destroy.   40

                                        (*The Rover*, 4, i, 1–40)

This scene follows two action-packed sequences. In Act 3, scene v,
Florinda, awaiting Belvile in the garden, is accosted by a drunken
Willmore, who, mistaking her for a courtesan, attempts to make
love to her. Despite Belvile's arrival, she flees, because she hears her

brother. In the subsequent scene, Willmore, entering Angellica's house, finds a masked man doing the same, and assaults him and his men with swords. Belvile assists Willmore and on the arrival of the city soldiers, is seized for wounding the masked man.

What does this extract tell us about Belvile's character? Combined with the cumulative narrative of the previous scenes, we see Belvile (like Florinda) as a victim of a series of accidental events, precipitated in each case by Willmore's carelessness and impulsive temper. Although Belvile curses 'fortune' (l. 1), the audience have seen his lack of fortune to be directly attributable to Willmore's behaviour. Despite the dramatic device of the reflective soliloquy here, Belvile's introspection is not critically analytical, although he calls Willmore 'that mad rogue', and likens him to the devil (l. 3). Behn often uses two contrasting gallant figures: one a rake, one more moderate. Throughout the play, debates between Willmore and Belvile emphasise this point, Belvile as the courtly gallant, Willmore as a boorish, drunken wit. Yet parallels are also continually made between the two characters (for example, the masquerade scenes in Act 2). This combined contrasting and paralleling enables the audience to consider what courtly gallantry and witty libertinism have in common. We never see Belvile treating Florinda as Willmore treats all women. But Belvile views courtesans as commodities.

However, here we meet Belvile the ideal courtly gallant. Despite his imprisonment, and his bewailing of fate whilst alone on stage, once Antonio enters, he assumes the language and self-possession of a gentleman, and there is a noticeable change in his language. In the first nine lines, he bewails fate, rues his friend, and is frank about his feelings for Florinda. The soliloquy offers the audience a glance into his private thoughts, which are contrasted with his public persona, through the change in the mode of delivery after line 9. The scene's structure, the situation, and the language therefore neatly epitomise the dual nature of identity, and the particularities of Belvile's own character.

In dialogue, both characters use the register of polite society: each addresses the other as 'sir', and the grammatical structures are correct and formal (for example, 'You are not only he who drew on me last night, but . . .', ll. 17–18). This register is supplemented by Antonio's claim that he recognises 'something in your face and mien' (l. 20) which he shares: and this is the mutual acknowledgement of gentlemanly status. Belvile's account of his actions reinforces his status as a man adhering to the gentleman's code of honour: he was fighting on behalf of a friend. Antonio equally behaves according to this code: he commends Belvile's courage, and offers therefore to waive punishment. Courage, gallantry, and a masculine code of honour are represented, both defining character and enabling men to find a common language and shared identity which then determine their actions. Yet the scene also sets divergent views of this gallantry before the audience, using Belvile's character and what we know him to be.

What are these divergent views? First, as we have seen, Belvile is presented to us alone, angry and to some extent frightened about his fate, grieving his loss of Florinda. We view the apparently private man. These are supposedly his 'true' feelings, which are contrasted with both the language and content of his public presentation to Antonio. This contrast asks the audience to see the constructedness of social identity, an important theme of the whole play. Secondly, the polite register marking the exchanges of the two men is rapidly exposed as simply an artifice. Once Antonio reveals his identity, Belvile returns to the revelatory mode and content of the opening of the scene, speaking in an aside to the audience (ll. 38–40), and cursing fortune once again. Gallantry is thus exposed both as a sham, and as an ineffective mode of achieving results. The only way in which Belvile can win Florinda is through trickery, of both Antonio and Pedro, as to his identity. Deception, rather than codes of honour and gallantry, produces successful sexual conquest and comic closure.

This scene shows us that masculine codes of honour and mutual politeness are crucial external markers of social conduct, but that they belie actual masculine behaviour and conduct. Both characterisation and scenic structure show such gallantry to be out-moded, ineffective, and always linked to an underlying self-interest. Let us now consider a second extract from *The Rover*.

* * *

[Act 2, scene ii]

Willmore. [*Offering money to Moretta*] Here, good forewoman of the
shop, serve me, and I'll be gone.   30
Moretta. Keep it to pay your laundress (your linen stinks of the gun
room), for here's no selling by retail.
Willmore. Thou hast sold plenty of thy stale ware at a cheap rate.
Moretta. Aye, the more silly kind heart I, but this is an age wherein
beauty is at higher rates. In fine, you know the price of this.   35
Willmore. I grant you 'tis here set down, a thousand crowns a
month: pray, how much may come to my share for a pistole?
Bawd, take your black lead and sum it up, that I may have a
pistole's worth of this vain gay thing, and I'll trouble you no more.
Moretta. [*Aside*] Pox on him, he'll fret me to death. – Abominable   40
fellow, I tell thee, we only sell by the whole piece.
Willmore. 'Tis very hard, the whole cargo or nothing. [*To Angellica*]
Faith, madam, my stock will not reach it, I cannot be your
chapman. Yet I have countrymen in town, merchants of love like
me: I'll see if they'll put in for a share; we cannot lose much by it, 45
and what we have no use for, we'll sell upon the Friday's mart, at
'Who gives more?' I am studying, madam, how to purchase you,
though at present I am unprovided of money.
Angellica. [*Aside*] Sure, this from any other man would anger me;
nor shall he know the conquest he has made. [*To Willmore*] Poor   50
angry man, how I despise this railing.
Willmore. Yes, I am poor; but I'm a gentleman,
And one that scorns this baseness which you practise.
Poor as I am, I would not sell myself,
No, not to gain your charming high-prized person.   55
Though I admire you strangely for your beauty
Yet I contemn your mind.
And yet I would at any rate enjoy you,
At your own rate, but cannot: see here
The only sum I can command on earth;   60
I know not where to eat when this is gone.
Yet such a slave I am to love and beauty,
This last reserve I'll sacrifice to enjoy you.
Nay, do not frown, I know you're to be bought,
And would be bought by me, by me,   65
For a mean trifling sum, if I could pay it down:

Which happy knowledge I will still repeat,
And lay it to my heart; it has a virtue in't,
And soon will cure those wounds your eyes have made.
And yet, there's something so divinely powerful there –   70
Nay, I will gaze, to let you see my strength.
Holds her, looks on her, and pauses and sighs.
By heaven, bright creature, I would not for the world
Thy fame were half so fair as is thy face.

(*The Rover*, 2, ii, 29–73)

This is one of the play's central scenes. Willmore has entered Angellica's chamber at the end of the previous scene, having fought off Antonio for the first time, and pulled down and kept a picture of her. This exchange displays his consummate linguistic and performative skills. His aim is to find a woman willing to go to bed, with no financial or marital obligations. The manner in which he achieves this is an admirable theatrical coup. He uses three strategies in this extract: he combines a ridiculing of the economics of Angellica's system (charging by the month) with a self-presentation as a poor, honest and honourable gentleman, and an assertion of the language of true love.

Let us look at each of these strategies in turn. From his opening statement, and in his treatment of Moretta, Willmore implies a disdain for, and critique of, the introduction of economics into sex ('Here, good forewoman of the shop'). We know this is a strategic performance to achieve his ends, so we view this as pure self-interest. Yet, his delivery is witty and amusing. He uses a conventional rhetorical device of *reductio ad absurdam*, the pursuing and reducing of one element of an argument to an absurd literalism: he ought to be able to possess Angellica for the number of minutes that a pistole can purchase, relative to her price of a thousand crowns for a month. Or, he could form a limited company to buy shares in her. By anatomising Angellica as a commodity and exposing the method as a logical costing and pricing market, Willmore effectively belittles Angellica. By reducing her supposedly high status as a courtly courtesan to the price and economics of a prostitute on the streets, he also implicitly calls on her to reject this characterisation. This is a clever, witty and underhand strategy, appealing to her vanity and self-respect, whilst simultaneously presenting himself as an honest, poor gentleman who believes that love should not be subject to economics. This is partly achieved by the *reductio ad absurdam*, but also by his disdainful tone, which needles Angellica into the response he has engineered.

This first strategy occupies the first 20 lines of this extract, punctuated by Angellica's aside to the audience, underlining her capitulation. However, because we are not so deceived, this raises dramatic tension. Willmore's second strategic rhetoric is his speech from line 52, and in verse. Although the rhythm is not regular, it is mainly in iambic pentameters, with a silent syllable at the end of the line. The sudden assumption of verse-speaking by Willmore tells the audience that this is an additional role he is playing: that of the poor humble gentleman (evident in the speech's content). The change in delivery enables us further to see him as manipulative, however much we may objectively admire his strategy. In this delivery, he contrasts the ethos of the gentleman (who disdains to sell himself) with that of the courtesan. Yet we already know that he is ready to marry for money, and the combination of economic and sexual needs drives his actions throughout the play. Our knowledge is an important and controlled background to this scene: Behn ensures that we are critical of Willmore's character.

His third strategy is to move into devotional language. The supposed confession of his devotion is enhanced by his manner and delivery: he introduces this stage with an 'And yet . . .' (l. 70), implying that he cannot help himself, despite his disdain for her status. By combining this linguistic shift with an exaggerated praise for her person and beauty ('something so divinely powerful'), and his own submission to this ('I will gaze'), he insinuates that love has overwhelmed him. This is reinforced by physical movements, described by the stage directions ('*Holds her, looks on her, and . . . sighs*'). The exaggerated enactment of unrequited desire again tells the audience that Willmore is acting: but Angellica submits to the act. The perceptual gap – between the audience's ability and Angellica's inability to see Willmore as a cad – is a crucial dramatic and narrative ploy. By playing on this gap, Behn enables us to criticise Willmore's ethics and values, whilst nevertheless admiring them.

We also sympathise with Angellica: we see her as an individual rather than as a function. The courtesan is thus presented as a victim of masculine ideology, as much as a manipulator of it.

Moretta's role here is crucial in guiding the audience: she does not trust Willmore, and her warnings make our views explicit on stage, reinforcing them through the only uninvolved character. Such commentator characters are used by dramatists to reinforce an analytical and critical view of action and plot, and as a means of enabling the audience to form a judgement.

* * *

Let us now consider the gallants of *The Feigned Courtesans*.

[Act 4, scene i]

Fillamour.	No, I would sacrifice a nobler fortune,	
	To buy thy virtue home.	85
Marcella.	What should it idling there?	
Fillamour.	Why, make thee constant to some happy man,	
	That would adore thee for't.	
Marcella.	Unconscionable! Constant at my years?	
	Oh, 'twere to cheat a thousand,	90
	Who, between this and my dull age of constancy,	
	Expect the distribution of my beauty.	
Galliard. (*Aside*)	'Tis a brave wench.	
Fillamour.	Yet charming as thou art, the time will come	
	When all that beauty, like declining flowers,	95
	Will wither on the stalk; but with this difference –	
	The next kind spring brings youth to flowers again,	
	But faded beauty never more can bloom.	
	If interest make thee wicked, I can supply thy pride.	
Marcella.	Curse on your necessary trash, which I despise, but as	100
	'tis useful to advance our love.	
Fillamour.	Is love thy business: who is there born so high,	
	But love and beauty equals?	
	And thou mayst choose from all the wishing world.	
	This wealth together would enrich one man,	105
	Which dealt to all would scarce be charity.	

Marcella.	Together? 'Tis a mass would ransom kings!
	Was all this beauty given for one poor petty conquest?
	I might have made a hundred hearts my slaves,
	In this lost time of bringing one to reason. 110
	Farewell, thou dull philosopher in love;
	When age has made me wise, I'll send for you again.
	[*Marcella*] *offers to go; Galliard holds her.*
Galliard.	By this good light, a noble glorious whore!
Fillamour.	Oh, stay.
	[*Aside*] I must not let such beauty fall: a whore! 115
	[*To Marcella*] Consider yet the charms of reputation;
	The ease, the quiet and content of innocence;
	The awful reverence all good men will pay thee,
	Who as thou art, will gaze without respect,
	And cry 'what pity 'tis she is – a whore'. 120
Marcella.	Oh, you may give it what coarse name you please;
	But all this youth and beauty ne'er was given,
	Like gold to misers, to be kept from use.
	Exit Marcella.
Fillamour.	Lost, lost, past all redemption.

(*The Feigned Courtesans*, 4, i, 84–124)

This scene takes place in what is supposed to be La Silvianetta's apartment. Marcella, having convinced Fillamour that she is the courtesan Euphemia, is testing his love for her by tempting him. It is night time, and Marcella is '*richly and loosely dressed*' (l. 13). The scene and setting are a conventional dramatic device, the disguise trick in which a lover tests the commitment and love of their beloved through illicit sexual temptation. Here the woman is the active partner, Fillamour presented as the relatively passive male who follows but does not quite succumb to his lust.

What does this extract tell us about Fillamour's character? Although tempted by 'Euphemia's' beauty, he remains true to the principles he avowed in Act 1: that virtue should dominate erotic relationships. He offers her money to prevent 'Euphemia' having to sell her body, showing himself to be both generous and foolhardy, but nearly tempted by her offers. Masculine desire is represented as a fusion and conflict of desire for the forbidden and the sanctioned.

Language and semantic register reflect his philosophic outlook:

for example, 'sacrifice' (l. 84), 'innocence' (l. 117), and 'awful rever-ence' (l. 118) construct women as precious objects of adoration. This sacred language markedly contrasts with both 'Euphemia's' arguments and Galliard's known views. 'Euphemia' deliberately opposes his language with the secular language of business, in a strategic attempt to elicit his views. To his argument that virtue should remain at home, she uses the conventional arguments of the libertine: beauty should be put to use rather than 'idling' (l. 86); constancy is a virtue for the old; and beauty should be distributed (l. 92) for all to admire. Such ideas belong to Galliard, and his presence ('Tis a brave wench') reminds us that, unlike him, she is playing a game. This scene echoes the first scene where Galliard and Fillamour discuss these very issues: here that debate is transposed to one between a man and woman, and inverted, in that 'Euphemia' speaks the masculine argument.

For example, Fillamour inverts the imagery often used by the lib-ertine to persuade a woman to have sex: that her beauty will soon fade and wither. By contrast Fillamour uses this image (ll. 94–9) to suggest that virtuous beauty will bloom continuously. When this fails to persuade, he moves to claiming that money can buy her status, and a good marriage. Yet, by using economic arguments, he effectively capitulates to her linguistic and philosophic register, reducing his more philosophic arguments about iconic women and virtuous sexuality to the language of the market-place.

'Euphemia' effectively acknowledges this in her response (ll. 107–12), returning to the discourse of the market-place, and inverting his argument: one purchase in return for her beauty is a poor exchange, when she may have a hundred; beauty is like gold, to be used. Fillamour's virtuous arguments seem rather pedestrian, compared with the wit of the libertine's. Having failed in mar-shalling anti-libertine and economic arguments, Fillamour returns explicitly to the language of morality: a good reputation will bring reverence, whilst 'as thou art' will bring shame. His moral argument ends the exchange (Marcella exits here), and Fillamour sees her as 'Lost, lost, past all redemption', (l. 124).

Much of this exchange takes place in verse, suggesting that this couple are the idealised pair, by contrast to Galliard and Cornelia who mainly speak in prose except where Behn wants to draw our attention to falsity through an erotic poetic register (which we shall see below). The archaic verse gives Fillamour's views and arguments an archaic air amidst the play's more urban and urbane sexual environment.

This extract therefore plays out in argument, character, and physical movement, the stages of erotic temptation faced by Fillamour, and his decision to reject such temptation. The scene is paradigmatic of his character and actions throughout the play. He remains virtuous, committed in practice and theory to his principles, split and tempted, but finally true to Marcella.

Nevertheless, 'Euphemia's' arguments and presence on stage are far more lively than his, a view reinforced both by the comments made by 'Euphemia' and Galliard, and by the moralised language Fillamour himself uses. 'Euphemia' calls him a 'dull philosopher' (l. 111) and (indirectly) a 'miser'. Galliard's asides, which link his views directly with ours, are complimentary exclamations (ll. 93, 113) about her. Fillamour's moralised language sits uncomfortably with our own sympathies with the more libertine characters. We may applaud his constancy: but we find Galliard's wit more amusing. Let us now turn to look at his character.

*   *   *

[Act 3, scene i]

> *Galliard.* And have you no kind message to send to my heart?
>   Cannot this good example instruct you how to make me happy?
> *Cornelia.* Faith, stranger, I must consider first; she's skilful in the   185
>   merchandise of hearts, and has dealt in love with so good success
>   hitherto, she may lose one venture, and never miss it in her stock;
>   but this is my first, and should it prove to be a bad bargain, I were
>   undone for ever.
> *Galliard.* I dare secure the goods sound –   190
> *Cornelia.* And I believe will not lie long upon my hands.
> *Galliard.* Faith, that's according as you'll dispose on't, madam: for
>   let me tell you, gad, a good handsome proper fellow is as staple a
>   commodity as any's in the nation; but I would be reserved for your

own use! Faith, take a sample tonight, and as you like it, the whole   195
piece, and that's fair and honest dealing I think, or the devil's
in't.

Cornelia.   Ah, stranger, you have been so over-liberal of those same
samples of yours, that I doubt they have spoiled the sale of the
rest. Could you not afford, think ye, to throw in a little love and   200
constancy, to inch out that want of honesty of yours?

Galliard.   Love? Oh, in abundance!
            By those dear eyes, by that soft smiling mouth,
            By every secret grace thou hast about thee,
            I love thee with a vigorous, eager passion;   205
            Be kind, dear Silvianetta, prithee do,
            Say you believe, and make me blest tonight!

(*The Feigned Courtesans*, 3, i, 183–207)

This short encounter between Cornelia as La Silvianetta and
Galliard, with her aloft in a balcony, and him below in the street
(stage directions, ll. 166, 215), is stage-managed by the woman,
although her intentions differ from Marcella's in the previous
extract. Cornelia is trying to tempt Galliard through the promise of
sex, but later to inveigle him to marriage. She deliberately displays
herself as a courtesan to the view of the street to tempt him to an
assignation.

Galliard's language and self-presentation are responsive to the cues
she gives him: emphasising his chameleon nature, able to shift identity and language to suit circumstances and needs. Where she uses
the language of economics (ll. 185–90), he responds similarly: 'I
dare secure the goods sound', with an implied sexual pun (he is free
from syphilis), and discoursing on his own body as a commodity to
be sampled, used and priced (ll. 192–7).

Cornelia then shifts to a different register: given he has been so
'liberal' with his 'samples', perhaps he should 'throw in a little love
and constancy' (ll. 198–201). His response is amusing and swift: he
shifts to verse, but in a self-conscious manner. The audience know
that this is a highly polished act: his enthusiastic, exaggerated, 'Love?
Oh, in abundance!' is accompanied by a physical flourish beneath
her balcony. He adopts the courtly lover's discourse, a register reinforced visually by the scenic situation (she above in a balcony, he

below as supplicant lover). The first three lines of his avowal use a conventional rhetorical figure of accumulating examples, 'By those dear eyes, by that soft smiling mouth, / By . . .', emphasising this through repetition of the first word. This usually produces a sense of intensity and commitment. Here, by contrast, since we watch his deliberate adoption of the unrequited lover's pose, and Cornelia's demand for such a pose, the repetition of examples becomes parodic and funny. Iambic pentameters are used to register archaic concepts of love. Cornelia's sceptical over-view informs that of the audience: the language and actions of courtly love are seen as problematic. We learn not to trust the rake heroes at face value.

Despite Galliard's witty self-presentation and responsiveness to Cornelia's lead, we remain suspicious about his motives. We are never completely clear when, if ever, the real Galliard steps forward. To reach a view on this, it is useful to contrast his characterisation here, with that when he is with Fillamour alone, as he is in Act 1. In the latter, he is less performative and changeable, less malleable to circumstances and suggestion. This contrast tends to make the audience more sceptical of his sincerity with Cornelia. Let us now turn to a final short extract from this play, in which the third hero appears.

*   *   *

[Act 3, scene i]

    Julio. A curse upon the sex! Why must man's honour
           Depend upon their frailty?   50
           Come, give me but any light which way they went,
           And I will trace 'em with that careful vengeance –
    Octavio. Spoke like a man that understands his honour;
                              (*The Feigned Courtesans*, 3, i, 49–53)

At the beginning of Act 3 the separate plot lines begin to converge. Julio, finding the woman he was pursuing is supposedly a courtesan, also now overhears his uncle complaining about the escape of his sisters. On discovering this, he reveals himself, and makes the above observation. The Julio/Laura story acts as a dark counterpoint to the happier tale of Cornelia/Galliard and Marcella/Fillamour. Its continued presence as a plot strand reminds us of the deliberately idealised situation and outcome with which we are presented. Julio's character is therefore an important commentary on that of the other heroes.

As the brother of the two main heroines, who advocates the status quo for their future arrangements, he functions as a blocking character with his uncle, linking him to the older patriarchal generation. But in pursuing Laura, and wanting to end his own arranged marriage (as he believes), he is linked with the younger couples. By this double function, Behn suggests that patriarchal attitudes to women cross generations. This link provides the dark commentary on Fillamour and Galliard, which is supplemented both by Galliard's unabashed libertine philosophy and by the similarities between all the men's views of courtesans as natural and commodified objects of exchange.

Julio's views here, applied both to his sisters and to Laura, are revealing and paradigmatic of the male view of women throughout the play. He curses the whole sex: implying all women are the same, and all are the cause of men's downfall. This overt misogyny is echoed by the elder men in the play, and endorsed by Octavio. His question, 'Why must man's honour / Depend upon their frailty?' is taken at face value by his companions, as a cry of solidarity with other men, against women as another species. Yet the audience takes this question in a different way. We are encouraged to ask ourselves that very question both by the unreasonable behaviour of the older men, and by the explicit questions and actions of Cornelia and Marcella. Why should there be a social system where men's 'honour' depends upon the women in their family? Why can't women be independent? Why should women be owned by men?

Julio's characterisation as an unsympathetic and misogynistic patriarchal figure has a key critical function. It reinforces the audience's view of male social and familial dominance by making explicit the nature of that dominance as the intersection of masculine honour with female chastity, and asks us to question whether this is either natural or right.

* * *

Let us now look at a short extract from *The Lucky Chance*.

[Act 5, scene i]

> *Sir Cautious his house*
>
> *Enter Belmour alone, sad.*
>
> Belmour.   The night is come: oh, my Leticia!
>   The longing bridegroom hastens to his bed,
>   Whilst she, with all the languishment of love
>   And sad despair, casts her fair eyes on me,
>   Which silently implore I would deliver her.   5
>   But how? Aye, there's the question. – Ha – (*pausing*)
>   I'll get myself hid in her bed-chamber,
>   And something I will do may save us yet;
>   If all my arts should fail, I'll have recourse
>   ([*Belmour*] *draws a dagger.*)
>   To this: and bear Leticia off by force.   10
>   But see, she comes.
>
>   (*The Lucky Chance*, 5, i, 1–11)

Act 5's opening situation and language feel potentially tragic: the stage directions tell us about Belmour's frame of mind ('*alone, sad*'), his words draw attention to nightfall and to the fact that Leticia's marriage is about to be consummated. Stage directions name the setting (Sir Cautious's house) and Belmour's hidden presence. This sets up a dramatically tense situation: will Belmour be discovered? Will he manage to free Leticia? The situation (a lover hidden in the bedroom, whilst husband and wife prepare for bed) is replicated in the forthcoming discovery scene at Sir Feeble's house in Act 5, scene iv.

The unusually regular iambic pentameters echo the heroic register to which Belmour strives. Apart from the final line, acting as a stage direction, only two lines are not regular (ll. 5 and 6). The eight beats of line 6 give rhythmic space for the actor to pause at the abrupt first question, along with the 'Ha', at the end of the line. Line 5 contains twelve syllables, but the first and last carry no emphasis, giving a five-beat line. Equally unusually, the final two lines of the speech (ll. 9 and 10) rhyme; but the delivery of these two lines is not a smooth couplet, as is indicated by their textual separation by a stage direction, the sense echoing the stage business. He draws his dagger, simultaneously saying, 'I'll have recourse / To this.' The physical movement and intimate setting make the rhyme seem more incidental, although it still underlines his declarative statement. Despite the formal structure, the speech's grammar flows naturally: there are two run-on lines, and the one question comes within a line. The combination of formal structure with informal content and setting helps ensure that we both believe in his tragic situation and sympathise intimately with his dilemma.

Belmour's verse does not carry connotations of parody: this is his natural speech. We believe that his situation is genuinely that of a victim of circumstances. Belmour's self-presentation here as both tragic victim and heroic saviour (of Leticia from the horrible Sir Feeble) is therefore credible. His stance of grieving lover is reinforced by the sudden interjection to his argumentative flow in the first line ('oh, my Leticia!'), grammatical irregularity replicating his thought process. This speech gives a sense of the natural movements of thought, partly because of the interjections, but also because of the combined use of an apparent stream of consciousness with self-posed questions and answers. The metaphorical subtext throughout the speech links darkness and night with risk and danger, as well as sexual fulfilment: a referential pattern recurring throughout the play.

The soliloquy, as a theatrical device to relate a character's state of mind and action to come, is used to present Belmour's character as a conventional hero in a potentially tragic romance. Let us now consider Gayman.

* * *

[Act 2, scene i]

> *Gayman's lodging*
>
> *Enter Gayman in a night-cap, and an old campaign coat tied about him; very melancholy.*
>
> Gayman. Curse on my birth! Curse on my faithless fortune!
> Curse on my stars, and cursed be all – but love!

That dear, that charming sin, though 't have pulled
Innumerable mischiefs on my head,
I have not, nor I cannot find repentance for.   5
No: let me die despised, upbraided, poor;
Let fortune, friends, and all abandon me,
But let me hold thee, thou soft smiling god
Close to my heart while life continues there,
Till the last pantings of my vital blood.   10
May the last spark of life and fire be love's!
   Enter Rag.
   – How now, Rag, what's o'clock?
Rag.   My belly can inform you better than my tongue.
Gayman.   Why, you gourmandising vermin you, what have you done
   with the threepence I gave you a fortnight ago?   15
Rag.   Alas, sir, that all gone, long since.
Gayman.   You gutling rascal, you are enough to breed a famine in a
   land. I have known some industrious footmen, that have not only
   gotten their own livings, but a pretty livelihood for their masters
   too.   20
Rag.   Aye, till they came to the gallows, sir.
Gayman.   Very well, sirrah, they died in an honourable calling. But
   hark'ee, Rag: I have business, very earnest business abroad this
   evening; now, were you a rascal of docity, you would invent a way
   to get home my last suit that was laid in lavender, with the
   appurtenances thereunto belonging, as periwig, cravat, and so   25
   forth.
Rag.   Faith, master, I must deal in the black art then, for no human
   means will do't; and now I talk of the black art, master, try your
   power once more with my landlady.   30
Gayman.   Oh! name her not, the thought on't turns my stomach. A
   sight of her is a vomit, but he's a bold hero that dares venture on
   her for a kiss, and all beyond that, sure, is hell itself.
                              (*The Lucky Chance*, 2, i, 1–33)

This presents two different images of the same man: first, on his
own, '*very melancholy*' (opening stage direction); and then in more
enlivened and witty conversation with his servant. This enables the
audience to see that his social persona differs from his private one,
and that the character of the rake is an adopted one. How do the
two aspects of his character differ?

The first 11 lines are delivered in iambic pentameters, suggesting a more heroic and noble self-image than that delivered to others (where he usually speaks in prose). The imagery and grammar are also rhetorically sophisticated: he, like Belmour, uses the device of accumulation (by repeating the 'curse on' phrase) to create a sense of unbearable anguish and frustration. This accumulation is defused slightly by the final words of that accumulation: 'cursed be all – but love!' The break in rhetorical regularity and logic ('**but** love') gives a sense of genuine thought processes developing as he speaks. This is reinforced by the way his words logically follow on from his last thought. So, once he has shifted from cursing all, because he remembered love, he goes on to talk about love, rather than returning to cursing. Gayman additionally uses accumulation in two subsequent lines (6 and 7). In each case he uses three words where one might do, connected through the 'let': 'let me die despised, upbraided, poor', and 'Let fortune, friends, and all, abandon me.' The effect of this accumulation, in three different phrases, is one of exaggerated feelings, supposedly typical of the frustrated lover.

The speech's content, then, appears to follow a natural thought process: he digresses on the nature of love. He represents love as two different things, first as 'that charming sin', suggesting an active transgression within a Christian framework ('I cannot find repentance for', l. 5). Secondly, he introduces pagan imagery, where love becomes a 'soft smiling god', whom he holds until death. Gayman embraces both discourses about (adulterous) love: he won't repel the sin, and he welcomes the pagan god.

In the second part of this extract, his manner and mode of delivery are very different. As soon as Rag enters, his register is jolly ('How now, Rag, what's o'clock?'), and informally insulting. Their exchange sounds like the natural jostling between two friends: mutual teasing and insults convey intimacy, but no real insights. The relationship reveals Gayman as far more dependent on his servant for his everyday needs (food, money and clothes) than he is on any other character in the play. Economic necessity is shown to dominate men's minds and identities as much as erotic interest.

Finally, in this masculine atmosphere of master and servant, where they discuss the master's intimate needs, Gayman gives voice to a surprising misogyny. His aversion to his landlady is expressed as a physical repulsion, through his characteristic exaggeration ('all beyond that, sure, is hell itself', l. 33), and looks forward to his later unknowing characterisation of Julia as 'a canvas bag of wooden ladles' (4, i, 84). The rake's success in the pursuit of beauty and love is linked to economic success, to status, to youth and to appearances. If he has no money he will be reduced to courting his landlady, but he is prepared to do even that to achieve his desires. Gayman is thus presented as a character prepared to abuse women to his own ends, a prophetic warning about his future game with Sir Feeble.

Conclusions

1. The rakes in Behn's plays exhibit all the conventional and typical rake characteristics. Whilst not all the young male heroes are rakes, both rake and gallant philosophy are questioned by the play's plots.
2. Masculine ideologies of love, whether libertine or courtly, are shown to conflict with the desires and views of the women. Such ideologies are allied to the play's more clearly patriarchal characters through character parallels, thus linking gallants with blocking figures.
3. However, any moral message about rakes is delivered with a light touch. Whilst we laugh at the antics of such characters, and tend to sympathise with the women, the young men still remain immensely more attractive to the audience than the uncles, brothers and old husbands with whom the rakes are both paralleled and contrasted.
4. Through the doubling and tripling of both characters and plot elements, Behn draws particular, and often parodic, attention to certain characteristics of the rake characters. For example, in *The Rover*, repeated violence by the rake hero in similar situations makes us recognise and judge this characteristic. All the rakes are repeatedly seen in situations where self-interest dominates their decisions, dialogue and character. Through plot repetition and parallels the rakes are objectified and offered up for audience criticism.

5. By using a trio of heroes (as she does with the heroines), Behn
   provides different and alternative models and scenarios for the
   conventional comic characters. Thus in *The Rover*, Willmore and
   Belvile provide alternative models of masculine ideology, whilst
   Frederick acts as a bridge between them and Blunt. In *The
   Feigned Courtesans*, Fillamour and Galliard represent respectively
   the courtly and libertine lover, whilst Julio provides the bridge to
   both the older generation, and a more explicitly rapacious pursuit
   of women. In *The Lucky Chance*, Belmour and Gayman play the
   courtly and libertine respectively, whilst Bearjest appears as a contrast whose views echo more closely the criticisms of the women.
   The use of characters in this way helps deepen our response to
   the themes and conflicts which construct the drama. It stops us
   from sympathising too deeply with the witty rake heroes.
6. All the male characters have allegorical names (unlike the women
   characters). The rakes' names help tell us how these characters are
   to be interpreted morally. Willmore and 'the rover' tell us that free
   will and a roving manner will dominate his actions. Belvile,
   meaning 'belle of the town', names him as an attractive gallant.
   Fillamour, meaning 'fine love', and Galliard, a lively dance, suggesting a courtly and a fun-loving character respectively, Belmour,
   a beautiful love, and Gayman, a man the epitome of frivolity, are
   all names which infect and inflect our interpretations of their
   characters. The names are a guide as to how the characters will
   and do act within the play, and a guide to Behn's satirical aim.

Methods of Analysis

This chapter builds on the previous chapter on characterisation, but
in addition we have:

1. considered the way in which characterisation is bound up with
   an author's moral or didactic intention;
2. further considered the way in which the doubling, tripling and
   paralleling of characters complicates the way themes and debates
   are presented to the audience;

3. introduced concepts of how comic and dramatic stereotypes can be manipulated to both humorous and critical effects;

4. shown how characterisation can be used in juxtaposition to plot, scene, setting, or other characters' views in order to set up the viewers' critical position;

5. made some judgements about Behn's dramatic intentions, but in doing so, we have returned to internal dramatic devices and content to justify our arguments about gender.

Suggested Work

We have examined only a few short extracts of the heroes' representation in each play. It is a good idea to have a look at their function in several other key scenes.

The Rover

Look at the contrasts between the characterisation of Belvile when with Florinda, compared with when with gallants, for example the opening of Act 2, scene i. When he is with Florinda (in Act 1, scene ii and Act 2, scene i) he never realises it is her until too late; their conversations are very limited (in length and content). Look at some of Willmore's exchanges with Hellena (for example, 1, ii, 126–98; 3, i, 131–95 and 230–64). How is the audience positioned by these exchanges and why? Consider the scenes where Blunt is gulled by Lucetta (Act 3, scenes ii and iii), and Blunt's overall function in the play.

The Feigned Courtesans

Consider the male characters of the sub-plot, Tickletext and Sir Signal. What is their overall function within the play? Act 2, scene i is a key scene in which the views and characters of the gallants are exposed. How does the structure and content of the scene help us understand their character? Comment on the number of fights with swords during the play. What is the audience led to think about these? What is the role of Petro in the play?

The Lucky Chance

Consider Gayman's self-presentation in his discussion with Lady Fulbank in 2, ii, 165–267. How does this differ from the extract we analysed? Apply your conclusions to the next scene in which he appears subject to her (Act 3, scene iv). Finally, look at the gambling scene (4, i, 346–485). How are we to think about both characters?

For Belmour, look at 3, i, 1–97. What is the audience's view of him? How is that view constructed? Count the number of scenes and lines in which Belmour and Gayman appear: who is the most dominant character in terms of appearances on stage and why? Does this affect our view of the play's endings?

Fathers, brothers and older husbands

One of the common features of openings and endings of Behn's plays is the presence and commented-upon absence of father figures, or their proxies in uncles and brothers. In *The Lucky Chance*, father figures are supplanted by the two elderly husbands. Older men in comedies frequently play figures of paternalistic and authoritarian resistance to change and youth, called 'blocking figures'. You should consider some of the following extracts in order to both parallel and differentiate these men from the younger rakes and gallants.

The Rover, 2, i, 147–93

- Comment on the structure and setting of this scene, particularly the way the male discourse sandwiches Angellica.
- Comment on the focalisation, genre and content of the song: how does it make us view the men in the scene?
- How and what are we asked to think about masculine competition, and the role of the brother and husband-to-be?
- Comment on the intersection of divine and sacred language.

The Feigned Courtesans, 2, i, 1–28

- How does this scene structure the audience's response against the men who control Cornelia's and Marcella's futures?

- What is the effect of us watching the men's misogyny at the same time as we see Marcella and Cornelia in disguise? Comment on their failure to recognise the women, and its invocation of themes of disguise and recognition.
- What effect does the representation of men making agreements about women have on our views?

The Lucky Chance, Act 1, scene iii and Act 4, scene i

- In what ways do setting and situation (the marriage celebration in the first case, and Sir Cautious's gambling of his wife in the second) contrast with the covert content? What is the significance of this in our judgements of the men?
- Comment on Leticia's silence and Julia's ignorance.
- Comment on Sir Feeble's infantilised language and his song.
- Comment on Sir Cautious's application of financial language to his wife.
- How and why is gaming linked to masculinity?

You will note that Behn adapts conventional comic stereotypes, the old men who block progress, to unconventional ends. Their ideas are specifically linked to those of some of the men in the younger generation (for example, Julio, or Pedro and Antonio). Patriarchal values are seen to be handed across generations, and shared by both bourgeois city men, and gentry. Brothers, uncles and fathers are involved in dynastic marriages, whereas gallants are seen to marry for love. Behn thus sets up a dramatic critique of arranged marriages.

6

Multiplying Plots

In any comedy, plotting is essential to theme and action. Characters devise plots to achieve their own ends and desires, and to defeat the blocking characters. Additionally, the playwright's plotting enables and encourages the audience to perceive and understand the action and themes in very particular ways. Behn frequently uses structural repetitions and parallels, to which our attention is explicitly drawn.

*   *   *

Let us turn first to *The Rover*, in which there are three near-rapes of one woman: Florinda. The first of these rapes happened prior to the play's action, but is nevertheless structurally central to it, introducing Belvile to Florinda, and enabling him to adopt the role of saviour. The play's other two threatened rapes, in Acts 3 and 4, should be read side by side, and are set out below without any commentary to interrupt them.

[Act 3, scene v]

> *The garden in the night*
>
> *Enter Florinda in an undress, with a key and a little box.*
> Florinda.   Well, thus far I'm in my way to happiness: I have got
>   myself free from Callis; my brother too, I find by yonder light, is
>   got into his cabinet, and thinks not of me; I have by good fortune
>   got the key of the garden back-door. I'll open it to prevent Belvile's

knocking; a little noise will now alarm my brother. Now am I as   5
fearful as a young thief. (*Unlocks the door.*) Hark, what noise is that?
Oh, 'twas the wind that played amongst the boughs. Belvile stays
long, methinks; it's time. Stay, for fear of a surprise I'll hide these
jewels in yonder jessamine.

     [*Florinda*] *goes to lay down the box. Enter Willmore, drunk.*

Willmore.   What the devil is become of these fellows, Belvile and   10
   Frederick? They promised to stay at the next corner for me, but
   who the devil knows the corner of a full moon? Now, whereabouts
   am I? Ha, what have we here, a garden! A very convenient place
   to sleep in. Ha, what has God sent us here? A female! By this light,
   a woman! I'm a dog if it be not a very wench!   15

Florinda. [*Aside*]   He's come! – Ha, who's there?

Willmore.   Sweet soul! let me salute thy shoe-string.

Florinda [*aside*] 'Tis not my Belvile. Good heavens! I know him
   not. – Who are you, and from whence come you?

Willmore.   Prithee, prithee, child, not so many hard questions. Let   20
   it suffice I am here, child. Come, come kiss me.

Florinda.   Good gods! What luck is mine?

Willmore.   Only good luck child, parlous good luck. Come hither.
   [*Aside*] 'Tis a delicate shining wench; by this hand, she's perfumed,
   and smells like any nosegay. – Prithee, dear soul, let's not play the   25
   fool, and lose time, precious time; for as Gad shall save me, I'm as
   honest a fellow as breathes, though I'm a little disguised at
   present. Come, I say; why, thou mayst be free with me, I'll be very
   secret. I'll not boast who 'twas obliged me, not I: for hang me if I   30
   know thy name.

Florinda.   Heavens! what a filthy beast is this!

Willmore.   I am so, and thou ought'st the sooner to lie with me for
   that reason: for look you, child, there will be no sin in't, because
   'twas neither deisgned nor premeditated; 'tis pure accident on both
   sides, that's a certain thing now. Indeed, should I make love to   35
   you, and vow you fidelity, and swear and lie till you believed and
   yielded, that were to make it wilful fornication, the crying sin of
   the nation. Thou art therefore, as thou art a good Christian,
   obliged in conscience to deny me nothing. Now, come, be kind
   without any more idle prating.   40

Florinda.   Oh, I am ruined! – Wicked man, unhand me.

Willmore.   Wicked! Egad, child, a judge, were he young and
   vigorous, and saw those eyes of thine, would know 'twas they gave

the first blow, the first provocation. Come, prithee let's lose no
time, I say; this is a fine convenient place.   45

Florinda.   Sir, let me go, I conjure you, or I'll call out.

Willmore.   Aye, aye, you were best to call witness to see how finely
you treat me, do.

Florinda.   I'll cry murder, rape, or anything, if you do not instantly
let me go.   50

Willmore.   A rape! Come, come, you lie, you baggage, you lie: what,
I'll warrant you would fain have the world believe now that you
are not so forward as I. No, not you! Why, at this time of night,
was your cobweb door set open, dear spider, but to catch flies? Ha,
come, or I shall be damnably angry. Why, what a coil is here!   55

Florinda.   Sir, can you think –

Willmore.   – That you would do't for nothing? Oh, oh, I find what
you would be at. Look here, here's a pistole for you. Here's a work
indeed! Here, take it I say.

Florinda.   For heaven's sake, sir, as you're a gentleman –   60

Willmore.   So – now, now – she would be wheedling me for more. –
What, you will not take it then, you are resolved you will not?
Come, come, take it, or I'll put it up again, for look ye, I never
give more. Why how now mistress, are you so high i'th' mouth a
pistole won't down with you? Ha, why, what a work's here! In   65
good time! Come, no struggling to be gone; but an y'are good at a
dumb wrestle, I'm for ye, look ye, I'm for ye.

> [*Florinda*] *struggles with* [*Willmore*]. *Enter Belvile and Frederick.*
>
> (*The Rover*, 3, v, 1–67)

[Act 4, scene v]

Blunt.   Talk on, talk on, and weep too, till my faith return. Do,   40
flatter me out of my senses again. A harmless virgin with a pox!
As much one as t'other, 'adsheartlikins. Why, what the devil, can
I not be safe in my house for you; not in my chamber? Nay, even
being naked, too, cannot secure me: this is an impudence greater
than has invaded me yet. Come, no resistance.   45

> [*Blunt*] *pulls* [*Florinda*] *rudely.*

Florinda.   Dare you be so cruel?

Blunt.   Cruel? 'Adsheartlikins, as a galley-slave, or a Spanish whore.
Cruel, yes: I will kiss and beat thee all over; kiss, and see thee all

over; thou shalt lie with me too, not that I care for the enjoyment,
but to let thee see I have ta'en deliberated malice to thee, and will   50
be revenged on one whore for the sins of another. I will smile and
deceive thee, flatter thee, and beat thee, kiss and swear, and lie to
thee, embrace thee and rob thee, as she did me; fawn on thee, and
strip thee stark naked, then hang thee out at my window by the
heels, with a paper of scurvy verses fastened to thy breast, in praise   55
of damnable women. Come, come along.
Florinda.   Alas, sir, must I be sacrificed for the crimes of the most
infamous of my sex? I never understood the sins you name.
Blunt.   Do, persuade the fool you love him, or that one of you can
be just or honest; tell me I was not an easy coxcomb, or any strange   60
impossible tale: it will be believed sooner than thy false showers or
protestations. A generation of damned hypocrites! To flatter my
very clothes from my back! Dissembling witches! Are these the
returns you make an honest gentleman, that trusts, believes, and
loves you? But if I be not even with you – come along, or I shall –   65
       Enter Frederick.

                                                    (*The Rover*, 4, v, 40–65)

These two extracts are almost exact replicas of each other, occurring
in subsequent Acts. Let us first consider precisely their parallels and
then why Behn doubles her plot.

The setting and timing of each scene are similar, both are at night
and in supposedly private places. Setting and time are used and read
by both men to judge Florinda as a whore looking for sex (for
example, 3, v, 53 and 4, v, 43–4). Yet for the audience both place
and time are read in a different way. We see Florinda's greater vulnerability than in her own home or during the day: in other words, we
see both how the men might misunderstand her character and how
such misunderstanding is inequitable to women. This understanding
is intensified by the fact that it occurs twice.

The situation of both encounters is also similar. Florinda is
looking for Belvile and the men who threatens her are both drunk
and violent, although Willmore arrives unexpectedly whilst she
approaches Blunt willingly. The contrasting nature of each
encounter only serves to underline the similarity of the men's
response to her. The mixing of parallel situations, with a slight varia-

tion on the initial agency of the action, suggests to the audience that male behaviour is generic: this dramatic structure suggests that any encounter with a vulnerable woman results in masculine violence. Doubled plotting thereby ensures criticism of a certain type of masculinity.

Characterisation within each episode is also eerily similar. Florinda is represented as virtuous but powerless. Her initial appearance in the scene suggests a woman in control of her destiny, who has arranged to elope with her lover and conspired with her servant to organise the financial and logistical means to do so. This self-determination is completely destroyed the moment the unpredictable happens. Willmore's sudden appearance in the garden, his drunkenness and his lechery illustrate the failure of Florinda's self-sufficiency. Women's powerlessness is figured in Florinda's successively ineffective resorts to salvation: in Act 3, scene v, her pleas to the gods (l. 22), exclamations to the audience (l. 32), and exclamations of helpless woe (l. 41). Her pleas to Willmore use archaic language ('Wicked man, unhand me', l. 41), threaten his exposure for rape (ll. 49–50), or express disbelieving outrage (ll. 56, 60). In each case her linguistic register is literally meaningless to Willmore, and it only makes sense to us because we know her. Willmore, seeing a woman in a state of undress in a garden, understands her language solely within that context: that she must be bargaining for money. The exposure of two ways of 'reading' women's behaviour and language in this context is crucial. The gap between Willmore's perceptions and Florinda's and ours enables us to see the sexual double standard at work. By making Willmore drunk, Behn intensifies this gap because he is allowed to be much more exaggeratedly verbal about his intentions (ll. 61–7).

In the second extract, Florinda's pleas for sanctuary are similarly interpreted as a pretence: Blunt 'reads' all women as sinful whores, ignoring the specifics of the individual situation. In this way Behn exposes masculine assumptions about femininity as ignorant, self-absorbed, self-interested and plain wrong. Blunt's madness echoes Willmore's drunkenness. At one level, their behaviour can be seen to be extreme because they are out of their minds. But equally, their characters as drunk or mad are merely intensifications of their characters elsewhere in the play. Parallel plotting thereby intensifies our perception of this conclusion and of masculinity as a way of mis-perceiving and misconstruing women.

Both men use language which constructs Florinda as an object without her own will or desires. For example, Willmore's triple exclamation 'A Female! By this light, a woman! I'm a dog if it be not a very wench!' (ll. 14–15) reduces Florinda to a generic function, although he kneels to 'salute thy shoe-string' (l. 17). This bathetic mock-veneration is converted to a direct appeal for sex (ll. 29–30), and then to violence when Florinda refuses (l. 41). Blunt's manic monologues bear no relation to the Florinda we see on stage, and by slotting her into the category of all-women-are-whores, Blunt is used to suggest that misogyny (which universalises all women as the cause of all evil) is irrational and indiscriminate. Both men claim that it was Florinda who initiated their desire: Willmore that it was her eyes that 'gave . . . the first provocation' (l. 44), and Blunt that her arrival is an act of provocation and impudence (ll. 41–5). The audience do not interpret the scene in this way, and, whilst acknowledging the dangerous comic potential, we also see that blaming women for male lust is both misogynist and part of the sexual double standard.

Stage directions and blocking further underline the violence the two men use as though it were natural, when Florinda resists their demands for sex. Their rapid appropriation of physical force reinforces our perception that certain types of masculinity, violence and misogyny are interlinked: Willmore has grabbed Florinda by line 40, and she 'struggles' as Belvile and Frederick arrive; and Blunt '*pulls Florinda rudely*' at line 45. The physical violence emphasises Florinda's fragility and vulnerability, underlining visually the power assumed by the men. This visual underlining distances the audience from both men. Florinda is the main character in both scenes, who addresses the audience directly through her asides, and combined with her situation and the characterisation of the men, this gains our sympathies. She acts as a commentary character on their misogyny. This commentary function is also literally expressed through her words to Blunt 'must I be sacrificed for the crimes of the most infamous of my sex?' (l. 57). The audience is thereby given the visual, empathetic and intellectual tools with which to condemn violent masculinity.

Finally, in both cases the situation is only resolved because a third character enters to prevent violence. Tragedy is only just averted in each case. Rape is therefore seen to be potentially inherent in situations where women's status is ambiguous, and open to exploitation by men. Equally, women are shown to be powerless to resolve their own vulnerable status.

Doubled plotting reinforces and universalises the exposure of violent masculinity in *The Rover*. Let us now turn to a more overtly comic usage of double plotting in *The Feigned Courtesans*.

* * *

[Act 3, scene i]

> *Exeunt Petro and Tickletext. Enter Fillamour and Marcella,*
> *with their swords drawn; Galliard after them.*

Galliard. A plague upon 'em, what a quarter's here for a wench, as   560
if there were no more i'th' nation. Would I'd my sword again.
(*Gropes for it.*)

Marcella. [*Aside*] Which way shall I direct him to be safer? [*To*
Fillamour] How is it, sir? I hope you are not hurt?

Fillamour. Not that I feel; what art thou ask'st so kindly?   565

Marcella. A servant to the Roman courtesan, who sent me forth to
wait your coming, sir; but finding you in danger, shared it with
you. Come, let me lead you into safety, sir.

Fillamour. Thou'st been too kind to give me cause to doubt thee.

Marcella. Follow me, sir; this key will give us entrance through the   570
garden.

> *Exeunt [Marcella and Fillamour]. Enter Octavio with his sword*
> *in his hand.*

Octavio. Oh, what damned luck had I, so poorly to be vanquished!
When all is hushed, I know he will return: therefore I'll fix me
here, till I become a furious statue, but I'll reach his heart.

Sir Signal. Oh, *lamentivolo fato*, what bloody villains these popish   575
Italians are!

> *Enter Julio.*

Ocatvio. Ha; I hear one coming this way. Ha, the door opens, too;
and he makes towards it. Pray heaven he be the right, for this I'm
sure's the house. Now, luck, an't be thy will.

>   [*Octavio*] *follows Julio towards the door, softly.*
> Julio.   The rogues are fled, but how secure I know not   580
>   And I'll pursue my first design of love;
>   And if this Silvianetta will be kind –
>   *Enter Laura Lucretia from the house in a nightgown.*
> Laura Lucretia.   Whist; who is't names Silvianetta?
> Julio.   A lover, and her slave.
>   [*Laura Lucretia*] *takes* [*Julio*] *by the hand.*
> Laura Lucretia.   Oh, is it you; are you escaped unhurt?   585
>   Come to my bosom, and be safe for ever.
> Julio. [*Aside*]   'Tis love that calls, and now revenge must stay. This
>   hour is thine, fond boy; the next that is my own I'll give to anger.
> Octavio.   Oh, ye pernicious pair; I'll quickly change the scene of love
>   into a rougher and more unexpected entertainment.   590
>   [*Laura Lucretia*] *leads Julio in. Octavio follows close.* [*They*]*shut*
>   *the door* [*behind*] *them. Sir Signal thrusts out his head to harken,*
>   *hears nobody, and advances.*
> Sir Signal.   Sure the devil reigns tonight; would I were sheltered,
>   and let him rain fire and brimstone, for pass the streets I dare not.
>   This should be the house; or hereabouts, I'm sure 'tis. Ha, what's
>   this? A string; of a bell, I hope. I'll try to enter; and if I am
>   mistaken, 'tis but crying *con licenzia*!   595
>   [*Sir Signal*] *rings* [*the bell*]. *Enter Philippa.*
> Philippa.   Who's there?
> Sir Signal.   'Tis I, 'tis I; let me in quickly.
> Philippa.   Who, the English cavalier?
> Sir Signal.   The same. [*Aside*] I am right; I see I was expected.
> Philippa.   I'm glad you're come. Give me your hand.   600
> Sir Signal.   I am fortunate at last; and therefore will say with the
>   famous poet:
>   No happiness like that achieved with danger,
>   Which once o'ercome, I'll lie at rack and manger.
>   *Exeunt.*

                              (*The Feigned Courtesans*, 3, i, 560–604)

Here we encounter a tripled plot, involving the main characters
from each of the three plots of the play, repeated successively within
the space of forty lines. This whole scene focuses on the attempts of
two of the gallants and Sir Signal to bed the woman of their dreams.
This extract is the culmination of those attempts, and the outcome

for at least two of them is not what they expect. In each case the men believe that they are pursuing La Silvianetta. Laura Lucretia has tried to distract Julio by pretending to be La Silvianetta, whilst she herself can pursue Galliard, so Julio believes he is entering her house. Cornelia has feigned an identity as La Silvianetta, and Galliard and Fillamour are admitted to her door by Marcella, disguised as a boy. Sir Signal is simply following the hot gossip about the best courtesan in town, and is allowed to enter by the maid, who has mistaken him for Galliard. The plot strands meet in this scene as all three men converge on the address at the same moment. The setting is a street at night, with three doors off the back of the set, which should look alike.

The setting and timing are used to suggest confusion and the possibility of natural mistakes. Nevertheless, the plotting and set are also constructed so that the audience are not confused. The first retreat behind a door is that of Galliard and Fillamour. We know who Marcella is, and having been privy to Cornelia's disguise as La Silvianetta, know that the door to which she leads the gallants, will lead to Cornelia. The audience is not troubled by this night-time encounter: we want these lovers to be satisfied.

The second departure, that of Julio, is behind a different door. We know that Julio has really been pursuing Laura, and that when he chooses what he believes to be La Silvianetta's door, it is in fact Laura's. Laura, however, is expecting Galliard to enter. The darkness conceals identity, allowing her to mistakenly welcome Julio as Galliard. This welcome is ironic and potentially disastrous, since we also know two things of which all the other characters are ignorant. The first is that Laura is not interested in the man who has been pursuing her from the opening of the play, and the second is that, unbeknownst to both, Julio and Laura have been betrothed in an arranged marriage, although they have never met. The audience therefore have a more complex response to this second departure. At one level, we can see that Behn is using plot confusion to ensure that one arranged marriage is consummated, albeit by trickery, and that the pursued Galliard is thereby freed up for the heroine Cornelia. However, we know that Laura is submitting to the wrong lover. This is both comic and potentially tragic. It is comic at a farcical level, featuring multiple doors and multiple identities which play with deliberate mis-recognition and confusion of identities. It is also comic in that this particular mis-recognition leads directly to one of the marriages which resolve the play. It is tragic for the same reason: we know, and later Laura explicitly says, that she is unhappy in this arranged marriage. Julio's language, of uncontrollable passion (ll. 587–8), and Octavio's of promised revenge (ll. 589–90), both use linguistic registers from tragedy, rather than comedy.

By placing this encounter immediately after the happier exit to Cornelia's house, Behn proposes a contrasting outcome for women's freedom. Cornelia and Marcella take on new identities (of boy and courtesan respectively) and are both liberated and fulfilled in their choice of lover. However, Laura, assuming her own fictional identity, is foiled by circumstance and accident. Behn thereby enables the audience to feel a sense of satisfaction in that one fantasy is consummated, but simultaneously underlines this as fantasy by showing us a very different potential outcome of such freedom. Instead of liberation, Laura is potentially chained, both by her own loss of status (for her possible loss of virginity) and by the husband she does not desire.

The third departure is clearly comic, although the audience can anticipate further intrigues as a result of Sir Signal's departure into Cornelia's house. The sub-plot of Sir Signal and Tickletext interrogates the main plot. Sir Signal's sexual buffoonery and exaggerated expressions of lust draw our attention not only to his character, but to the motives and desires of the other men who have wanted to enter La Silvianetta's door. This reminds the audience that illicit erotic desire fuels the actions of Julio in particular, whose desire is not reciprocated by Laura, and it acts as a shadowed commentary and reminder of Galliard's views on libertine sexuality. Sir Signal's incorporation into the main narrative acts as a warning to the audience about the motives of the gallants. Finally, Sir Signal's admittance to Cornelia's house also promises further plot complications and a potential postponement of her desired private encounter with Galliard. Sir Signal therefore acts as a plot device to postpone illicit sex and a subsequent fall for the heroine. In that sense he indirectly maintains the main character's chaste reputation. His final couplet, which ends the scene and the Act, functions simultaneously as both a promise and a warning. Happiness, danger, success and wealth are all inter-linked in the meanings, particularly of the two rhyming words (danger/manger). As the third and most minor character to enter one of the doors, he is both inside and outside the plot on stage, and thus best positioned to deliver this moral commentary without disturbing our involvement with the other characters.

The internal structuring of these three encounters is also critical. The potentially tragic encounter, and the one the audience can predict the least, is sandwiched between two more conventionally comic ones. The audience does not focus solely on the possible tragic outcome: but equally we are reminded that the romantic love of the first encounter is more than counterweighed by the two other examples of forced sex: arranged marriage and purely carnal desire. Thus plot and scenic structure force the audience to acknowledge the fictionality of romantic comedy, and to recognise the forces which dominate the sexual and marriage markets which romantic comedy attempts to deny. Such reminders give Behn's comedy a darker, more satirical edge than would a single-plot romantic comedy.

* * *

Let us now turn to our final play, where we find two paralleled characters undergoing a similar gulling for similar purposes in successive Acts of *The Lucky Chance*.

[Act 4, scene i]

> *Sir Cautious.* . . . Sir,
>   I wish I had anything but ready money to stake. Three hundred
>   pound: a fine sum!
> *Gayman.* You have moveables sir, goods; commodities –
> *Sir Cautious.* That's all one, sir; that's money's worth, sir; but if I   380
>   had anything that were worth nothing –
> *Gayman.* – You would venture it; I thank you, sir. I would your lady
>   were worth nothing.
> *Sir Cautious.* Why so, sir?

Gayman.   Then I would set all this against that nothing.   385
Sir Cautious.   What, set it against my wife?
Gayman.   Wife, sir; aye, your wife.
Sir Cautious.   Hum, my wife against three hundred pounds? What,
    all my wife, sir?
Gayman.   All your wife? Why, sir, some part of her would serve   390
    my turn.
Sir Cautious. (*Aside*)   Hum, my wife. Why, if I should lose, he could
    not have the impudence to take her.
Gayman.   Well, I find you are not for the bargain, and so I put up.
Sir Cautious.   Hold, sir, why so hasty? My wife? No: put up your   395
    money, sir; what, lose my wife, for three hundred pounds!
Gayman.   Lose her, sir! Why, she shall be never the worse for my
    wearing, sir. [*Aside*] The old covetous rogue is considering on't, I
    think. [*To Sir Cautious*] What say you to a night? I'll set it to a
    night. There's none need know it, sir.   400
Sir Cautious. [*Aside*]   Hum, a night! Three hundred pounds for a
    night! Why, what a lavish whore-master's this: we take money to
    marry our wives, but very seldom part with 'em, and by the
    bargain get money. [*To Gayman*] For a night, say you? (*Aside*)
    Gad, if I should take the rogue at his word, 'twould be a pure jest.   405
Sir Feeble.   You are not mad, brother?
Sir Cautious.   No, but I'm wise, and that's as good; let me consider –
Sir Feeble.   What, whether you shall be a cuckold or not?
Sir Cautious.   Or lose three hundred pounds: consider that. A cuckold:
    why, 'tis a word, an empty sound, 'tis breath, 'tis air, 'tis nothing; but 410
    three hundred pounds: lord, what will not three hundred pounds do!
    You may chance to be a cuckold for nothing, sir.
Sir Feeble.   It may be so; but she shall do't discreetly then.
Sir Cautious.   Under favour, you're an ass, brother: this is the
    discreetest way of doing it, I take it.   415
Sir Feeble.   But would a wise man expose his wife?
Sir Cautious.   Why, Cato was a wiser man than I, and he lent his
    wife to a young fellow they called Hortensius, as story says; and
    can a wise man have a better precedent than Cato?
Sir Feeble.   I say Cato was an ass, sir, for obliging any young rogue   420
    of 'em all.
Sir Cautious.   But I am of Cato's mind; – [*to Gayman*] well, a single
    night, you say.
Gayman.   A single night: to have, to hold, possess, and so forth, at
    discretion.   425

Sir Cautious. A night; I shall have her safe and sound i'th' morning.

Sir Feeble. Safe, no doubt on't: but how sound?

Gayman. And for non-performance, you shall pay me three hundred pounds; I'll forfeit as much if I tell. 430

Sir Cautious. Tell? Why, make your three hundred pounds six hundred, and let it be put into the *Gazette*, if you will, man; but is't a bargain?

Gayman. Done. Sir Feeble shall be witness, and there stands my hat.

(*The Lucky Chance*, 4, i, 376–434)

[Act 5, scene ii]

Leticia. I am ashamed to undress before you, sir; go to bed.

Sir Feeble. What, was it ashamed to show its little white foots, and 30 its little round bubbies? Well, I'll go, I'll go. ([*Aside*] *going towards the bed*) I cannot think on't, no I cannot.

> *Belmour comes forth from between the curtains, his coat off, his shirt bloody, a dagger in his hand, and his disguise off.*

Belmour. Stand.

Sir Feeble. Ha!

Leticia and Phillis. (*Squeak*) Oh, heavens! 35

Leticia. (*Aside to Phillis*) Why, is it Belmour?

Belmour. Go not to bed; I guard this sacred place,
And the adulterer dies that enters here.

Sir Feeble. Oh, why do I shake? Sure I'm a man! What art thou?

Belmour. I am the wronged, the lost and murdered Belmour. 40

Sir Feeble. [*Aside*] Oh, lord! It is the same I saw last night. [*To Belmour*] Oh! hold thy dread vengeance: pity me, and hear me. – Oh! a parson, a parson! What shall I do? Oh! Where shall I hide myself?

Belmour. I'th' utmost borders of the earth I'll find thee,
Seas shall not hide thee, nor vast mountains guard thee. 45
Even in the depth of hell I'll find thee out,
And lash thy filthy and adulterous soul.

Sir Feeble. Oh! I am dead, I'm dead; will no repentance save me?
'Twas that young eye that tempted me to sin; oh!

Belmour. [*To Leticia*] See, fair seducer, what thou'st made me do; 50
Look on this bleeding wound: it reached my heart,
To pluck thy dear tormenting image thence,

>   When news arrived that thou hadst broke thy vow.
> *Sir Feeble.*   Oh lord! Oh! [*Aside*] I'm glad he's dead though.
> *Leticia.*   Oh, hide that fatal wound; my tender heart faints with a   55
>   sight so horrid! (*Seems to weep*)
> *Sir Feeble.* [*Aside*]   So, she'll clear herself, and leave me in the devil's
>   clutches.
> *Belmour.*   You've both offended heaven, and must repent or die.
> *Sir Feeble.*   Ah, I do confess I was an old fool, bewitched with   60
>   beauty, besotted with love, and do repent most heartily.
> *Belmour.*   No, you had rather yet go on in sin:
>   Thou wouldst live on, and be a baffled cuckold.
> *Sir Feeble.*   Oh, not for the world, sir; I am convinced and mortified.
> *Belmour.*   Maintain her fine, undo thy peace to please her, and still   65
>   be cuckolded on; believe her, trust her, and be cuckold still.
> *Sir Feeble.*   I see my folly, and my age's dotage, and find the devil
>   was in me; yet spare my age, ah! Spare me to repent.
> *Belmour.*   If thou repent'st, renounce her, fly her sight.
>   Shun her bewitching charms, as thou would'st hell: 70
>   Those dark eternal mansions of the dead,
>   Whither I must descend.
> *Sir Feeble.*   Oh, would he were gone!
> *Belmour.*   Fly; be gone; depart; vanish for ever, from her to some
>   more safe and innocent apartment.   75
> *Sir Feeble.*   Oh, that's very hard!
>   [*Sir Feeble*] *goes back trembling; Belmour follows in, with his*
>   *dagger up; both go out.*
>   (*The Lucky Chance*, 5, ii, 29–76)

Here the situations echo each other: both husbands are in the process of being tricked out of their wives by the man whom their wives love. The gallants choose different ways and times of doing this. In the first extract, the gulling takes place at the end of an afternoon or evening of festive and social celebration. The whole Act is a succession of small peripatetic encounters between characters: Gayman following Julia in desperation; Sir Cautious refusing him a further mortgage; Diana and Bredwell planning and executing their elopement; and the beginning of the card game, which ends here. The scenic structure is an accumulation of key incidents, providing an atmosphere of a large party in which many different encounters can occur, and in which, because of its very size, small pockets of intimacy and intrigue can take place. Viewed without the rest of the scene, this extract condemns Gayman; viewed in the context of the play, we see two things. First, that Julia's trick on him in the previous act, conjuring up a temptress figure whom she does not acknowledge was herself, shows that she is not completely innocent. Secondly, that Sir Cautious's miserliness towards Wasteall (ll. 142–5) and jealousy of the 'young stallion' (l. 124) Gayman remind us of his suspicious, miserly character. Consequently we feel less pity than we might as he becomes the victim of these very characteristics in wagering his wife.

Similarly, the bedroom scene of the second extract comes at the end of several desperate attempts by Leticia to avoid the consummation of her marriage. The situation and setting have been the anticipated climactic end of each scene since Act 1, and the audience have had copious opportunities to observe Sir Feeble's trickery in blackening Belvile's name and his lecherous and misogynist treatment of Leticia. By the time the extract opens, the audience's sympathies and allegiances are clearly aligned against the old husband.

The characterisation in each of the extracts echoes the other. First, both gallants are trickster figures, taking on a dramatic identity which masks their true identity and intentions. Sir Cautious does not know that Gayman is the long-time beloved of his wife, merely that he is a gallant winning at cards. Gayman plays that role in order to blind him to his true aim, that of obtaining Julia. Belvile dresses up as a ghost, and manipulates Sir Feeble's guilt and fear in a mock scene from a Jacobean revenge play. By playing on the husband's respective weaknesses (greed and timidity), the trickster achieves his ends and credibly stays within his enacted role.

These two extracts demonstrate how characterisation of the old men is used to deny them sympathy: for example, Sir Cautious's cumulative references to his attachment to money over his wife (ll. 381, 388, 401–2, 409–11, 429–30). The doubling of the plot therefore ought to intensify the audience's distaste for their characters. In fact, and interestingly, the opposite effect is at least intimated. By doubling the trickery, and in each case taking it to the furthest extreme, of tricking the men out of their wives, Behn asks us to focus on its method. Although the audience is sympathetic to the outcome (the true lovers can be united), there are discordant notes.

The first of these is the positioning of the wife. In the first extract, Cautious's wife is absent from the negotiations about her, and even when she enters (after this extract ends), she is kept in the dark about the true meaning of their language. This clarifies for the audience the ways in which Sir Cautious and Gayman think of her: as a mere commodity. The encounter, whilst providing a showcase for Gayman's wit and improvisational ability, also intimates that he may think of Julia in a way that is uncannily similar to her husband's views. Thus, despite our admiration for the way Gayman manipulates Cautious here, by piling suggestion on top of suggestion, and playing to his greed, such rhetorical legerdemain places Gayman firmly within the masculine culture of gaming and winning, where women are the stake and prize.

In the second extract, Leticia is present at the gulling of her husband, although ignorant about what is yet to happen. It is clear that her servant Phillis has been privy to Belmour's intentions, whilst Leticia has to adapt to the situation to act her part. Her relatively active participation encourages the audience to sympathise more with this couple than with Gayman's trick. Such sympathy is further encouraged by the fact that Feeble has clearly engaged in nefarious and illegal tactics to win his wife from Belmour. The parallels between the two scenes thus help to remind us that the situations are different, and to encourage the audience to judge the participants differently. Julia's absence from the action in the first underlines and symbolises her absence as an equal in Sir Cautious's life. Equally, although Leticia is present in the second episode, she is only responsive to male leads: either that of her husband, or Belmour's. Both extracts therefore literally display through physical action the disempowerment and displacement of women.

Both extracts utilise images and language from games and economics. In the first extract the wagering of a wife in a card game is the most overt example, but additionally, Gayman and Sir Cautious talk about contracts, bargains, and the witnessing of agreements. In using gaming and market-place language to win his beloved, Gayman both succeeds and fails in his main objective. He succeeds, because he uses a language and game which Sir Cautious recognises and accepts sufficiently for him to abandon his cautious nature and wager his wife. However, he fails because Julia, as we see in Act 5, does not accept the logic of their bargain and wager, nor does she accept her designation as a piece of property. Thus, through displaying how the language of gaming and bargaining functions to enable men and to dis-able women, Behn once again shows an audience both the inequitable gender system and a way for women to resist it.

The second extract uses the game model more parodically, and it is Leticia's over-acting which draws this to our attention. Behn indicates this through the stage directions, and the actor by the exaggerated mock-tragic language she uses and her physical engagement in the performance (for example, ll. 55–6). Equally, Belmour's language must read as parody. The archaic and formal linguistic register and rhythm of his words, which echo those of Jacobean revenge tragedies and revenge ghosts, alerts the audience to the scene's parodic status. The fact that Sir Feeble takes such bombastic fiction seriously further underlines his folly. The mock-tragic acting reminds us that Sir Feeble has seriously wronged Belmour and Leticia, but it provides a way of turning such a wrong into a comic ending, rather than a tragic one. Role-playing in this extract therefore moves from the mock-tragic to the comic, whilst in the first extract it moves from the comic to the satiric.

Finally, the different setting of each extract (a public place and a private bedroom) point to the different interpretations the audience might make of each trick. By negotiating his wife away as part of a social game in public, both Sir Cautious and Gayman may be seen to consider Julia as no more than a bargaining counter between men. The setting of the bedroom in the second extract clarifies that the wrong done Belmour by Sir Feeble was both a private matter, and intimately related to their love for Leticia. By resolving it privately, both men are represented as resolving it in front, in the presence, and with the consent, of Leticia. A private setting fully incorporates the woman's participation.

Conclusions

1. Behn typically doubles or triples actions, events and characters. This is a plotting device enabling the audience to understand and literally see on stage the similarities and differences between characters, actions and situations. The replicative violence of *The Rover*, applied successively by different men to the same woman, makes the actions, ideology and characters of the gallants appear dangerous and endemic rather than amusing or comic. When you see the play on stage this cumulative replication becomes very disturbing. Florinda's near rape on three occasions (albeit one occurs prior to the play's opening) enables the audience to see that disguise and public rambling can be disastrous for women, whilst liberating for men. Replication reinforces our perception of some of the bases of gender inequality.

2. Her use of sub-plots which echo and reinforce the characterisation and themes of the main plot enables her to darken our perception on some of the supposedly liberating and fun-filled actions of the gallants and heroines. For example, in *The Feigned Courtesans*, the Julio/Laura plot and the Sir Signal sub-plot act as darker commentaries on the adventures of Cornelia, Marcella, Fillamour and Gayman. This is also true of the parallel plots of Hellena and Willmore, and Angellica and Willmore in *The Rover*.

3. Improvisation is an attractive trait. However, by doubling or tripling plots, Behn shows how such improvisation may be read or understood in different ways. Thus Gayman's brilliant improvised strategy does not endear Julia to him, whilst Belmour's is recognised and taken up by Leticia, and frees her from her marriage.

4. The plotting and paralleling of events, including slight divergences, reveals Behn's intelligent approach to her drama. In doubling and tripling events, she is concerned to alert her audience to the complexities and nuances of her subject, but she does so via dramatic rather than didactic means. We shall return to the subject of her professional dramaturgy in the next chapter.

5. Each plot teeters on the brink of tragedy, but finally moves towards a comic resolution. In each play the multiplying of plots

brings the outcome closer to tragedy, raising audience tension about potential outcomes. The proximity of potential tragedy ensures that Behn's comedies retain a darkness which deepens the audience's engagement and enables us to both laugh at comic invention, and ponder at the serious issues raised by the near-tragic denouement.

Methods of Analysis

We have introduced some additional modes of analysis, most of which ask you to consider structure as an integral part of dramatic writing, including:

1. structural analysis and perception of the interweaving of main and sub-plots;
2. the noting of the tripling of characters and events, and consideration of the ways in which such paralleling offers different or similar perspectives on the themes of the play;
3. the interlinking of structural devices with content;
4. consideration of the relationship between plot, structure and audience response.

Suggested Work

The Rover
Look at Willmore's flirtation and attempted seduction of the three women: first of Hellena (1, ii, 123–95; and Act 3, scene ii), then of Angellica (Act 2, scene ii) and finally of Florinda (Act 3, scene v). Note the similarities of language and approach. Why does Behn draw attention to this? What is the effect of tripling Willmore's seductions? Look at the parallels between the Hellena/Willmore and the Angellica/Willmore plots. Why are there similarities between Hellena and Angellica? What is the effect of the ending of the Angellica episode in Act 5 on our perception of the relationship between Willmore and Hellena?

The Feigned Courtesans

Consider the parallels between Marcella and Cornelia on the one hand, and Laura Lucretia on the other. What are the similarities between them? Why is our attention drawn to such parallels? The outcomes of their desires and pursuits are very different:

We have already considered some of the major doublings and triplings of *The Lucky Chance* in previous chapters: remind yourself of your conclusions.

7

Staging

Behn's theatrical and visual sense of how her plays should work on stage is clear from both the way the text performs and the authorial stage directions. We have not the space here to consider all the examples in each play of her theatrical facility: one example from each demonstrates Behn's use of the spatial and visual dimensions of the stage to build tension, aid characterisation and deepen the drama. Throughout our previous analyses this approach has been implicit: now we need to make it explicit.

*   *   *

The scenes we shall look at from *The Rover* are the quick succession of short episodes where Blunt is gulled by Lucetta (Act 3, scenes ii–v). We shall include only those parts of those three scenes illustrating explicit staging issues. You should return to the full text to understand how the three scenes work as a whole.

[Act 3, scene ii]

> *Lucetta's house*
>
> *Enter Blunt and Lucetta with a light.*
>
> Lucetta.   Now we are safe and free: no fears of the coming home of my old jealous husband, which made me a little thoughtful when you came in first, but now love is all the business of my soul.

Blunt.   I am transported! (*Aside*) Pox on't, that I had but some fine
    things to say to her, such as lovers use. I was a fool not to learn   5
    of Fred a little by heart before I came . . .

        Enter Sancho.
Sancho.   Sir, my lady has sent me to conduct you to her chamber.
Blunt.   Sir, I shall be proud to follow.
        Exit Sancho.
Here's one of her servants too! 'Adsheartlikins, by this garb and   30
gravity, he might be a justice of the peace in Esssex, and is but a pimp
here.
        Exit.

[Act 3, scene iii]

        The scene changes to a chamber with an alcove bed in it, a table, etc.
        Lucetta in bed.

        Enter Sancho and Blunt, who takes the candle of Sancho at the door.
Sancho.   Sir, my commission reaches no farther.
Blunt.   Sir, I'll excuse your compliment.
        Exit Sancho
 – What, in bed, my sweet mistress?
Lucetta.   You see, I still out-do you in kindness.
Blunt.   And thou shalt see what haste I'll make to quit scores.   5
    [*Aside*] Oh, the luckiest rogue!
        [*Blunt*] *undresses himself.*
Lucetta.   Should you be false or cruel now!
Blunt.   False! 'Adsheartlikins, what dost thou take me for? A Jew?
    An insensible heathen? A pox of thy old jealous husband; an he
    were dead, egad, sweet soul, it should be none of my fault, if I did   10
    not marry thee.
Lucetta.   It never should be mine.
Blunt.   Good soul! I'm the fortunatest dog!
Lucetta.   Are you not undressed yet?
Blunt.   As much as my impatience will permit.   15
    Goes towards the bed in his shirt, drawers, etc.
Lucetta.   Hold, sir, put out the light, it may betray us else.
Blunt.   Anything; I need no other light, but that of thine eyes!
    [*Aside*] 'Adsheartlikins, there I think I had it.

[*Blunt*] *puts out the candle; the bed descends* [*by means of a trap*]; *he gropes about to find it.*

Why – why – where am I got? What, not yet? Where are you, sweetest? – Ah, the rogue's silent now, a pretty love-trick this: how   20
she'll laugh at me anon! – You need not, my dear rogue, you need not! I'm all on fire already. Come, come, now call me in pity.–
Sure I'm enchanted! I have been round the chamber, and can find neither woman, nor bed. I locked the door, I'm sure she cannot go that way; or if she could, the bed could not. – Enough, enough, my   25
pretty wanton, do not carry the jest too far. – Ha, betrayed! Dogs! Rogues! Pimps! Help! help!

[*Blunt*] *lights on a trap, and is let down. Enter Lucetta, Philippo, and Sancho with a light.*

Philippo.   Ha, ha, ha, he's dispatched finely . . .

[Act 3, scene iv]

The scene changes, and discovers Blunt, creeping out of a common-shore, his face, etc., all dirty.

Blunt. (*Climbing up*)   Oh Lord! I am got out at last . . . !

(*The Rover*, Act 3, scenes ii–v)

There are several aspects of staging to consider in analysing plays. As we shall see, not all of these will apply to each extract, although we shall use all of them in the chapter. First, we should consider the way our chosen scenes achieve significance in relation to the surrounding scenes and action. Secondly, how stage directions, including both explicit authorial ones and those placed within dialogue, illuminate the visual and physical choreography of dramatic meaning. Thirdly, how dialogue, action and stage business illustrate and illuminate the blocking and choreography of characters, and the manipulation of stage space to engage the audience. Fourthly, how characters manipulate the audience and consequently how Behn expects her dramatic writing to be interpreted. Fifthly, how technical effects (including lighting, stage properties and mechanical devices) enhance dramatic meaning and understanding.

How do these scenes fit in with the rest of the play, and what do they look like on stage? The answers to these questions help us to

understand how Behn makes her writing and staging dramatic. This
succession of scenes comes between scenes in which the love affairs
of Florinda and Hellena are explored: in Act 3, scene i, the women
roam the street in '*antic*' attire, looking for adventure, and Hellena
both observes Willmore emerging from Angellica's house in the early
hours, and flirts on the streets with him. In the scenes immediately
following this one (scenes v and vi), we observe Florinda in the
garden accosted by Willmore, and the consequent fall-out between
him and Belvile. What then is the dramatic significance of this interlude between Blunt and Lucetta? By sandwiching this extract
between examples of Willmore's sexual voraciousness (we see him
with three different women in the framing scenes), our attention is
drawn to the parallels between Blunt and Willmore. Blunt's experience is placed on a continuum with Willmore's and Belvile's. Whilst
Willmore is more adept at seduction, and more street-wise, all see
women as usable commodities. Conversely, the women in all these
scenes are far cleverer, more sexually active, and intelligent than the
men. By staging a juxtaposition between the main and sub-plots,
Behn ensures the audience literally sees both masculine pomposity as
generic, and how female sexuality can be appropriated as a mode of
self-determination. These are key themes, which are dramatically
realised in three-dimensional staging and scenic structure.

What do the stage directions tells us about Behn's dramatic intelligence? First, she is greatly concerned to convey an exact sense of
place and space. The first scene is in a reception room in Lucetta's
house, the next changes to a chamber '*with an alcove bed in it, a
table etc.*', and the final one '*discovers Blunt, creeping out of a
common-shore*'. These invoke an exact visual imagining of physical
environment, and suggest a relationship to dramatic meaning. The
first two scenes progress visually as Blunt expects: he moves from the
more public space of Lucetta's house into the inner chamber of her
bedroom. The setting then replicates his expectations, and those of
the audience, since we are not privy in advance to the trick. The
intimacy of the bedroom setting is indicated both by the props listed
and intimated (bed, table and 'etc.'), and by the candles exchanged
between Blunt and Sancho (Act 3, scene iii). Lighting, stage directions and stage props therefore create an atmosphere of sensual and

sexual expectation, lulling both Blunt and audience. Implicit stage directions in the dialogue enhance character and atmosphere: Blunt's commentaries on Lucetta's behaviour in scene ii reinforce his gullibility, but do not necessarily warn of what is to come. In scene iii Blunt remarks that she is already in bed, while Lucetta comments on his slow undressing.

The explicit stage directions mean that the audience realise before Blunt that he has been gulled ('*puts out the candle; the bed descends*'), if the overall lighting enables us to see this. Blunt's understanding does not come for another six lines. The stage directions in this part of the scene relate to technical effects, which we shall discuss in a moment. With its intimate lushness, and victorious crowing, the end of scene iii is then contrasted visually with the opening of scene iv, where the shutters for the bedroom pull away, the furniture is removed (the stage direction '*discovers Blunt*'), and we see a '*common-shore*', in other words a sewer. The physical delineation of Blunt, '*his face, etc., all dirty*', contrasts both with the luxury of the previous scene and with his original expectations. He is visually as well as physically humiliated, and an object of ridicule for the audience.

What about other aspects of the choreography of these scenes? Blunt speaks several asides (3, ii, 4–6; 3, ii, 30–2; 3, iii, 6; and 3, iii, 18). These imply that he is quite near the front of the stage, and able to deliver these as though to the audience. However, unlike the usual intimacy engendered by asides, they do not endear him to us, but illustrate his pomposity, lack of experience and potential gullibility. The entrances and exits of Sancho help create an illusion of normality up until the point of the descent of the bed. Similarly, Lucetta's positioning in bed, implicitly undressed, sets up an expectation that she is passive and motionless, so that we (and Blunt) do not expect her to engineer a trick. Explicit stage blocking, then, helps set up the surprise denouement. Conversely, the arrival of Lucetta's servants and Philippo (3, iii, 27), looking down the trap at Blunt, provides a momentary visual symbol of the inversion of Blunt's expectations (he is down below and mocked, rather than on top and celebrated) and of the real power relations of the whole three scenes. Philippo's triumphal words at the end of the scene (3, iii, 53–7) imply physical, exuberant dominance over the (literally) fallen man.

This scene contains the most spectacular technical effects of the
play: the descent and disappearance of the bed implies a large trap-
door and an effective pulley system, as well as proficient technicians.
The trap-door evidently serves a triple purpose, since Blunt '*lights on
a trap, and is let down*' after the bed disappears, and at the beginning
of scene iv comes out of the sewer, which is presumably from the
trap-door. By using a single technical function for this triple
purpose, Behn illustrates her dramatic economy and versatility. Stage
space and props can signify different functions depending on
context, setting and dialogue.

On a less spectacular level, the use of candles for lighting enables
two simultaneous effects crucial for the scenes' effectiveness. They
create an intimate atmosphere, but make it easier to deceive Blunt
(and the audience) by conveying only partial light, and being easily
extinguished. By specifying Blunt's dirty body (implicitly covered in
excreta), and leaving some of the representation of this up to the
director, actor and make-up team ('*his face, etc.*'), Behn draws attention to Blunt's total humiliation, and proposes him visually as a
figure for our disgust and mirth. Here visual effects combine with
other dramatic manipulation to suggest the blindness of masculine
pride. Visual and staging effects thereby reinforce dramatic themes.

*   *   *

Let us now turn to the staging of a key scene in *The Feigned
Courtesans*.

[Act 5, scene ii]

> *A chamber*
>
> *Enter Laura Lucretia, as before, in a night-gown.*
> *Laura Lucretia.*   Now for a power that never yet was known,
>   To charm this stranger quickly into love;
>   Assist my eyes, thou god of kind desires;
>   Inspire my language with a moving force,
>   That may at once gain and secure the victory.   5
> *Enter Silvio.*

Silvio.   Madam, your lover's here; your time's but short. Consider,
    too, Count Julio may arrive.
Laura Lucreta.   Let him arrive!
                    Having secured myself of what I love,
                    I'll leave him to complain his unknown loss   10
                    To careless winds, as pitiless as I.
                    Silvio, see the rooms be filled with lights,
                    Whilst I prepare myself to entertain him.
                    Darkness shall ne'er deceive me more.
            [*Exit Laura Lucretia*]. *Enter, to Silvio, Galliard, gazing about him,*
            [*followed by*] *Cornelia,* [*still in man's clothes*] *peeping at the door.*
Galliard.   All's wondrous rich, gay as the court of love,   15
            But still and silent as the shades of death.
        Soft music whilst they speak.
    Ha, music, and excellent! Pox on't, but where's the woman? I need
    no preparation.
Cornelia. [*Aside*]   No, you are always provided for such encounters,
    and can fall to sans ceremony; but I may spoil your stomach.   20
        A song tuning.
Galliard.   A voice, too, by heaven, and 'tis a sweet one;
            Grant she be young, and I'll excuse the rest,
            Yet vie for pleasure with the happiest Roman.
        The song as by Laura Lucretia, after which soft music till she enters.

THE SONG
by a person of quality

Farewell the world and mortal cares,
The ravished Strephon cried,
As, full of joy and tender tears,   25
He lay by Phillis' side:
Let others toil for wealth and fame,
Whilst not one thought of mine
At any other bliss shall aim,
But those dear arms, but those dear arms of thine.   30

Still let me gaze on thy bright eyes,
And hear thy charming tongue,
I nothing ask t'increase my joys
But thus to feel 'em long;
In close embraces let us lie,   35
And spend our lives to come;

> *Then let us both together die,*
> *And be each other's, be each other's tomb.*

Galliard.   Death, I am fired already with her voice.
Cornelia. [*Aside*]   So, I am like to thrive.   40
      Enter Julio.
Julio.   What mean these lights in every room, as if to make the day
    without the sun, and quite destroy my hopes? Ha, Galliard here!
Cornelia. [*Aside*]   A man! Grant it some lover, or some husband,
    heaven, or anything that will but spoil the sport. The lady! Oh,
    blast her, how fair she is.   45
      Enter Laura Lucretia, with her lute, dressed in a careless rich
      dress, followed by Sabina, to whom she gives her lute.
Julio.   Ha, 'tis the same woman!
    [*Laura Lucretia*] *sees Julio, and starts.*
Laura Lucretia. [*Aside*]   A stranger here! What art can help me now?
    (*She pauses.*)
Galliard.   By all my joys, a lovely woman 'tis.
Laura Lucretia. [*Aside*]   Help me, deceit, dissembling, all that's woman!
    She starts, and gazes on Galliard, pulling Silvio.
Cornelia. [*Aside*]   Sure I should know that face.   50
Laura Lucretia.   Ah, look, my Silvio! Is't not he? It is!
        That smile, that air, that mien, that bow is his!
        'Tis he, by all my hopes, by all my wishes!
Galliard.   He? Yes, yes, I am a he, I thank my stars,
        And never blessed 'em half so much for being so,   55
        As for the dear variety of woman.
Cornelia.   Curse on her charms, she'll make him love in earnest.
    [*Exit Silvio.*]
Laura Lucretia (*going towards* [*Galliard*])   It is my brother, and
    report was false!
Galliard. [*Aside*]   How, her brother? Gad, I'm sorry we're so near
    akin with all my soul, for I am damnably pleased with her!   60
                (*The Feigned Courtesans*, 5, ii, 1–60)

There are several bedroom scenes in this play, each involving an
assignation by one of the heroines with her gallant, which is postponed or disrupted by the arrival of several unwanted suitors or rela-
tives, or by the wrong man. The first is implied by the ending of Act
3, scene i (analysed in the previous chapter) in which Laura accepts

Julio into her chamber, believing it is Galliard. The second is the subsequent scene (Act 4, scene i), in which Marcella dresses as a courtesan, and attempts to seduce Fillamour, interrupted by both Sir Signal and Tickletext. The third is Act 4, scene ii, in which Cornelia has hoped to seduce Galliard, but this is foiled by the buffoonery of Signal and Tickletext, as well as by Cornelia's failure to persuade Galliard to love 'honourably'. This extract (Act 5, scene ii) is thus the fourth such scenario, and follows the structural pattern of those three in confounding its opening expectations. We know (from scene i) that Laura still believes it was Galliard with whom she slept. The audience alone know it was actually Julio. The framing and contextualisation of this scene is therefore crucial in understanding its meaning. The audience have come to expect such scenes to end in bathos and failure: women's desires are frustrated by accident, buffoonery, or masculine fighting. Desire is crowded out by fate and by the accidents attendant upon the multiplication of 'Silvianettas'. In addition, in the case of Laura, the audience anticipate disaster when she realises she has made her vows to Julio instead of to Galliard (her chosen beloved). This scene is therefore placed in a crucial structural position: it is the last bedroom scene, and thereby acts as a commentary on the previous failures. Equally, the previous failures intensify our feeling that there will be a potentially tragic outcome for Laura.

In what ways do the stage directions aid our dramatic under-standing and sense of the play as enacted? Stage directions are used to delineate appearance, attitude or response, setting and action. Such exactitude is unusual compared with the other plays studied here, suggesting the centrality of visual and spatial representation in *The Feigned Courtesans*. Laura is '*in a night-gown*', and later '*dressed in a careless rich dress*', establishing a visual sense of lush intimacy and vulnerability. Galliard's arrival and attitude ('*gazing about him*') are painted visually before being reinforced through his comments (ll. 15–16). Visual appearance and effect are therefore as important as verbal content. Attitude is signalled in the stage directions applied to Laura's response to seeing Julio ('*starts*' and '*she pauses*') and in her manufactured response to Galliard when Julio is the audience ('*starts, and gazes on Galliard, pulling Silvio*'). Once again, these visual cues are reinforced by her words, particularly the asides she makes (ll. 47 and 49), and effectively slow down the action, drawing the audience's attention to her self-conscious acting. The effect of this is to make her seem calculating, a judgement underlined by her plea, 'Help me, deceit, dissembling, all that's woman' (ll. 48–9). Visual cues work, then, to slow down action and help the audience judge characters. Implicit and explicit stage directions tell us about the setting, for example, the opening direction of 'A chamber', Laura's request for lights (l. 12), and Gayman's comments on the 'rich, gay' environment, which intensify the feeling of a bordello.

Finally, stage directions also direct action, for example, Cornelia's illicit arrival and observance of the scene are implied by the verb '*peeping*' (l. 15), whilst the delivery and enactment of the song are portrayed as seductively gradual ('*A song tuning*', l. 21), and slow moving ('*soft music till she enters*', l. 23). Once again this physical experience, through the stage directions and the song itself, is delivered simultaneously to audience and characters before any comment is made upon it (l. 39). The aural and visual enjoyment of the song predominates over any intellectual response. This is important dramatically, because it engenders sympathy for Laura through her singing and through the pathos attached to her desires (which we suspect will be thwarted). Staging devices thus establish our sympathies and manipulate our judgement, initially suspending it through sensory temptation, then bringing it back through explicit visual characterisation.

In what ways does the dialogue and action here illuminate Behn's attention to staging? Laura's opening invocation ('Now for a power that never yet was known') implies in both delivery and content the role of a tragic heroine. The verse is mainly iambic pentameter, the register and tone elevated (for example, using the synecdoche 'thou god of kind desires', l. 3, for Cupid). Such elevation posits a character who dominates the stage, and claims an ambiguous response from the audience. Laura's domination continues within this extract: she stage-manages the song, and even when Julio arrives unexpectedly, she explicitly tells us that she needs to find an 'art' that will help her deceive him. The audience thence know her actions are an act, and her exaggerated delivery as she exclaims over Galliard's fea-

tures is both visually humorous and strategically necessary, if ultimately disastrous. The visual delivery of this effect is crucial to our
full understanding of its complexity. Deception and self-deception
are key themes in the play, and by making these visually explicit,
Behn illustrates her understanding of dramatic form as a combination of the verbal, visual and physical.

Two characters act as direct channels of communication with the
audience, and help direct our interpretation. We have already
touched upon Laura's self-conscious and self-confessed stage-man-
agement and acting, and the way these both draw us to her, and
encourage us to see her as potentially deceitful. In addition, the presence of Cornelia as a commentary figure is a key way of manipulating audience opinion. She stands on the edge of the stage,
directing her comments to us on the action: like us, she is not
involved. Her physical place on the stage is a crucial visual indicator
of this, and helps to remind us that our strongest allegiance is to her,
and we therefore want Laura's seduction of Galliard to fail.

Finally, the technical effects aid our understanding of the play.
The delivery and playing of the song, supposedly by Laura, who is
described as holding a lute, are a key atmospheric and aesthetic
caesura in the overall pace of this scene. Music captures and silences
the audience, engages our sensory response, and tempts us, as it
tempts Galliard. Yet the singing of music by women was often erotic
on stage, and is here explicitly so. For Behn to specify that Laura
should hold a lute suggests her emphasis of Laura's sexual availability, since lutes were often used in seventeenth-century paintings
to signal female sexual organs or sexuality. Additionally, the song's
content is explicitly erotic, and expressed in the words of Strephon,
the man not the woman. Finally, the song's genre is the poetic pastoral, which was often used in Restoration verse as an explicit invitation to sex, despite its overtly innocuous context, the natural setting
invoking the naturalist arguments of libertines for free sexual expression and behaviour. This may be a further way in which the audience is encouraged to judge Laura's behaviour as inappropriate: she
is an active lover, appropriating masculine erotic discourses and
points of view and prepared to lose her virginity. In content, genre
and focalisation it is very similar to that sung from Angellica's

balcony in *The Rover*. The song, as with much of the other staging devices of this scene, is ambiguous: it simultaneously draws us to Laura, and pushes us away. This dual response to her character and dilemma is part of Behn's complex dramatic aim. She demands that we think about Laura's situation: both her forced marriage and the expressed views on how women should behave. Yet she also demonstrates that the actions Laura chooses result only in condemnation. Staging helps us experience this dilemma emotionally as well as intellectually.

*   *   *

Let us now turn to *The Lucky Chance*.

[Act 3, scene iii]

> *A wash-house, or out-house*

> *Enter, with [a] dark-lantern, Bredwell, disguised like a devil, leading*
> *Gayman.*

Bredwell. Stay here, till I give notice of your coming.
> *Exit Bredwell. [He] leaves his dark-lantern.*

Gayman. Kind light, a little of your aid. Now must I be peeping,
  though my curiosity should lose me all. Ha! Zouns, what's here, a
  hovel or a hog-sty? Hum, see the wickedness of man, that I should
  find no time to swear in, but just when I'm in the devil's clutches.   5
> *Enter Pert, [disguised] as an old woman, with a staff.*

[Pert]. Good even to you, fair sir.

Gayman. [Aside] Ha, defend me! If this be she, I must rival the devil,
  that's certain.

[Pert]. Come, young gentleman, dare not you venture? . . .

[Act 3, scene iv]

> *A chamber in the apartments of Lady Fulbank*

> *Enter [Pert, still as an] old woman, followed by Gayman in*
> *the dark. Soft music plays. She leaves him.*

[Gayman]. Ha, music – and excellent!

[SONG]

Oh, love, that stronger art than wine,
Pleasing delusion, witchery divine,
Want to be prized above all wealth,
Disease that has more joys than health, 5
Though we blaspheme thee in our pain,
And of thy tyranny complain,
We all are bettered by thy reign.

What reason never can bestow,
We to this useful passion owe. 10
Love wakes the dull from sluggish ease,
And learns a clown the art to please;
Humbles the vain, kindles the cold,
Makes misers free, and cowards bold.
'Tis he reforms the sot from drink, 15
And teaches airy fops to think.

When full brute appetite is fed,
And choked the glutton lies, and dead,
Thou new spirits dost dispense,
And 'finest the gross delights of sense: 20
Virtue's unconquerable aid,
That against nature can persuade,
And makes a roving mind retire
Within the bounds of just desire:
Cheerer of age, youth's kind unrest, 25
And half the heaven of the blessed.

[*Gayman*].   Ah, Julia, Julia! if this soft preparation
Were but to bring me to thy dear embraces,
What different motions would surround my soul
From what perplex it now. 30

    Enter nymphs and shepherds, and dance. Then two dance alone.
    All go out but Pert and a shepherd.

If these be devils, they are obliging ones. I did not care if I
ventured on the last female fiend.

Man. (*sings*)   *Cease your wonder, cease your guess,*
Whence arrives your happiness;
Cease your wonder, cease your pain, 35
Human fancy is in vain.

[*Enter nymphs and shepherds.*]

Chorus.   'Tis enough you once shall find,
                      Fortune may to worth be kind;

[*Man*] *gives* [*Gayman*] *gold.*

                      And love can leave off being blind.
[*Pert*] (*sings*)   You, before you enter here,   40
                      On this sacred ring must swear;
       [*Pert*] *puts* [*the ring*] *on* [*Gayman's*] *finger, holds his hand.*

                      By the figure, which is round,
                      Your passion constant and profound;
                      By the adamantine stone,
                      To be fixed to one alone;   45
                      By the lustre, which is true,
                      Ne'er to break your sacred vow;
                      Lastly, by the gold, that's tried,
                      For love all dangers to abide.

       They all dance about [*Gayamn*], *while* [*Pert and the man*] *sing.*

Man.   Once about him let us move,   50
                      To confirm him true to love. (*bis*)
Pert.   Twice with mystic turning feet,
                      Make him silent and discreet. (*bis*)
Man.   Thrice about him let us tread,
                      To keep him ever young in bed. (*bis*)   55

              Gives [*Gayman*] *another part* [*of gold*].

Man.   Forget Aminta's proud disdain:
                      Taste here, and sigh no more in vain,
                      The joy of love without the pain.
Pert.   That god repents his former slights,
                      And fortune thus your faith requites.   60
Both.   Forget Aminta's proud disdain:
                      Then taste, and sigh no more in vain,
                      The joy of love without the pain,
                      The joy of love without the pain.

       Exeunt all dancers. [*Gayman*] *looks on himself and feels about him.*
Gayman.   What the devil can all this mean?   65
                              (*The Lucky Chance*, 3, iii, 1 to 3, iv, 65)

This extract is framed by scenes of Leticia's wedding night, a story of near-tragedy and farce, in which consummation is avoided by Belmour's action of stealing Sir Cautious's watch, and using it to summon Sir Feeble to his house in the middle of the night. The scenes here take place somewhere in Sir Cautious's house, although Gayman is unaware of where he has been taken. Act 3 involves six changes of scene, and the efficient use of changing shutters to symbolise changing spaces and rooms. Such swift changes of place add to the feeling of fast-moving action and intrigue, as well as the potential danger of discovery of Belmour or of Gayman's intentions. In addition, these two scenes we are analysing, juxtaposed as they are with Leticia's powerless passivity on her marriage night, provide an inverse mirror image to that of Leticia. The two scenes are stage-managed and directed by Lady Fulbank (albeit off stage), and align her with active feminine agency, and indeed, with the dramatic powers and skills of the playwright herself. The audience is thus presented with two versions of how a woman might respond to a forced or arranged marriage: passive denial or active plotting.

Stage directions in these two scenes construct the details of the fictional masque. Thus, in the first scene they set the scene in '*A wash-house or out-house*', into which Bredwell, disguised as a devil, leads Gayman. The disguise of both Bredwell and Pert (as an old woman, with a staff) are specified, although Gayman's clothes are not. This illustrates that Behn's visual imagination focused on the nature of the trick, rather than on Gayman's response. The use of a dark-lantern in Act 3, scene iii, and the abandonment of Gayman in the dark at the beginning of scene iv, also point to an exact choreography of action and movement, although stage directions do not explicitly say at what point greater light is produced so that we can watch the dance. By the end of the dance when Gayman '*looks on himself and feels about him*', light is faint again, although 'feeling about him' may suggest he is patting himself down to see whether he has dreamed the experience. Gayman, moved around in the dark, hearing the sudden sound of 'excellent' (3, iv, 1) music, is disorientated before the song and dance begin. Stage directions mark the manner and our understanding of this disorientation.

Stage directions also direct the actions of the singer and dancers, and are integrated with the dialogue and actions of the performed masque. The contents of both the first song and the second duet focus on advice about love. The first is a conventional neo-platonic account of how love supersedes reason, reforms sin and refines gross senses. The second is a duet, less erudite, but an equally significant evocation of fairy love enchantment, achieved through the magical rhythms of the song, the invocation of magic circles, and the gift of fairy gold. It is important that we both hear and see this spell being woven: it makes it more evocative and more puzzling. The fusion of classical and magical traditions aids the atmosphere of fictional fantasy and playfulness, producing the feeling of an interlude from the intrigues of the main action. The rhyming couplets of both songs help build this sense of another world. The idealised pastoral world constructed in the masque is far removed from the economic transactions of the rest of the play, although ironically Julia uses it as a means of giving Gayman money, which he otherwise refused. Such idealisation is represented simultaneously as desirable and impossible.

Gayman himself is not a scripted part of the performance, and his comments on the action, as well his own reflections about his love for Julia, act as our own commentary on this play-within-the-play. He conveys a kind of child-like pleasure in the music, the dance and the gold. Although Bredwell is disguised as a devil, conjuring images of damnation and fall, there is nothing else in these scenes which reinforces this image: but he is a reminder of the adulterous nature of both Julia's and Gayman's desires. Nevertheless, the theatrical performance produces pleasure and sensory delight, with a subtext demanding men to be faithful in love. If we read the masque as a microcosm of Behn's own play, the explicitly constructed audience response here (through our observation of Gayman's response) might be applied to the overall play. Horace's dictum that poetry should be both pleasurable and didactic, a commonplace in Restoration literary and dramatic theory (as we shall see in Chapter 11), is evoked by Behn's dramatic manipulation of the masque.

Finally, the technical effects of this extract are a fusion of music, dance and audience on stage (Gayman). Whilst the nature of the dance is not specified, it is clear that Gayman is included when '*They all dance about Gayman*', and when he is the recipient of the ring and the gold. We can assume a round dance of some kind, combined with the music. Such a dance helps foster the sense of a magical fairy encounter, an out-of-this-world experience, which contrasts starkly with the intrigue and monetary negotiations of the play's other scenes. The key stage props (ring and gold) signal two key themes in the play: ideals about romantic, everlasting love and marriage, and financial exchange. Although Julia has attempted to introduce the idealised language and commitment of romantic love, gold is exchanged, and later further money is given, so that Gayman can continue his life as a gallant. The use of stage props thus displays the play's fundamental, and unresolved, opposition between economics and love. Staging thus acts as a key mechanism by which contrasts are established between scenes and characters, through which audience response is manipulated, and as a means of visualising and distilling many of the play's key themes and motifs. Let us move on to consider some overall conclusions about Behn's staging.

Conclusions

1. Behn has a clear three-dimensional understanding of how her texts will play on stage. This is obvious from analysis of her stage directions, which show her to be exactly concerned with key entrances and exits, the placing of certain key stage properties, actors' attitudinal responses at certain points, as well as stage business.
2. She uses all parts of the stage to give the audience a sense of a fully-rounded world, and this is clear from both stage directions and character blocking. We can see this when we look at a succession of scenes (for example, in *The Rover*) where scene changes are swift-moving, and shutters drawn back to reveal new scenes behind, or drawn forward to introduce a concept of the outside (in the '*common-shore*' scene, for example). Characters are required to use the edges of the stage, or the fore-stage, for eavesdropping and hiding, and such characters use this space for direct communication with the audience, or commentary upon the action. The '*long street*' in Act 2 of *The Rover* utilises the proscenium arch and shutters to give a sense of perspective and space.

3. By using all parts of the stage she is able to develop complex relationships and parallels between characters in a visual as well as thematic manner. Action and intrigue function effectively partly on the basis of our visual understanding of who is where and when.

4. Behn uses stage directions (which assume a spatial dimension to action) and character blocking (implicit in the dialogue) to confirm or contrast characters' senses of themselves and others. Thus, for example, in the extract we analysed from *The Rover*, Blunt's confident control of the spaces of the bedroom, symbolising his own self-regard and pomposity, are reduced and destroyed by the descent of darkness, the disappearance of the bed, and then his own fall into the sewer. His physical environment exactly echoes his disorientation and fall, and helps the audience to judge and understand him. Similarly in *The Feigned Courtesans*, Laura's initial supreme control of her environment and situation, in which she orders the room and lights to suit her needs, is undone by the arrival of Julio. Stage directions (or acting) show us the desperation with which she adopts an acting role, and gradually loses control of stage and situation. Physical movement and spatial control are therefore further indices of character, and of Behn's use of theatrical space as a means of deepening dramatic meaning.

5. Dramatic space is often used to represent power: in *The Rover*, Blunt's initial assumption of his own sexual and masculine power over the bedroom is denied by Lucetta's trick and self-assertion over the dramatic spaces. In our chosen extracts we have seen instances where women assume control over dramatic space, mainly in the form of engineering a performance to trick a man in some way. In each case, this is an inversion of the usual power relations. In other parts of the plays it is usually men who clearly own most of the stage space, and are seen to strut, declaim and appropriate space as they desire. You could consider some instances of this in the suggested work, below.

6. Music, song and dance are key aspects of Behn's theatrical repertoire, and are used partly as interludes in the action and intrigue, but also often as displaced commentaries on the main action, and

as a means by which we can observe key characters' responses to events.

7. As we saw in Chapter 3 ('Discovery Scenes'), Behn's sense of the theatrical in discovery scenes is structural, spatial, visual, and thematic.

8. Stage props are used symbolically, and are used to emphasise key themes and conflicts.

9. Women can be seen to engage in 'plotting' theatrical events within the plays: Behn suggests a meta-theatrical connection between her own writing and successful dramatisation by her characters.

10. Behn frequently uses the pastoral to symbolise a nostalgic, unobtainable sexual ideal.

Methods of Analysis

We have:

1. introduced, or re-used, some terms of theatrical analysis, such as 'character blocking', 'use of stage space', and 'scenic juxtaposition';

2. considered how stage props can be integrated with verbal themes to coalesce and deepen verbal meaning with visual representation;

3. used stage directions as a proxy in understanding how Behn envisages action on stage, and combined these with analysis of the content of the scene in order to establish a valid interpretation;

4. taken note of music, song and dance as integral parts of the overall meaning of the play.

Suggested Work

The Rover
Look at the staging of Act 1, scene ii. What is the significance of the setting? Comment on the men's perception of women in this context. How does Behn use the stage? How is the setting and use of

space a contrast to that in scene i? Is there a difference between gentry women and the courtesans when they are on the streets? Look for other scenes where you see space and setting used differently by men and women.

The Feigned Courtesans

Look at Act 2, scene i, and Act 4, scene i, where Marcella tries to tempt Fillamour. Consider, for example, the setting, dress and language and Fillamour's physical response. How do the visual prompts reinforce our interpretation of the scene?

The Lucky Chance

Look at the party and gambling scene (Act 4, scene i). Comment on how the dice game acts as a visual and aural counterpoint to the sexual bargaining. What is the effect of their juxtaposition? Where are each placed on the stage? Where is Julia whilst this happens?

Consider how and why certain stage props are used and reappear. In *The Rover* references to and appearances of the sword should be identified. Why are they so frequent? What other props are important, and why, and how?

Finally, consider the question of costume. All the plays use the motif of the disguised heroine, but also draw attention to dress and appearance through stage directions and dialogue. Comment on why Behn does this.

8

Carnival and Masquerade

Carnival, the celebration before the fasting of Lent, was both a physical festival in Catholic countries, and a state of mind. During Carnival the inversion of normal identities and activities could be celebrated and played with, and normality was mocked. Disguise, noise, sexual and bodily excess, were all features of Carnival entertainments. The Russian critic Mikhail Bakhtin has argued that Carnival can also be considered a literary or linguistic mode, in which inversion of normal hierarchies, celebration of the body and of the popular, may be used as a way of criticising the status quo. In *The Rover*, in particular, Carnival is central to setting, plot and theme, whilst in the other plays disguise is formalised as an essential part of both plot and structure. We shall examine the way in which Behn uses Carnival's modes (such as inversion, cross-dressing, disguise, grotesquerie, and darkness) in order both to celebrate aberrant behaviour and identity and to show how women are often punished more for such aberrance than men. Let us look at *The Rover* to explore this.

* * *

The play is set in Naples at Carnival time, and the following extract in the opening scene demonstrates one of the play's key class and gender themes.

[Act 1, scene i]

> *Callis.*   I must obey the commands I have; besides, do you consider
> what a life you are going to lead?
> *Hellena.*   Yes, Callis, that of a nun: and till then I'll be indebted a
> world of prayers to you, if you'll let me now see, what I never did,
> the divertisements of a Carnival.   170
> *Callis.*   What, go in masquerade? 'Twill be a fine farewell to the
> world, I take it; pray, what would you do there?
> *Hellena.*   That which all the world does, as I am told: be as mad as
> the rest, and take all innocent freedoms. Sister, you'll go too, will
> you not? Come, prithee be not sad. We'll outwit twenty brothers,   175
> if you'll be ruled by me. Come, put off this dull humour with your
> clothes, and assume one as gay, and as fantastic, as the dress my
> cousin Valeria and I have provided, and let's ramble.
> *Florinda.*   Callis, will you give us leave to go?
> *Callis.* (*Aside*)   I have a youthful itch of going myself. – Madam, if I   180
> thought your brother might not know it, and I might wait on you;
> for by my troth, I'll not trust young girls alone.
>
>   (*The Rover*, 1, i, 166–82)

The characters here recognise a dual division in their social world:
that between women of their class (who, according to Callis, are not
allowed out alone) and all other women; and that between women
and men, implicit in the appearance of their brother moments
before, carrying his vizard. He has forbidden them to go out (as
Callis reminds us), although he is free to go himself. However,
Hellena (literally) has the last word in the scene, and propels the
action in her decision to experience 'the divertisements of a Carnival'
(l. 170). The women's conversation illustrates their self-conscious
knowledge of the licence and opportunities provided by Carnival. It
is both a rebellion against authority (that of their brother) and a
time for celebration. Callis emphasises disguise (they 'go in masquerade', l. 171), whilst Hellena focuses on both licence ('be as mad
as the rest, and take all innocent freedoms', ll. 173–4) and the ability
to assume any identity (ll. 176–7). There are two further aspects of
Carnival to which she is attracted. She notes the 'fantastic' (l. 177)
humour she can adopt in Carnival, a sense of both an alternative

identity for herself, and a manner of being and space in which to act. The second aspect is implicit in her cry 'let's ramble' (l. 178), which, as we discussed in Chapter 4, invokes the language and freedoms of libertine men in Restoration London. By appropriating a gendered term for sexual and libertine freedoms, Hellena also suggests that Carnival might liberate her sexuality. Carnival to Hellena is a time and a space for alternatives, for inversion and disguise, for adventure and sexual discovery.

Yet such an exuberant opening introduction to Carnival from a woman's point of view is soon tested both by the play's action and by the contrasting behaviour of men during and because of Carnival. Let us move on to our next extract to see the beginnings of such a contrast.

[Act 1, scene ii]

> *Willmore.* But well, faith, I'm glad to meet you again in a warm
>   climate, where the kind sun has its god-like power still over the
>   wine and women. Love and mirth are my business in Naples, and
>   if I mistake not the place, here's an excellent market for chapmen
>   of my humour.   75
> *Belvile.* See, here be those kind merchants of love you look for.
>   *Enter several men in masking habits, some playing on music, others
>   dancing after, women dressed like courtesans, with papers pinned
>   on their breasts, and baskets of flowers in their hands.*
> *Blunt.* 'Adsheartlikins, what have we here?
> *Frederick.* Now the game begins.
> *Willmore.* Fine pretty creatures! May a stranger have leave to look
>   and love? (*Reads the papers*) What's here: 'Roses for every month'?   80
> *Blunt.* Roses for every month? What means that?
> *Belvile.* They are, or would have you think they're courtesans, who
>   here in Naples are to be hired by the month.
> *Willmore.* Kind; and obliging to inform us. [*To a woman*] Pray,
>   where do these roses grow? I would fain plant some of 'em in a   85
>   bed of mine.
> *Woman.* Beware such roses, sir.
> *Willmore.* A pox of fear: I'll be baked with thee between a pair of

sheets (and that's thy proper still), so I might but strew such roses
over me, and under me. Fair one, would you would give me leave   90
to gather at your bush this idle month; I would go near to make
somebody smell of it all the year after.

Belvile.   And thou hast need of such a remedy, for thou stink'st of
tar and ropes' ends, like a dock or pest-house.

> *The woman puts herself into the hands of a man, and* [*both begin
> to leave*].

Willmore.   Nay, nay, you shall not leave me so.   95

Belvile.   By all means use no violence here.

> [*Exeunt man and woman.*]

Willmore.   Death! Just as I was going to be damnably in love, to
have her led off! I could pluck that rose out of his hand, and even
kiss the bed the bush grew in.

Frederick.   No friend to love like a long voyage at sea.   100

Blunt.   Except a nunnery, Fred.

Willmore.   Death! But will they not be kind, quickly be kind? Thou
know'st I'm no tame sigher, but a rampant lion of the forest.

> *Advances, from the farther end of the scenes, two men dressed all
> over with horns of several sorts, making grimaces at one another,
> with papers pinned on their backs.*

(*The Rover*, 1, ii, 70–103)

Why does Behn place this scene in juxtaposition to the previous
one, and in what ways does the men's approach to the Carnival
differ from the women's? This extract, immediately subsequent to
the first scene's predominantly female environment, displays a masculine environment and point of view. The four friends are wan-
dering the streets during Carnival, having met up with Willmore by
accident, and looking for adventure. Willmore's welcoming celebration of Naples's character ('Love and mirth are my business', l. 73)
both establishes his acquisitive and ludic character, as well as linking
his own identity and conduct to the city's Carnival. Willmore's
excesses, from this first introduction to his character and actions, are
thereby linked explicitly to Carnival. This both connects him to
Hellena's welcoming of Carnival in the previous episode, but also
sets up the possibility of a contrast with her. From the opening Act
the audience will watch and judge their parallel Carnival experiences.

This extract also offers Behn the opportunity to use dance and costume as a way of setting the carnivalesque scene. Masking players enter and dance, some dressed as courtesans who offer their bodies for sale as part of the licence of Carnival. Behn structures this short episode in a critical way: first the men converse about Naples; then the women dressed as courtesans dance to the men's ongoing commentary; then Willmore's attempted seduction is interrupted; and finally we watch a short dance by men covered in cuckold's horns. This structural arrangement initially places the men in power: they observe and comment on the women, probably from down-stage, whilst the women performers move from up-stage towards and through the men. This establishes men's ability to both gaze on and comment on women's bodies at will ('May a stranger have leave to look and love?' ll. 79–80). Carnival thus provides an opportunity to free men from the civility of their normal behaviour towards women of quality, enabling sexual desire and lust to be fully and freely expressed. However, the final part of this spectacle (the arrival of the horned men) acts as a visual warning and commentary on this freedom: men may be humiliated or tricked by the sexual freedoms on offer. This is a warning that echoes throughout the play: for example, in Lucetta's gulling of Blunt, and in Hellena's witty management, and eventual snaring, of Willmore. Behn, in this short episode, manages to distil a visual image of the benefits and risks of Carnival to men and women. Carnival experience differs with gender.

Women out on the streets in Carnival are assumed by Willmore to be unambiguously available for sex. Belvile alone notes the potential ambiguities which Carnival may provide, in allowing anyone to take on any disguise: 'They are, **or would have you think**, they're courtesans' (ll. 82–3). This warning reminds us, just before the arrival of Hellena, Florinda and Callis disguised as gypsies, both that Willmore will believe they are sexually available, and that they themselves are playing with ideas about sexual availability. Thus whilst Carnival theoretically liberates, in Willmore's and Blunt's eyes it actually reduces all women to sexual objects. Although these women believe they are offering themselves for display and purchase, in doing so they conform to Willmore's ideas about women as free for his use. It is important that the audience are made critical of Willmore at this point through his attitude to Carnival: his impetuous expressions of desire are countered by the visual warning of the cuckolded maskers. An audience viewpoint is explicitly set up outside the Carnival experience on stage.

Men and women use different language about Carnival. As we saw in the analysis of the first extract, Hellena talks of being 'mad' and of 'rambling'. Willmore focuses much more explicitly on sex: even though he uses euphemisms, they are conventional and explicit ones. Thus, when he talks to successive women about looking for 'love', he means a night's sex. He picks up the women's euphemism ('Roses for every month'), and extends the metaphor into further explicit reference to sexual organs ('give me leave to gather at your bush this idle month', ll. 90–1). Being 'kind' (ll. 84 and 102) means obliging him with their bodies. Equally, the masculine banter about Willmore's expressions of desire acknowledges and encourages male lust as a natural expression and need ('No friend to love like a long voyage at sea', 'a rampant lion of the forest', ll. 100 and 103), and establishes a communal masculine camaraderie based on mutual acknowledgement of common desires. This explicit discussion and celebration of bodies and bodily function is typically carnivalesque. Yet Behn makes us aware that here it is gendered: in other words, Carnival provides men with the freedom to think and talk in this way, but this is at the cost both of women's autonomy, and of any ability they may have to think or act in the same way. Carnival is represented as inequitable and dangerous: all is not what it seems.

Let us now consider a final short extract from *The Rover*, before noting a few other uses to which Behn puts Carnival in the play as a whole.

[Act 2, scene i]

> *The long street*
>
> *Enter Belvile and Frederick in masking habits, and Willmore in his own clothes, with a vizard in his hand.*

> Willmore. But why thus disguised and muzzled?
> Belvile. Because whatever extravagances we commit in these faces,
> our own may not be obliged to answer 'em.
>
> (*The Rover*, 2, i, 1–3)

This Act opens with the whole stage turned into a long street, shutters pulled back to indicate house or shop fronts. The men are now in masks, although Willmore carries rather than wears his: he is the only character in the play who is never disguised. Unexpectedly, it is Belvile who notes the potential violence in Carnival, and indirectly forewarns the audience that mirth may turn to near tragedy. His defence of masking ('Because whatever extravagances we commit in these faces, our own may not be obliged to answer 'em', ll. 2–3) acknowledges disguise as central to Carnival, but equally suggests that their extravagances may be so excessive as to require disguise. This makes a critical contrast with the actions of the women during Carnival. The most obvious victim of the transition to Carnival identity is Florinda. Because she is in disguise, she opens herself to Willmore's, Blunt's, and then her brother's assumptions about women who are on the streets during Carnival. Thus, in marked contrast to the freedom assumed by the men, Behn demonstrates that Carnival constrains women's identity, opening them up to near-rape and demonstrating the need for women to be protected by men or to remain at home. In addition, she suggests that male freedoms in Carnival are actually only achieved at the expense of women's loss of freedom. The progress of the plot, its repetitive structure, and the lucid contrasts established between men and women in Carnival, display this to the audience's understanding. Critical accounts of Carnival argue that it can be either regenerative or sinister: Behn manages to suggest both.

However, Carnival provides Hellena, first as a gypsy and then as a boy, with the opportunities she hoped for in the opening scene. She chooses and wins Willmore, beating him at his own game of pursuing sexual desire, with a safe outcome for her in a negotiated marriage. Behn thus provides a happy ending for one part of her comedy: Hellena's sexual freedom appears cost-free. But Florinda's experiences always shadow Hellena's, acting as a less fantastic representation of how Carnival imprisons women as much as, if not more than, it liberates them.

*   *   *

Although Carnival is not explicitly invoked in the next two plays, they both use masking, disguise and performance structurally and thematically. Our next extract is from *The Feigned Courtesans.*

[Act 2, scene i]

> [*Marcella and Cornelia*] *walk down the garden. Enter Galliard,*
> *Fillamour, and Julio,* [*and*]*see the women.*
> *Galliard.*   Women! and by their garb for our purpose, too. They're
> courtesans; let's follow 'em.
> *Fillamour.*   What shall we get by gazing but disquiet? If they are   120
> fair and honest, we look and perhaps may sigh in vain; if beautiful
> and loose, they are not worth regarding.
> *Galliard.*   Dear notional knight, leave your satirical fopperies, and
> be at least good-humoured, and let's follow 'em.
> *Julio.*   I'll leave you in the pursuit, and take this opportunity to write   125
> my uncle word of my arrival; and wait on you here anon.
> *Fillamour.*   Prithee do so. Ha, who's that with such an equipage?
> > [*Exeunt*] *Julio, Fillamour and Galliard going after. Marcella and*
> > *Cornelia meet, just entering, Laura Lucretia with her equipage,*
> > *dressed like a man.*
> *Galliard.*   Pox, let the tradesmen ask, who cringe for such gay
> customers, and follow us the women!
> > [*Exeunt*] *Fillamour and Galliard down the scene, Laura Lucretia*
> > *looking after them.*
> *Laura Lucretia.*   'Tis he, my cavalier, my conqueror! Antonio, let   130
> the coaches wait! – And stand at distance, all! – Now, Silvio, on thy
> life, forget my sex and quality, forget my useless name of Laura
> Lucretia, and call me count of –
> *Silvio.*   What, madam?
> *Laura Lucretia.*   Madam! Ah, foolish boy, thy feminine courage   135
> will betray us all; but – call me – Count – Sans Coeur; and tell me
> > Silvio, how is it I appear?
> > How dost thou like my shape, my face and dress,

My mien and equipage; may I not pass for man?
Look it *en prince*, and masculine? 140

Silvio. Now, as I live, you look all over what you wish, and such as
will beget a reverence and envy in the men, and passion in the
women; but what's the cause of all this transformation?

Laura Lucretia. Love! Love! Dull boy, couldst thou not guess
'twas love? That dear *Inglese* I must enjoy, my Silvio. 145

Silvio. What, he that adores the fair young courtesan?

Laura Lucretia. That very he.
My window joins to hers, and 'twas with charms
Which he'd prepared for her, he took this heart,
Which met the welcome arrows in their flight, 150
And saved her from their dangers.
Oft I've returned the vows he's made to her
And sent him pleased away;
When through the errors of the night, and distance,
He has mistook me for that happy wanton, 155
And gave me language of so soft a power,
As ne'er was breathed in vain to listening maids.

Silvio. But with permission, madam, how does this change of
petticoat for breeches, and shifting houses too, advance that love?

Laura Lucretia. This habit, besides many opportunities 'twill give 160
me of getting into his acquaintance, secures me too from being
known by any of my relations in Rome.

(*The Feigned Courtesans*, 2, i, 118–62)

Although this play does not use the Carnival motif explicitly, it
explores many similar issues to those of *The Rover*, and uses both
mechanisms of disguise and plot devices of deception to raise those
issues. In what ways does this extract illustrate such techniques? It
divides clearly into three parts, each of which briefly explores a
different carnivalised motif.

Like *The Rover*, the opening of this extract sets groups of men
against groups of women visually on the stage, in order to display to
the audience the masculine habit of commenting upon women's
appearances and fashion. In this case we see both Marcella and
Cornelia walking in the garden, and closer to us, the men commenting upon their appearance. Women's visual appearance is
thereby set up as a key marker of their identity to men (and also us,

although we also criticise the masculine viewing of such signs as a rush to judgement). In this scene, this observation should go further, since these particular women's appearance is taken to signify their status as courtesans ('by their garb for our purpose, too. They're courtesans', ll. 118–19). The plot is driven by the women's disguise, because the men persist in following them as courtesans, and both women then attempt to use the disguise either to test or engage the men. Yet, equally, appearances are simultaneously questioned throughout the play, and in this extract this counterpointed questioning occurs in Fillamour's response to Galliard's simple equation of appearance and virtue. Fillamour argues that exterior beauty may signal virtue as much as vice (ll. 121–2). This sceptical questioning gives voice to the audience's view (established by our prior knowledge) that appearances are deceptive, whilst nevertheless maintaining a strict opposition between virtuous women and women of loose morals. As we have seen in some of the previous chapters, Cornelia's and Laura's words and actions attempt to break down that latter opposition through problematising how knowledge and judgement can be deceived by appearances.

The second part of this extract illustrates another key theme of identity and disguise, also common to Carnival, that of cross-dressing. Laura explicitly displays her boyish appearance to the audience as a disguise: we always know she is a woman dressed as a boy. This establishes her identity throughout the play as both dual and unstable ('forget my sex and quality', l. 132; 'Look it *en prince* and masculine?', l. 140). We literally see identity as determined by dress, acting and the perceptions of others, rather than as something innate. In addition, as Silvio makes clear, identity can be self-determined: 'you look all over what you wish' (l. 141). By playing with dress, identity, sexuality and gender in this way, the play disturbs conventional notions that these are fixed. 'May I not pass for a man?' (l. 139) posits a play world of carnivalesque disguise, of inverted gender, and 'passing' as a key means of social acceptability. Both the other women use cross-dressing as a means of disturbing conventional notions of what it is to be a woman, as you will have noted in the further work you did for Chapter 4.

It is possible to argue that these notions are closed off at the end of the play, when conventional marriage resolves such disturbing notions for all three women. However, the performance (or reading) of the play explicitly and repeatedly raises these issues, and draws the audience's attention to them. Behn thus uses the space and time of a performance to indulge in carnivalesque notions and use carnivalesque themes, raising radical ideas about identity, whilst returning via comic convention to the status quo at the end of the play. The play's Carnival content acts as a continued counterpoint to that conventional ending, holding it in oppositional suspension, so that the radical nature of the content is never quite erased by the conventional closure.

The third part of this extract shows us Laura discussing another aspect of her disguise: she has pretended to be La Silvianetta from the next-door balcony to Cornelia, in a variation on the comic bed-trick, substituting her voice and response from the balcony for Cornelia's. This characterises her as actively deceitful. Disguise in our other examples is shown to be benign, both within the action of the play, and in terms of the final happy outcome: disguise obtains their desired objectives for the heroines. This is, of course, not true for Laura Lucretia, as we have seen in Chapters 2 and 4. Although, like the other two heroines, she wants to escape her family, and pursue her lover (ll. 160–2), her Carnival 'habit' has darker consequences. Whilst they succeed in both, she fails in both. Through Laura's actions and destiny, Carnival disguise is demonstrated to be potentially destructive, of identity, trust and good name. This is set in deliberate opposition to the happier effects which disguise brings to Cornelia and Marcella, and serves to remind the audience from quite an early point in the play that playing with identity may have dangerous and real consequences for women. The fantastic, happy and radical effects of masquerade are set against the starker consequences experienced by Laura. The play thus incorporates and celebrates the liberating effects of masquerade, and yet, in critiquing it simultaneously, exposes its real dangers. It does so through character parallels and contrasts, and through the plot by illustrating divergent ends for the three heroines' use of carnivalised disguise.

* * *

Let us now turn to the final play, *The Lucky Chance.*

[Act 2, scene i]

Landlady.   Dear me no dears, sir, but let me have my money: eight
weeks' rent last Friday. Besides taverns, ale-houses, chandlers,   50
laundresses' scores, and ready money out of my purse; you know
it, sir.
Gayman.   Aye, but your husband does not; speak softly.
Landlady.   My husband! What, do you think to fright me with my
husband? I'd have you to know I am an honest woman and care   55
not this – for my husband. Is this all the thanks I have for my
kindness, for patching, borrowing, and shifting for you? 'Twas
but last week I pawned my best petticoat, as I hope to wear it again
it cost me six and twenty shillings, besides making; then this
morning my new Norwich mantua followed, and two 'postle   60
spoons; I had the whole dozen when you came first, but they
dropped, and dropped, till I had only Judas left for my
husband.
Gayman.   Hear me, good landlady –
Landlady.   Then I've passed my word at the George Tavern for   65
forty shillings for you; ten shillings at my neighbour Squab's for
ale; besides seven shillings to mother Suds for washing – and do
you fob me off with my husband?
Gayman. [*Aside to Rag*]   Here, Rag, run and fetch a pint of sack,
there's no other way of quenching the fire in her slabber chops.   70
        Exit Rag.
– But, my dear landlady, have a little patience.
Landlady.   Patience? I scorn your words, sir; is this a place to trust
in? Tell me of patience, that used to have my money beforehand!
Come, come, pay me quickly, or old Gregory Grime's house shall
be too hot to hold you.   75
Gayman.   Is't come to this, can I not be heard?
Landlady.   No, sir: you had good clothes when you came first, but
they dwindled daily, till they dwindled to this old campaign, with
tanned-coloured lining, once red, but now all colours of the
rainbow; a cloak to skulk in a-nights, and a pair of piss-burned   80
shammy breeches. Nay, your very badge of manhood's gone, too.
Gayman.   How, landlady! Nay then, i'faith, no wonder if you rail so.
Landlady.   Your silver sword, I mean: transmogrified to this two-

handed basket hilt, this old Sir Guy of Warwick, which will sell
for nothing but old iron. In fine, I'll have my money sir, or i-faith,   85
Alsatia shall not shelter you.

    Enter Rag [with the drink].

Gayman.   Well, landlady, if we must part, let's drink at parting; here
landlady, here's to the fool that shall love you better than I have
done.

    Sighing, [Gayman] drinks.

Landlady.   Rot your wine! D'ye think to pacify me with wine, sir?   90

    [Landlady] refusing to drink, [Gayman] holds open her jaws;
    Rag throws a glass of wine into her mouth.

What, will you force me? No, give me another glass, I scorn to be
so uncivil to be forced; my service to you, sir; but this shan't do,
sir.

    [Landlady] drinks; [Gayman], embracing her, sings.

        Ah, Cloris, 'tis in vain you scold,
        Whilst your eyes kindle such a fire.   95
        Your railing cannot make me cold,
        So fast as they a warmth inspire.

Landlady.   Well, sir, you have no reason to complain of my eyes,
nor my tongue neither, if rightly understood. (*Weeps.*)

Gayman.   I know you are the best of landladies, as such I drink your   100
health. (*Drinks.*) But to upbraid a man in tribulation, fie, 'tis not
done like a woman of honour – a man that loves you, too.

Landlady.   I am a little hasty sometimes, but you know my good
nature. (*She drinks.*)

Gayman.   I do, and therefore trust my little wants with you. I shall   105
be rich again, and then, my dearest landlady –

Landlady.   Would this wine might ne'er go through me, if I would
not go as they say through fire and water, by night or by day for
you. (*She drinks.*)

Gayman.   And as this is wine, I do believe thee. (*He drinks.*)   110

Landlady.   Well, you have no money in your pocket now, I'll
warrant you. Here, here's ten shillings for you old Greg'ry knows
not of. (*Opens a great greasy purse.*)

                        (*The Lucky Chance*, 2, i, 49–113)

Why does Behn use the stock-comic figure of the fat lady? How is
the audience positioned by this characterisation? The grotesque

dominates this episode. The landlady stands as a proxy representation of the seamier side of the play's sexual politics. Gayman is quite
explicit, with both his servant and the audience, about his financial
use of her desire for him. We gain a vivid picture of her physical
nature through Gayman's description of her as fat and lustful
('quenching the fire in her slabber chops', l. 70), her own characterisation as loud, rapacious, drunk, and lustful, and Behn's stage directions and use of stage props ('*Opens a great greasy purse*', l. 113). She
is the extreme caricature of the fat, greasy, lower-class woman, the
butt of so many comic jokes. We are clearly meant to feel physical
disgust, or distaste. Gayman's account of his fall from wealth in
pursuit of his beloved Julia, at the scene's opening, establishes sympathy for his point of view. However, his landlady's claims act as a
counterpoint to his self-justification. He has neglected to pay his
rent, his laundry or tavern bills, as well as borrowing 'ready money'
from the landlady to shower presents on Lady Fulbank. The actual
economics of his courtship are exposed by the landlady's words and
anger. It is clear that he has been living on borrowed money and
borrowed time, simply on the basis of his gentry status and his
ability to obtain money for sexual favours. The landlady's list of the
valuable commodities she has pawned for him (her best petticoat,
the mantua shawl, and apostle spoons, ll. 57–61) creates two opposite effects for the audience. At one level it renders the landlady
ridiculous for her excessive desire and credulousness. However,
equally importantly, Gayman's attitude to sex is displayed as purely
mercantile: he is prepared to trade sex for money and status.

Despite the landlady's physical grotesquerie, which is clearly exaggerated here for a comic-performance effect, we have a growing sympathy for her plight, as well as her folly. This sympathy is developed
in two ways: first, the list of items which Galliard has gulled and
conned out of her, and secondly, the description she gives of his
descent into poverty. She is the only voice in the play acting as an
independent commentary on his real state, because all the other
characters always see him dressed in his former wealth. Her description of him in 'a cloak to skulk in a-nights' and his 'pair of piss-
burned shammy breeches' (ll. 80–1) reduces Gayman from elegant
gallant to filthy, skulking, lustful man. By using the description of

'piss-burned' breeches, the landlady conjures up an image not only of poverty, but of shameful and shaming incontinence. Grotesque physical descriptions are thus visually transferred from the landlady to our image of Gayman, an image he continually tries to dispel through his adoption of new clothes and his fictional wealthy identity.

Our earlier sympathy for Gayman is thus rendered problematic. We are forced to ask questions about him: are we prepared to see his attitudes here as exceptional, or do we link it with his later bargaining for Julia over a card game? Ironically, the grotesque representation of the landlady makes us ask questions about the venality of Gayman, rather than her. Carnival excess thus becomes a technique for literally displaying all the basest human desires, physical functions, and our common animal impulses. Behn uses this technique in quite a sophisticated manner: she does not simply display Gayman as rapacious. In linking Gayman to the landlady, developing pathos for her, and linking his behaviour here to that later in the play, Behn suggests that all human desire may be reduced to the physical greed and naked sexual desire we witness in this woman.

The plot devised between Rags and Gayman to trick the landlady out of more money by plying her with copious drink and making love to her, furthers the masquerade motif. Gayman's actions are displayed as self-interested. From the beginning of the scene we are aware that Gayman acts to an economic purpose, and is prepared to do almost anything to achieve that. Masquerade is therefore shown to be not simply fun and liberating, but a calculating and selfish mask, linked to acquisitive wealth and lustful desire. Gayman's act includes a pastoral love song (ll. 94–7), excessive praise ('you are the best of landladies', l. 100), flattery ('a woman of honour', l. 102), declarations of love (l. 102) and suggestive silences, by which she may intimate further promises ('and then, my dearest landlady –', l. 106). The blatant excess of each of these tactics declares his self-conscious acting to the audience, although not to the landlady. This engenders further sympathy for her credulity. We are amused by their gulling of the landlady, particularly because of her blindness to their self-evident tactics of getting her drunk as quickly as possible. Nevertheless, we are also appalled, particularly by their physical manhandling of her ('*holds open her jaws . . . throws a glass of wine into her mouth*', l. 90). The slapstick nature of this latter act is visually humorous, and simultaneously disturbing. We laugh, and are appalled at our own laughter. Thus, while Gayman achieves his desired objective (the receipt of free money), he does so at the expense of our sympathy. Masquerade, linked to Gayman's acts of trickery, is problematised as a technique of social and economic success. Whilst it apparently liberates men, it imprisons women (both the landlady, and arguably, Julia and Leticia). Once again, Behn both utilises Carnival techniques, and problematises Carnival's potential politics: men are liberated more than women, and the gentry more than the lower classes. She exposes both a gender and a class divide in the society she represents. This is an issue to which we shall return in the next chapter.

Conclusions

1. The dramatic space of Carnival, both in its fictionalised realisation on stage and in the broader use of some of its techniques (such as masquerade, inversion of roles and gender, its celebration of frank sexuality) ostensibly allows both men and women freedom of autonomy and identity. In the extracts from *The Rover* we saw Hellena, Willmore and Belvile expressing this view at a variety of points. Similarly, Gayman in *The Lucky Chance* uses disguise and masquerade to liberate his true identity and situation from poverty.

2. However, as we have seen, this freedom is severely curtailed for women: it is shown either not to exist at all (in the case of the landlady or Florinda), or to be ineffective (in the case of Laura Lucretia), or temporary (in the case of the heroines, who all marry conventionally by the plays' endings).

3. This curtailment of Carnival freedom can be seen to take place during the action of the play, as part of the plot's demonstration of how temporary and deluded such freedom can be (in the case of Florinda in *The Rover*, for example); or at the end of the time of Carnival during the play's action.

4. In *The Feigned Courtesans*, female agency and autonomy are

given greater freedom, and not curtailed to the same extent during the action as in *The Rover*, with the exception of the characterisation and fate of Laura Lucretia. In this play, women control both the inside and outside spaces represented (the gardens and the houses) as well as the action (they have the men running over the city in pursuit of them, and they achieve their desires).

5. Disguise and masking are seen to be coincident with social identity and social success. Gender itself is displayed as a social and costumed performance. Depending upon the production, or the audience's interpretation, this can be read as a critique of the falsity of polite society, or a liberating expression of how all identity can be moulded and manipulated at will.

6. Carnival is used to make a utopian political critique of contemporary codes of conduct for men and women, a stance we noted particularly in *The Rover*, where women are liberated, but in a much more compromised way than men are.

7. Self-conscious role-playing is shown to be usually socially and politically successful, and morally acceptable, so long as it does not compromise the values of romantic love. The representation of Gayman's treatment of the landlady acts as a bass counterpoint to this.

8. Disguise and costuming integrate with action and theme in the setting of Carnival in *The Rover*, and in the invocation of the afternoon and then night-time setting of *The Feigned Courtesans*.

9. Disguise and deception are not necessarily negative, but can be interpreted as such.

Methods of Analysis

We have:

1. considered how an understanding of the practice and theory of Carnival helps illuminate some of the political and dramatic effects of the plays;

2. introduced terms such as 'Carnival' and 'carnivalesque' to

describe dramatic and formal techniques of plotting, theme and
action, to understand why Behn foregrounds disguise and deception within her plays;

3. tried to integrate a focus on the carnival with other elements of
   our analysis, including plotting, setting, character, and dramatic
   space;
4. considered the ways in which the audience's response is invoked
   by differing uses of masquerade and disguise;
5. paid attention to gender differences in attitudes to Carnival and
   disguise, and in plot outcomes as a result of the liberations of
   Carnival.

Suggested Work

1. We can judge how the play asks us to think about the carnivalesque elements, by considering what happens to them at the end
   of the play. You could return to your notes and thoughts about
   Chapter 2. How far is Carnival celebrated and how far condemned by the closures? To what extent are the loose ends, or the
   unhappy resolutions, determined by action taken during
   Carnival or as a result of disguise or deception? To what extent
   are the liberations afforded women in Carnival maintained at the
   end? How many of the women characters are aware that the
   play's closure brings with it a return to convention? What is the
   significance of their awareness or lack of awareness?
2. Disguise and deception dominate theme and action in all three
   plays. Identify parts of the plot driven by disguise or deception.
   What attitudes are taken towards disguise (either by the characters' own comments, or by the nature of the action or dialogue)?
   Relate this to cross-dressing.
3. Identify other moments which are carnivalesque, or which raise
   issues about masking. Look at Lucetta's gulling of Blunt in *The
   Rover*, or the card game at the end of Act 4 in *The Lucky Chance*.
   What is the audience's attitude to the events? Is this constructed
   by the way the scenes work?
4. Carnival is essentially a performative act and occasion. Think

about how the setting of Carnival in *The Rover*, and its sugges-tion in *The Feigned Courtesans*, are self-consciously staged throughout the performance. Why does Behn draw our attention so explicitly to Carnival playfulness? Does this underline the utopian, fantastic quality of her version of romantic comedy, and conversely the ugly materiality of Restoration mercantile London, with which we are left at the play's end? Or does it suggest that she offers a utopian way of thinking about identity, gender and love?

9

Politics and Society

Behn dramatises social and political issues and conflict indirectly through intrigue comedy which focuses on romantic love. Yet within the conventions of the genre she draws our attention quite explicitly to issues of class, gender and politics which resonate out into Restoration London. In this chapter we shall draw together some of the insights of previous chapters by focusing on extracts which raise, directly or indirectly, social and political questions central to each play. We shall consider whether Behn manipulates staging and comic convention to direct or question our views on key themes, and whether she simply mirrors or actively criticises the social and political structures she represents.

* * *

Let us turn first to *The Rover.*

[Act 2, scene i]

> *Enter two bravos [Biskey and Sebastian], and hang up a great picture of Angellica's against the balcony, and two little ones at each side of the door.*

Belvile.   See there the fair sign to the inn where a man may lodge
    that's fool enough to give her price.
> *Willmore gazes on the picture.*
Blunt.   'Adsheartlikins, gentlemen, what's this?

Belvile. A famous courtesan, that's to be sold. 95

Blunt. How, to be sold! Nay then, I have nothing to say to her. Sold! What impudence is practised in this country! With what order and decency whoring's established here by virtue of the Inquisition! Come, let's begone, I'm sure we're no chapmen for this commodity. 100

Frederick. Thou art none, I'm sure, unless thou couldst have her in thy bed at a price of a coach in the street.

Willmore. How wondrous fair she is. A thousand crowns a month? By heaven, as many kingdoms were too little. A plague of this poverty, of which I ne'er complain but when it hinders my 105 approach to beauty, which virtue ne'er could purchase.

[*Willmore*] *turns from the picture.*

Blunt. What's this? (*Reads*) 'A thousand crowns a month'! 'Adsheartlikins, here's a sum! Sure 'tis a mistake. [*To Bravo*] Hark you, friend, does she take or give so much by the month?

Frederick. A thousand crowns! Why, 'tis a portion for the Infanta. 110

Blunt. Hark'ee, friends, won't she trust?

Bravo. This is a trade, sir, that cannot live by credit.

Enter Don Pedro in masquerade, followed by Stephano.

Belvile. See, here's more company; let's walk off awhile.

Exeunt [*Belvile, Willmore, Frederick, and Blunt*]; *Pedro reads.*

Pedro. Fetch me a thousand crowns, I never wished to buy this beauty at an easier rate. 115

[*Pedro*] *passes off* [*the stage*]. *Enter Angellica and Moretta in the balcony, and draw a silk curtain.*

Angellica. Prithee, what said those fellows to thee?

Bravo. Madam, the first were admirers of beauty only, but no purchasers; they were merry with your price and picture, laughed at the sum, and so passed off.

Angellica. No matter, I'm not displeased with their rallying; 120 their wonder feeds my vanity, and he that wishes but to buy gives me more pride, than he that gives my price can make my pleasure.

Bravo. Madam, the last I knew through all his disguises to be Don Pedro, nephew to the general, and who was with him in Pamplona. 125

Angellica. Don Pedro, my old gallant's nephew! When his uncle died he left him a vast sum of money; it is he who was so in love with me at Padua, and who used to make the general so jealous.

Moretta. Is this he that used to prance before our window, and take

    such care to show himself an amorous ass? If I am not mistaken,   130
    he is the likeliest man to give your price.

Angellica.   The man is brave and generous, but of an humour so
    uneasy and inconstant that the victory over his heart is as soon lost
    as won: a slave that can add little to the triumph of the conqueror;
    but inconstancy's the sin of all mankind, therefore I'm resolved   135
    that nothing but gold shall charm my heart.

Moretta.   I'm glad on't: 'tis only interest that women of our
    profession ought to consider, though I wonder what has kept you
    from that general disease of our sex so long, I mean that of being
    in love. ·   140

Angellica.   A kind, but sullen star under which I had the happiness
    to be born. Yet I have had no time for love: the bravest and noblest
    of mankind have purchased my favours at so dear a rate, as if no
    coin but gold were current with our trade. But here's Don Pedro
    again; fetch me my lute, for 'tis for him, or Don Antonio the   145
    viceroy's son, that I have spread my nets.

                                (*The Rover*, 2, i, 92–146)

This extract divides neatly into two mirror-imaged parts: that of the two groups of men discussing Angellica; and then the inverse, she and her servants discussing the men. This both separates women from men (they are seen to belong to different spheres), and sets up a thematic opposition between masculinity and femininity. As we have observed elsewhere, Behn structures scenes, or parts of scenes, to provide a visual ordering and image of the structure of social or familial relationships. This is clear in both the scenic structure and the physical staging of the event: the men exit before Angellica speaks, they are below and she is above on her balcony. What links the two separate groups, acting as a bridge between them, is sexual desire. By separating the two groups, Behn offers the possibility that each may have different views on sexual desire. By loosely lumping all the men together Behn also suggests that all men have generic desires and a generic 'masculine' identity. Thus, even before we examine either content or characterisation in this extract, it is possible to see that Behn's dramatic structure, staging and blocking of characters already begins to suggest social and political interpretations to the audience.

There are two further ways in which staging makes political themes a physical presence. The first is the way in which the staging of the balcony arrangement works. Visually, it places Angellica on high, an object of adoration for men, who literally look up to her. Her portrait is hung against the balcony, and at the doors below, forcing our eyes upwards to the apex of a triangle. This arrangement seems to empower her, particularly since it is set up in this manner by her design (as the initial stage directions make clear). By contrast, the men below appear smaller, and are seen to be drawn to the trap she has set. At one level, then, the balcony arrangement suggests that women (or this woman) have power over men. However, this leads to our second point about staging, which is the way the characters move about the stage. All the men have the freedom to move across the stage, or back and forth, as they wish. The gallants walk up and down in front of the pictures, and turn to the audience. They walk off by choice when Don Pedro arrives, who also parades down the street in masquerade. By contrast, Angellica and Moretta are confined to the balcony above, an enclosed and an interior space, with only a view on the outside world of the street and men. Staging thus acts as a visual means of displaying a contradiction in sexual politics: women's power is dependent on sexual allure and the ability to engender veneration, and only functions in a confined interior space. Whilst the men are drawn by sexual desire, their physical and political power is prevalent in the world outside the domestic, and they control both the streets and their own volition.

Let us look at the men's characterisation and attitudes to widen this analysis. At first, the men's attitudes to Angellica seem to be distinguishable from each other. Belvile despises men who pay for sex ('that's fool enough to give her price', l. 93); Blunt cannot believe prostitution is so blatant in Italy (ll. 96–7), that she is charging so much (ll. 107–8), and that she won't take credit (l. 111); Frederick allies her price with a princess's dowry (l. 110); Willmore is struck by her beauty, and bemoans his poverty; and Pedro makes the decision to find money immediately. What are we asked to think about each of their responses? The key answer to this lies in Angellica's and her bravo's subsequent commentary (ll. 117–22). What they note, as we should too, is that the men still all share a common fascination with

both her sexuality and her price. The language of trade and the
market-place is common to all five men's expressed attitudes: Belvile
refers to her 'price' (l. 93), Blunt to 'this commodity' (l. 100),
Frederick to her 'price' (l. 102), comparing it to a dowry ('portion', l.
110), Willmore speaks of his need to 'purchase' beauty (l. 106), and
Pedro commands her purchase, claiming it to be an easy 'rate' (l.
115). The prospect of purchasing women, and thereby conceiving of
them as marketable commodities, is common to all men, and is here
applied by them to both courtesans and aristocratic women (the
Infanta, l. 110). Masculine attitudes to women thus diverge slightly in
moral terms, but merge in their reduction to an economic currency.

Additionally, there is a crucial and discernible hierarchy between
the men, which is dependent upon wealth and status. Whilst the
gallants observe and admire, and bemoan the cost of buying
Angellica, Pedro is able to sweep on to the stage, gaze and buy
immediately. Financial liquidity equals power, both between men,
and for men over women. But this power is represented as negative
in two ways. First, Willmore's successful courting of Angellica suggests that romantic charm can be more powerful than money. Behn
thus suggests that economics can be subverted and may not rule
women's actions and decisions. Secondly, Pedro's characterisation
and his role as a blocking figure in the play's romantic comic genre
provide an alternative model of gender relationships. Pedro is avaricious, uncaring and selfish. His power, though absolute here in both
economic and political terms (as Angellica's commentary makes
clear), is critiqued directly by and through Hellena elsewhere.
Pedro's unchallenged exertion of power is rendered problematic
because it is literally seen to debase and reduce women to economic
counters. A political perspective on his power is engendered by the
emphasis on women's viewpoints, Pedro's function as a negative
blocking figure and the comic plot which celebrates the love matches
at the end of the play.

Let us now turn to the final part of the extract. Angellica makes
clear the workings of the market-place for her body: wonder feeds
her credit and price. Her credit is dependent upon the continued titillation of masculine desire, through the displaying of her pictures
(ll. 117–22, 142–4). This displays both her dependence on this eco-

nomic system and her manipulation of it, simultaneously suggesting and denying (or setting limits to) her power. Her subsequent discussion about Don Pedro emphasises his high political, martial and economic status (ll. 125–8). She analyses both his character and her political relationship to him by imagining how her status will change once he has conquered: 'a slave that can add little to the triumph of the conqueror' (l. 134). This acknowledges his power over her: once she submits to her purchaser, she will be a slave. Despite this self-knowledge, however, the end of this extract shows that she is completely dependent on, and actively seeks, such relationships: 'for 'tis for him, or Don Antonio the viceroy's son, that I have spread my nets' (ll. 145–6). Behn suggests therefore that sexual slavery is both the inevitable end and the inevitable choice for women like Angellica.

The most explicit political dimension here is the opposition between Blunt, with his disdain for Catholic Italian and Spanish practices, and the English gallants and their support for, and eventual marriage into, the Spanish gentry. Blunt is represented throughout as narrow-minded, bigoted and hypocritical, characteristics applied to puritans by Tory writers. By contrast, the gallants are witty and attractive cavaliers. Behn replicates in Carnival Naples the central political and social conflict of her day: between libertine Tory cavaliers and mercantilist, Whig puritans, the former supporting an absolute monarchy, and the latter parliamentary reform. By demonising Blunt and making the cavaliers romantic heroes, Behn suggests that Tory aristocratic values provide a social climate less dominated by money and greed than that advocated by the new mercantilists. Consequently, she suggests greater freedom for women under an aristocratic regime than under a bourgeois capitalist one. Nevertheless, all the men here still reduce women to economic counters.

Finally, it is worth remembering that the Naples of the play is occupied by Spanish rulers. The theme of an occupied country and imperial attitudes is implicit throughout the play and thematically raised through both Lucetta (the only Italian woman in the play) and Florinda's proposed husband (who gained his wealth in the slave and sugar trades). Naples itself is thus both a place of liberation (for cavaliers) and yet a place of occupation. The city serves as a proxy metaphor for the paradoxical position of women in the play: political occupation and sexual slavery are discursively linked by both Hellena's and Angellica's speeches on freedom. Conversely, their pleas for sexual equality gain a political dimension. However, the play suggests that the women's ability (or inability) to negotiate their freedoms determines their destiny, not just a political ideology.

*   *   *

Let us now turn to our next extract, from *The Feigned Courtesans.*

[Act 1, scene ii]

Tickletext.   How mean you sir, a courtesan, and a Romish courtesan?

Sir Signal.   Now my tutor's up, ha, ha, ha; and ever is when one   105
names a whore. Be pacified, man, be pacified; I know thou hat'st
'em worse than beads or holy water.

Tickletext.   Away, you are such another knight; but leave this
naughty discourse, and prepare for your fencing and civility-
masters, who are coming.   110

Sir Signal.   Aye, when, governor, when? Oh, how I long for my
civility-master, that I may learn to out-compliment all the dull
knights and squires in Kent with a '*Servitore, Hulichimo*'; – no:
'*Signora Bellissima, base le mane de vossignoria, scusa mi, Illustrissimo,
cospetto de Bacco*', and so I'll run on; ha, governor, ha! Won't   115
this be pure?

Tickletext.   Notably ingenious, I profess!

Sir Signal.   Well, I'll send my *staffiere* for him *incontanente*. Hey
Jack – a – *cazzo*, what a damned English name is Jack? Let me see;
I will call him – Giovanni, which is as much as to say John. – Hey,   120
Giovanni!

          Enter Jack.

Tickletext.   Sir, by your favour, his English Protestant-name is
John Pepper; and I'll call him by ne'er a Popish name in
Christendom.

Sir Signal.   I'll call my own man, sir, by what name I please, sir; and   125
let me tell you, Reverend Mr Tickletext, I scorn to be served by any
man whose name has not an -*acho* or an -*oucho*, or some *Italiano* at

the end on't; [*to Jack*] therefore, Giovanni Peperacho is the name by
which you shall be distinguished and dignified hereafter.

Tickletext.   Sir Signal, Sir Signal, let me tell you, that to call a man   130
out of his name is unwarrantable, for Peter is called Peter, and
John, John; and I'll not see the poor fellow wronged of his name
for ne'er a Giovanni in Rome.

Sir Signal.   Sir, I tell you that one Italian name is worth any two
English names in Europe, and I'll be judged by my civility-master.   135

Tickletext.   Who shall end the dispute, if he be of my opinion?

Sir Signal.   *Molto volentieri*, which is as much as to say, with all my
heart.

Jack.   But sir, my grandmother would never own me if I should
change the cursen name she gave me with her own hands, an't   140
please your worship.

Sir Signal.   Hey, *bestia*! I'll have no more of your worship, sirrah,
that old English sir-reverence; let me have you call me Signor
Illustrissimo, or *padrone mio* – or –

Tickletext.   Aye, that I like well enough now: but hold, sure this is   145
one of your masters.

     Enter Petro, dressed like a French dancing-master.

                         (*The Feigned Courtesans*, 1, ii, 104–46)

This extract humorously delineates some of the explicit social and
political themes addressed by the play. *The Feigned Courtesans*, as we
have discussed in previous chapters, deals explicitly with issues such
as forced marriages, sexual politics, patriarchal control of women
and libertine masculinity. However, we have touched on these issues
when discussing heroines, rakes and heroes, and brothers and husbands (Chapters 4 and 5), as well as in the extract from *The Rover*.
In the present extract we shall concentrate on how the sub-plot's politics comment upon or contrast those of the main plot.

In this extract, Sir Signal and his tutor Tickletext discuss his
preparations for his forthcoming civility lessons. Characterisation is
crucial to an audience's understanding. Sir Signal's exaggerated buffoonery is indicated via several means. The first is through his gratu-
itous misuse of Italian (ll. 113–15, 118–19), which one imagines is
accompanied by extravagant gestures as he attempts to enact his self-
image as man-about-the-continent. The second indication is his attitude to his servant Jack. His insistence on completely re-naming him

betrays Sir Signal's slavish adherence to a fashionable (if inappropriate) love of all things Italian: 'I scorn to be served by any man
whose name has not an -acho or an -oucho' (ll. 126–7). By taking
such adherence to a ridiculous and bathetic extreme, Behn pushes
his character into caricature, and invites us to simultaneously laugh
and condemn. Both her method (exaggerated bathos producing caricature) and her aim (our disapproval) are key aspects of successful
satiric writing.

Sir Signal is the archetypal foolish and self-important puritan
Englishman abroad (ll. 1 and 2), continually exposing his ignorance
at the point at which he thinks he is displaying his sophistication.
Interestingly, Behn does not offer us alternative views of
Englishmen, as she does in *The Rover* (where Blunt is the ingénue,
and the other gallants show how aristocratic Englishmen may be
witty and sophisticated). However, class and political attitudes are
clearly part of her attack here: for Sir Signal betrays his lack of aristocratic origins both in his peremptory attitude to his servant and in
his lack of civil education, which he is forced to purchase from the
rogue, Petro. By marking himself as one of the *nouveau riche*, in
need of social and civil improvement, he condemns himself as a
target for satire.

Tickletext is also set up as a patsy. His prudish attitude towards
sex, combined with his insistence on Jack's 'English Protestant-name'
in contrast to a 'Popish' one, marks him as a stereotypical stage
puritan. We suspect, at this early point in the play, that such pomposity is going to be exposed as hypocritical or punctured as a false
pride. Behn actually does both, as Tickletext later attempts to court
La Silvianetta secretly, on the flimsy justification that he is trying to
convert her. His enthusiastic welcoming of Sir Signal's inept Italian
(for example, ll. 117 and 145–6) suggests here that he may be
sucked into the pleasures of Italy, and that he is a hopeless tutor,
since he knows no more Italian than Sir Signal.

Characterisation of both men sets up an opposition that is not
just between the sophisticated gallants about town and the bumbling
Englishmen, but between sophisticated Italy and backward England,
and between a civilised catholicism (in its broadest sense) and a
narrow-minded and hypocritical puritanism. Indirectly, then, Behn

offers up a political critique of a certain kind of Englishness which was most often associated with puritan views and the new Whig politics linked to city money. By reducing the latter's views to bathos and satirising their beliefs, Behn suggests by contrast that the older paternalistic values of the English aristocracy (and linked to that, those of the monarchy) were far more civilised than those of the new bourgeoisie.

The representation of Jack does not participate in this demonisation: the plain English servant is manipulated and used by the new political men in a way that emphasises their abuses of power and inhumane attitudes. Behn suggests that class conflict originates with the bourgeoisie, because all other class relationships in the play are represented as benign. Petro is a key example. He is given near total freedom by his mistresses (Cornelia and Marcella), just as long as he makes money as well. Their relationship with their servant is represented as one of genuine *noblesse oblige*, whilst that of Sir Signal to Jack as one of master and slave. Behn uses sets of contrasting characters to make a political point: in supporting the sympathetic characters and laughing at those whom the action satirises, we end up indirectly supporting aristocratic rather than bourgeois politics.

* * *

Let us now move on to our last play, *The Lucky Chance*.

[Act 1, scene i]

> *Gayman.*   I see you're peevish, and you shall be humoured. You know   115
> my Julia played me e'en such another prank as your false one is
> going to play you, and married old Sir Cautious Fulbank here i'th'
> city; at which you know I stormed, and raved, and swore, as thou
> wilt now, and to as little purpose. There was but one way left,
> and that was cuckolding him.   120
> *Belmour.*   Well, that design I left thee hot upon.
> *Gayman.*   And hotly have pursued it. Swore, wept, vowed, wrote,
> upbraided, prayed and railed; then treated lavishly, and presented
> high, till between you and I, Harry, I have presented the best part
> of eight hundred a year into her husband's hands, in mortgage.   125

Belmour. This is the course you'd have me steer, I thank you.

Gayman. No, no, pox on't, all women are not jilts. Some are honest,
and will give as well as take; or else there would not be so many
broke i'th' city. In fine, sir, I have been in tribulation, that is to
say, moneyless, for six tedious weeks, without either clothes or   130
equipage to appear withal; and so not only my own love affair lay
neglected, but thine too, and I am forced to pretend to my lady
that I am i'th' country with a dying uncle, from whom, if he were
indeed dead, I expect two thousand a year.

Belmour. But what's all this to being here this morning?   135

Gayman. Thus have I lain concealed like a winter fly, hoping for
some blessed sunshine to warm me into life again, and make me
hover my flagging wings; till the news of this marriage (which fills
the town) made me crawl out this silent hour, to upbraid the fickle
maid.   140

Belmour. Didst thou? Pursue thy kind design. Get me to see her,
and sure, no woman, even possessed with a new passion, grown
confident even to prostitution, but when she sees the man to
whom she's sworn so very, very much, will find remorse and
shame.   145

(*The Lucky Chance*, 1, i, 115–45)

This extract explicitly discusses and exemplifies in its dramatic situation and content the political and class opposition which we discussed in the second extract. Belmour has just learned from Gayman
that Leticia, 'your contracted wife', is 'to be married to old Sir Feeble
Fainwould, induced to't I suppose by the great jointure he makes
her' (ll. 96–8). Since Gayman has not seen her for the six weeks he
has been skulking in the country, because he is too poor to be seen
(ll. 129–31), both men assume that wealth has tempted her to
renounce the poorer, disgraced, if aristocratic, Belmour (l. 111). The
scene therefore sets up dramatically a situation in which the audience are asked to sympathise with Belmour's plight. He has lost his
mistress unfairly, he has a legal right to believe her promised to him
('your **contracted** mistress'), and the man she is to marry is described
in such physically unattractive terms (old, and probably impotent, as
implied in his name, 'Fainwould'). The play promises to tell the
story of two young lovers prevented from their desires by an older
man, a conventional comic device, but here complicated and politi-

cised by Behn's casting of the husband, and one of a particular class, as the blocking figure to successful romance. Let us consider how this casting politicises the usual comic convention.

In the first place, the replacement of the conventional blocking figure of father or uncle by a potential elderly husband, suggests that neither youth nor new love can necessarily succeed. This sets up greater tragic potential for the play. Secondly, the replacement creates a more fixed link between fathers and husbands as men who arrange women's lives and marriages, rather than in the conventional form, which offers the possibility that a young lover might liberate a woman from paternalistic dictates. Thirdly, it sets up an opposition between the values represented by the elderly husband-to-be and those of the young gallant. Given that audiences are predisposed to support young lovers in comedies, we are here complicit in wanting the norms of marriage to be disrupted and violated. By these means Behn positions the audience as radical sympathisers with, marital generational, economic and gender rebellion. We sympathise with youth against age, with poverty not wealth, and with a free choice of sexual partner rather than forced or economic marriages, and with gallants rather than citizens. This sympathy and political viewpoint is established first through simple manipulation of comic structural convention.

It is reinforced and expanded by the content of the gallants' conversation and by their characterisation, in opposition to that of Fainwould and Sir Cautious. Gayman makes clear the economic basis of Sir Cautious's wealth and of his marriage to Julia. By naming him from 'here i'th' city' (l. 117) he implies that his business is in trade or money, and the source of his attractiveness to Julia. He explains his own situation as a parallel to that of Belmour, allying them both against old and wealthy men of the city, willing to use large amounts of money to attract women formerly affianced to gentlemen such as themselves. Gayman's personal animosity to Sir Cautious for stealing his lover is converted into a fourfold political and social opposition. First, it sets up a political opposition between men in the city and those whom Gayman represents. Secondly, it extends this to the economic and geographic field: his poverty forces him to retreat from city to country, wealth belongs to the city and to the bourgeoisie under this new regime. Thirdly, bourgeois money and trade are shown to possess the ability to buy women and force marriages, in contrast to the romantic and free love offered by the gentry. Gender rights are implicitly greater under an aristocratic order. Finally, the opposition encompasses class: Gayman will inherit wealth once his uncle dies (ll. 133–4), emphasising that he belongs clearly to the old landed gentry as opposed to the new wealth makers of the city.

These oppositions are further elaborated in Gayman's self-description as generous and of Sir Cautious as his mortgager. Their relationship is therefore literally held in economic opposition, with Julia poised between as the cause of that economic relationship.

Gayman also makes explicit the relationship between sex, sexuality and politics. He shows how marriage is determined by economics in the new city order he berates. However, conversely and consequently, he then effectively claims that cuckolding is an act of political resistance: 'There was but one way left, and that was cuckolding him' (ll. 119–20). Libertine masculine sexuality is posited as a way for the gentry to indirectly reclaim both their lost wealth, and their lost power over their women. Yet once again, it is clear from this play that despite this gallant masculine perception, the women are men's pawns in both political camps.

Gayman's justification of cuckolding and trickery as a political act, combined with our sympathies for the younger lovers, means that the comic business of intrigue and trickery is endued with a covert political agenda. The audience again become complicit in supporting the old gentry and libertine values against those of the new bourgeoisie. Yet this is tempered to some extent by the characterisation of the two main women, and by the closures of the play, as we discussed in Chapter 2. In the end Julia does not submit to either of the men whose views, outlook and economic background set them up as opposed political representatives. She divorces her husband, and refuses to acknowledge that she will submit to Gayman. Women's freedom is shown to be separate from either political agenda.

Let us now consider some overall conclusions we may draw from these analyses.

Conclusions

1. Behn continually interlinks sexual and gender politics with those of class and economics. We noted this most particularly in *The Rover* and in *The Lucky Chance*, although you may also look at *The Feigned Courtesans* in this light via the suggestions for further work below. Masculine sexuality is celebrated at its most free under aristocratic regimes, and seen at its most debased and avaricious under bourgeois ones. However, masculinity is not celebrated uncritically: under both regimes, it is shown to be potentially rapacious (of both women's bodies and women's potential wealth). Furthermore, women are literally seen to be pawns of both economic systems and both classes: for maintaining a pure genealogy, in the case of aristocratic fathers, or for the purchase into such a line for bourgeois husbands. Women who are seen to succeed (like Hellena in *The Rover* or Cornelia in *The Feigned Courtesans*) do so because they are conscious of negotiating their own personal and economic autonomy within this market.

2. Structural, spatial staging and thematic techniques together provide a unified critique of the double sexual standard, which is shown to be political because it is intimately linked to how power ultimately functions in the plays. This is clearest in the extract from *The Rover*. At the end of Act 4 of *The Lucky Chance*, for example, Julia's visual and verbal marginalisation on stage replicates the men's economic and sexual manipulation of her. By making us see this, Behn encourages us to condemn it. Similarly, in *The Feigned Courtesans*, Marcella's temptation of Fillamour, particularly in Act 4, scene i, visually displays the masculine confusion between love and lust. The conflict between men's views of women as desirable sexual objects and their need for chaste wives is shown to determine how women are treated and thought about.

3. Questions of how identity and autonomy may be retained in a hierarchical and patriarchal society recur in each play. Wit, intrigue and trickery are validated as means of expression and fulfilment, and are utopianly posited as able to conquer wealth and established interests. Comic structure is used to reinforce this social and political message.

4. Each play examines questions about marriage in Restoration London. Courtship conventions, economic necessity, patriarchal control, a lack of female autonomy and desire, and arranged marriages are all raised dramatically as themes and as essential triggers for plot and intrigue. By continually focusing on the viewpoints and plots of women, Behn's plays produce a woman's view on these issues. We have suggested in previous chapters that her dramatic method forces us to judge masculine conduct as both generic and to be questioned.

5. Comic conventions, of character, caricature, stereotype and structure, are used both conventionally (as in the case of the buffoon as satiric butt) and unconventionally (as in the case of older husbands becoming critical blocking figures). This illustrates both Behn's admirable technical grasp of her dramatic heritage and her ability to adapt it to her own original and critical ends.

6. Contemporary politics are represented through caricatures representing bourgeois or puritan men as foolish, stupid, grasping and hypocritical, thereby setting up a binary opposition to members of the old gentry. Religion and class are seen as clear social and political dividing lines. Whilst economics may determine new power relationships, this is something which Behn decries in men. However, the wealthy women (who coincidentally all belong to the gentry) possess thereby their only means of self-determination. There is thus a small contradiction in her work, since wealth seems to be bad when held by the city men, but good when held by aristocratic women.

Methods of Analysis

1. We have focused on dramatic techniques (such as staging, space, symbolism, and comic conventions) to illustrate how Behn makes us think about broader issues of politics and society.

2. We have considered how she uses character parallels to set up political or social contrasts, and uses our sympathy with certain characters to make political allegiances.

3. We have broadened our understanding of the dramatic workings

of a scene to consider how it resonates both with the broader themes and issues raised in the play, and with the social and political issues, events and themes of Behn's time. We have implicitly asked questions: How does dramatic structure reflect or critique the social and political structures represented in the fictional world we see? What implications does this scene have for our understanding of the politics of the rest of the play? What does Behn ask us to think about political issues?

4. We have tried to integrate our previous insights with an explicit consideration and discussion of social and political engagement.

Suggested Work

1. What happens to the political and social issues discussed in this chapter at the ends of the plays? Are they resolved, or do they remain in opposition? Is the audience asked to have a political view? Comment on the way gender politics work in the endings.

2. Look at Act 4, scene i of *The Feigned Courtesans*, and the succession of courtiers who appear for La Silvianetta. In what ways are they distinguished from each other, what is the nature of these distinctions, and how would you describe them in social and political terms? Look at how gender, sexual politics and class politics intersect.

3. Look again at Blunt in *The Rover*. What is the nature of his opposition to the gallants? Why and how is he demonised by the play? What is the converse effect on our judgement of the gallants?

4. Lucetta and Angellica (in *The Rover*), and the landlady (in *The Lucky Chance*) are the only working women represented in these plays. Comment on the way in which Behn represents and asks us to think about prostitution as a necessary or acceptable way of earning money and independence for women.

5. Look at *The Lucky Chance*, Act 3, scene v. Comment on the satirising of Sir Feeble.

6. Look at the names of all the men again: comment on how these give indicators of social class and political viewpoint.

General Conclusions to Part 1

1. Comedy is conventionally definitively social: issues about identity, love and marriage are represented as processes which involve all members of a community. This is true for Behn, but additionally her women have an explicitly active role. Although the comic world posits a fantasy of community coherence, Behn draws attention to its fictionality, usually by leaving at least one key woman or couple out of the conventional happy ending of love resolved. This sets up a dialogue between romantic resolutions and other possibilities, and enables the audience to both enjoy the utopian elements of the comic world, and recognise Behn's engagement with 'real world' issues.

2. Gender is central to the problems which trigger comic action in Behn's plays: marriage, arranged marriage, mistaken identity, and cross-dressing. It is also problematised through combining both conventional and unconventional endings, which ask us to focus on how both masculinity and femininity function as socially constructed and constraining ideologies

3. Her use of comic form is sophisticated, combining simultaneous celebration of conventional comic themes (love and marriage) with satiric and critical accounts of that same material. Caricature and satire blend with romantic representation.

4. Her heroines are dramatically stronger and more attractive characters than the heroes, and they direct and conduct the plot's action. The plays are thus structured to engender sympathy for the women's point of view.

5. Staging and dramatic space are used with great versatility and skill, for spectacular and symbolic ends and to emphasise gender politics in the use of symbolic and psychic space and geography.

6. Carnival is used as a dramatic mode and a setting to make concrete the conundrum of juxtaposing the ideal with the real, combining celebratory utopian possibilities with a necessary return to the status quo. Behn always acknowledges and demonstrates Carnival as a time of both danger and opportunity.

7. Behn's plays are dialogic: questions are asked through dramatic means but the use of multiple or parallel plots demonstrates both the complexity of the questions and the possibility of numerous answers. This gives the plays an open-ended feeling: the audience are left to decide and debate.

8. Behn's dramaturgy is sophisticated and technically thoughtful: she knew, as a working dramatist, how her plays could be performed and how they work in a three-dimensional space. They are still eminently performable.

PART 2

CONTEXT
AND CRITICS

10

Behn's Literary Career

Aphra Behn's first play to be performed, *The Forc'd Marriage*, was at the Duke's Theatre in early 1670. At this point, she was a woman of thirty, with no previous publication history, and from a relatively humble, and certainly obscure, background. How did such a woman emerge and go on to become one of the leading and most prolific playwrights of her generation? That question cannot be answered completely satisfactorily, partly because Behn herself fictionalised and disguised her own past life, and partly because sufficient records do not exist about women of her class to verify suppositions made about her education, background and personal views. This chapter examines what we know about her plays and other literary works, first in the context of the theatrical and literary world in which she moved and wrote, and then briefly in the context of what we do know, and may guess, about her biography. The range and nature of the plays she wrote, which spanned a writing and performance career of nearly twenty years, illuminates the comedies we have analysed and discussed in this book. Her thematic concerns remained remarkably constant, focusing frequently on questions of identity, marriage, female autonomy, and gender and sexuality, within a social, familial and political context. Equally, her use of theatrical modes and genres can be seen as a developmental trajectory, moving from romantic tragicomedies and two tragedies, towards the more assured intrigue and farcical comedies of her middle and later period. However, before we consider these in greater detail, let us look at the theatrical world and milieu in which she worked.

On Charles II's return to England in 1660, he restored the old form of the monarchy and government to England and Scotland, but also re-opened the theatre. However, the theatre of Restoration London was very different from that of Jacobean and Caroline London in the earlier part of the seventeenth century. In the first place, in the earlier period there were numerous outdoor and indoor theatres, owned by and performed in by three or four companies. In 1660 Charles II first licensed only one theatre, the Cockpit at Whitehall Palace, at which his own company (the King's Company) had a performing monopoly. They were managed by Thomas Killigrew, a playwright who had shared Charles II's political exile, participated in aborted uprisings during the inter-regnum, and later managed spies for Charles II. This company obtained the performing and copy rights to the major Jacobean dramatists' works: Shakespeare, Beaumont and Fletcher, and Jonson. A second company and theatre were then also licensed, the Duke of York's Company, based at Lincoln's Inn Fields and then Dorset Garden, and under the direction and management of William Davenant, a playwright and royal political supporter. These two companies and managers had an absolute monopoly of theatrical production and performance in Restoration London. Both the ability to perform, and the question of what could be performed, were strictly controlled by the monarch and the court. In 1682 the two companies merged to form the United Company, performing at both Drury Lane and Dorset Garden, thereby intensifying the effect of the monopoly.

The nature of the audience and the stage changed. The two new theatres were indoors rather than outdoors, and this in combination with their royal patronage, affected both the price of seats and the size of the auditorium, and consequently the type of audience who attended. In order to pay for the cost of lavish buildings, the price of seats was far higher than it had been in Jacobean London, and this, in combination with the overall reduction in the number of seats in the smaller theatres, comparatively narrowed the audience base. Such a narrowing chimed with royal and court patronage of the theatre, perceived now as solely an upper-class and courtly cultural pursuit, and certainly a wealthy one.

Additionally, both theatres were built to new specifications, similar to the type Charles II had admired at Louis XIV's court in France during his exile. The two theatres had a proscenium arch, a thrust stage, and side shutters and back-cloths to aid painted scenic changes, and discoveries of persons or scenes behind the last performed scene. The thrust stage enabled actors to speak asides or engage in action close to the audience, while the proscenium arch distanced the audience from the actors in a way in which playing in the round did not. The effective use of both kinds of space, the spectacular and the dialogic, characterises Behn's work, as we have seen in this book.

Finally, unlike Jacobean theatre, where women's parts were played by boys and young men, Charles II licensed women actors, and women appeared for the first time on the public stage in England in 1661. The appearance of women on stage explicitly sexualised theatrical performance in the eyes of many in the audience, as Samuel Pepys's Dairy accounts of theatrical visits make abundantly clear. Many men perceived women actors to be potential whores, seeing a link between performing on stage, and selling their bodies on the street. Male playwrights took advantage of the novelty of women on stage to dramatise female vulnerability in a titillating manner, and to use discovery scenes as a way of visually focussing on erotic encounters and erotic glimpses of ankles and breasts. Conversely, male bodies could also be more explicitly sexualised: and Behn herself takes advantage of this in *The Lucky Chance*, most famously where Sir Feeble is attempting to consummate his marriage to Leticia. The stage directions say he *'throws open his gown'*, at which all Leticia's attendant women *'run away'* (3, ii, 13). For such a visually explicit rendering of male sexuality, Behn was much criticised on the grounds of lewdness.

Behn's writing and theatrical productions drew on, and were conscious of, each of these material changes to the theatre. Examples we have noticed in this book include the *'long street'* in *The Rover*'s Act 2; the gulling of Blunt in Act 4; the display of women's bodies as La Silvianetta in *The Feigned Courtesans*, as well as their shifting and playful disguises; and the masque organised by Lady Fulbank in *The Lucky Chance*.

Where do Behn's productions fit into this context? The following chronology shows the first production dates, company, major actors, and genre of her plays. I have also included dates for her main published non-dramatic works, so we can understand the overall patterning of her career. Take time to familiarise yourself with her literary career before moving on to the rest of the chapter.

What can we learn from this chronology? As we have already remarked, Behn's literary career spanned the last nineteen years of her life, and apparently made her financially independent. In that time she wrote across a range of dramatic, poetic and prose genres, just as, for example, did the poet laureate, John Dryden. Her versatility, prolific production and range are testament both to her own ability to respond to different audiences according to demand, and to her need to earn her living through her writing. This is clearer if we match her writing with other contextual dates. For example, the increased number of translations (or modernising of previous translations) and prose works in the 1680s coincides with several changes in the theatrical and political world. First, the two theatre companies had merged in 1682, reducing the overall number of plays commissioned. This affected commissioning of her work within a year. Secondly, Charles II's death and James II's accession in 1685, and the growing opposition to the monarch, may have divided even court audiences, resulting in fewer commissions for an overtly royalist playwright. Thirdly, fashions in drama were already beginning to change: more objections were made to what was considered 'bawdy' comedy, and Behn in particular fell foul of such attacks. Fourthly, Behn herself was attacked over her epilogue to her political Roman tragedy *Romulus and Hersilia*, in which she directly attacked Monmouth, the King's illegitimate son, who had been inciting rebellion against his father. Charles II did not appreciate such a direct attack, and no new political plays were commissioned: she wrote nothing for the stage between 1682 and 1686, although she did produce Rochester's play *Valentian* in 1684.

In such a changed climate Behn had need of additional income, and as her dramatic commissions fell off, so she turned her attention to other marketable literary forms. Conversely, during the period of greatest political ferment under Charles II, from 1679 to 1682, when the Popish plot triggered a resurgence of party politics, Behn was most active as a political dramatist. She wrote nine plays in three years, all of which to a greater or lesser extent support authoritarian monarchy and configure parliamentary democracy as the threat of mob rule. It is clear, then, that both the genre and content of Behn's writing was dependent upon the political climate, available patronage, and the literary market. In other words, as she herself frequently makes clear in prefaces and prologues to her plays, she knew herself to be a professional writer, necessarily embedded in the economics and politics of her time. Yet this is not to say that what she wrote was dramatic propaganda. Her plays are more complex than blatant political propaganda, although on occasion she did write propaganda, for example a Coronation Ode to James II in 1685. As we have seen in our analysis of her plays, her manipulation of comic conventions to engender a critical audience stance on Restoration rakes and on fathers and husbands, means that we cannot simply categorise her as a mouthpiece for Stuart patriarchalism.

If we look at the nature of genres in which she wrote across the whole of her career, we can also see that she gradually developed a feel for the genre in which she clearly worked best, that of comedy. Her first plays were tragicomedies, a genre in which romantic improbability closes off and prevents potential tragic conflict. As a genre it was particularly popular with Restoration audiences and patrons of the 1660s, which was one reason the Jacobean collaborative playwrights Beaumont and Fletcher were so popular. In 1672 Dryden's *Marriage à la Mode* was first performed, a play Behn greatly admired, and which both set the fashion for farcical intrigue comedy and caught the mood of the time in its focus on sexual and gender politics. Two other key writers of this genre were Wycherley and Etherege, whose *The Country Wife* and *The Man of Mode*, respectively, followed in 1675 and 1676.

Behn's conversion to comedy began in 1676 with an adaptation of a Jacobean city comedy, a genre to which she returns consistently throughout her career for inspiration and source material. Her move into this type of comedy, undoubtedly influenced by her contemporaries and by her own reading, nevertheless matched her personal interests more exactly. In comedy, in contrast to tragicomedy, she

Date	Theatre company	Authors	Genre	Title	Source
1670	Duke's at Lincoln's Inn Fields	Behn	Tragicomedy	*The Forc'd Marriage*	
1671	Duke's at Lincoln's Inn Fields	Behn	Tragicomedy	*The Amorous Prince, or The Curious Husband*	
1672		Various, edited by Behn	Selected verse	*The Covent Garden Drollery*	
1673	Duke's at Dorset Garden	Behn	Tragicomedy	*The Dutch Lover*	
1676	Duke's at Dorset Garden	Behn	Tragedy	*Abdelazar, or The Moor's Revenge*	*Lust's Dominion* (performed 1620/1)
1676	Duke's at Dorset Garden	Behn	Comedy	*The Town Fop; or Sir Timothy Tawdry*	Wilkins' *Miseries of an Enforced Marriage* (1637)
1677	Duke's	Behn and others (Betterton)	Comedy	*The Debauchee*	Brome's *A Mad Couple Well Match'd*
1677	Duke's	Behn	Comedy	*The Counterfeit Bridegroom*	Middleton's *No Wit, No Help like a Woman*

Year	Company	Author	Genre	Title	Source
1677	Duke's at Dorset Garden	Behn	Comedy	The Rover	Killigrew's Thomaso
1678	Duke's at Dorset Garden	Behn	Comedy	Sir Patient Fancy	Molière's Le Malade Imaginaire
1679	Duke's at Dorset Garden	Behn	Comedy	The Feigned Courtesans	No known source
1679	Duke's at Dorset Garden	Behn	Tragicomedy	The Young King	Revision of play she wrote in 1660s
1680	Duke's at Dorset Garden	Behn and Marston	Tragicomedy	The Revenge	Marston's The Dutch Courtesan
1681	Duke's at Dorset Garden	Behn	Comedy	The Rover, Part 2	
1681	Duke's at Dorset Garden	Behn	Comedy	The False Count	Molière's Les Précieuses Ridicules
1681	Duke's at Dorset Garden	Behn	Political comedy	The Roundheads	Tate's The Rump
1682	United Company at Dorset Garden	Behn	Comedy	Like Father, Like Son	

Table continued overleaf

Date	Theatre company	Authors	Genre	Title	Source
1682	United Company at Dorset Garden	Behn	Political comedy	*The City Heiress*	Middleton's *A Mad World My Masters*
1682	United Company	Behn	Roman tragedy	*Romulus and Hersilia*	
1684	United Company	Behn	Novel	*Love Letters Between a Nobleman and His Sister*	
1684		Behn	Translation	Tallemant's *Voyage to the Island of Love*	
1684	United Company	Behn prepared Rochester's play for stage		Rochester's *Valentian*	
1684		Behn	Poems	*Poems Upon Several Occasions* (published with the Tallemant)	
1685		Behn	Poems and translation	*Miscellany* (including translation of Rochefoucauld as *Seneca Unmasked*)	
1686	United Company at Drury Lane	Behn	Comedy	*The Lucky Chance*	Original to Behn

Year	Company	Author	Genre	Title
1687	United Company at Dorset Garden	Behn	Comedy	The Emperor of the Moon
1687		Behn	Translation	Aesop's Fables
1688		Behn	Translation	A Discovery of New Worlds
1688		Behn	Poems	Lycidus: Together with a Miscellany of New Poems
1688		Behn	Novella	Oroonoko, or The Royal Slave
1688		Behn		The Fair Jilt
1688		Behn	Translation	The History of Oracles, including 'Essay on Translated Prose'
1688		Behn	Translation	Agnes de Castro
1689	United Company at Drury Lane	Behn	Comedy	The Widow Ranter
1689		Behn	Novella	The History of the Nun
1689		Behn	Short story	The Lucky Mistake

could exercise her skill for theatrical farce with a satirical edge. In addition, the conventional subject matter of such comedy (romantic intrigue, young lovers, and difficult fathers) enabled her to address the questions of sexual politics she had already raised in the tragi-comedies and her poetry, more explicitly, playfully and yet critically. She wrote only two tragedies in her whole career, and although the first, *Abdelazar*, made good money for the theatrical shareholders, she did not return to this genre voluntarily. Perhaps comedy's mixed potential, for critical perception in combination with laughter and hope for renewal attracted her more. We shall turn to the issue of her theatrical philosophy and ideas about comedy in the next chapter.

To a modern reader one of the most remarkable features of this chronology is the frequency with which Behn adapted or borrowed source material from other plays. Although on occasion she was accused of plagiarism by her critics, such borrowing was common practice amongst dramatists of the period, and indeed, of the earlier seventeenth century. None of Shakespeare's plays was 'original': he always used other sources, either a combination of earlier plays and histories, or prose romances. Equally, Dryden, Shadwell and other Restoration writers adapted many Jacobean plays for the stage and the taste of Restoration London. Behn's plays range from plots devel-oped from her own newspaper reading (such as *The Widow Ranter*), through free adaptations of previous works (for example, from those of Marston and Middleton, or her closer contemporary, Molière), and to wholly original works, indebted only to the theatrical climate in which she worked, such as *The Feigned Courtesans*, *The Lucky Chance* and *The Emperor of the Moon*. It is clear that she learned much through her understanding of other playwrights. Thus, from Middleton and Marston she learned the arts of tight comic plotting, of using an ambiguous trickster figure as hero, and how to manipu-late comic conventions to critical ends. From Molière she learned how to keep a balance between harsh satire and a comedy of humours, whilst keeping her audience both critical and amused. From Dryden, Etherege and Wycherley she learned how to merge contemporary social and political characters and issues with older comic conventions and plot.

Yet despite these observable debts, Behn's work plays and reads as freshly original: her own slant on the issues of the day is demonstrably different from that of many of her contemporaries, particularly on issues of gender and sexuality. For example, in her collaborative play *The Debauchee*, the women are far less witty and independent than in plays wholly scripted by Behn. It is also clear that in her adaptations she gives greater agency and freedom to women during the action of the play than her sources do, for example her adaptation of Marston's *The Dutch Courtesan* as *The Revenge*, where the courtesan becomes an explicitly more active and empathetic character than in Marston's play. Finally, in her original intrigue comedies, she focuses explicitly on two issues which have a different emphasis, if similar subject matter, to the plays of her male contemporaries. The first is female empowerment and the social and economic constraints working against such empowerment, such as arranged marriages and the intersection of patriarchal family arrangements with those of a wider society. Secondly, she clearly places masculinity, rather than femininity, under critical scrutiny: most particularly the philosophy and actions of the cavalier rake. In doing so, she does not markedly change the genre from that in which Dryden, Wycherley and Etherege wrote, but she manipulates it to create a different viewpoint, both on stage and in her audience. In achieving this, she demonstrates theatrical ingenuity and an assured understanding of theatrical conventions and audiences.

It is often argued that criticism of the male rake figure did not emerge until the late 1680s and 1690s, in particular in the work of Congreve, but partly discernible in Behn's *Second Part of The Rover*. Recent critics have begun to argue that Etherege's *The Man of Mode* initiates a far more caustic view of the rake as early as 1676. However, as we have noted in our analyses, Behn is also clearly critical at a far earlier stage, and this is something we can discuss further in our chapter on critical views and performances. Most viewers and readers ascribe this emphasis and interest to her being a woman in an overtly masculine world, both politically and theatrically. This is an opinion which you will need to determine for yourself, with the help of the analyses of previous chapters.

Behn's life history, particularly in her early years, is obscure. She was probably the daughter of a Bartholomew and Elizabeth Johnson, christened Eaffrey Johnson in Canterbury on 14 December 1640. Her mother was wet-nurse to Thomas Colepepper, who later wrote one of the few sources we have of Behn's life. This would have meant that she was in contact with his family in her early years, and possibly later. His family was connected to the Sidneys, and it is possible that she received both some education through this connection, and some knowledge of previous women writers, since both Mary Sidney and her niece Lady Mary Wroth, had published poetry and prose in the early seventeenth century. Her father was a barber, whose work and geographical position put him in contact with some of the leading political figures in Kent. Barber shops were places where music was played and performed, and Behn's theatrical usage and interest in music is discernible throughout her plays. It has been suggested that during her late teens (in the late 1650s) many of the men who supported Charles II's return may have conspired in Canterbury, and even used young women such as her as couriers. It is possible that she went to Flanders in 1659 on such a mission, and the details of such plots in her play *The Roundheads* make this a plausible hypothesis.

Evidence for the next stage in her life comes mainly from her fictional novel *Oroonoko*, written in the first person, and in which she claims that her family travelled to the West Indian colony of Surinam, her father having been appointed as lieutenant-general, but that he died on the way. There is no corroborative evidence of this appointment, but from the details about the then colony and its politics in *Oroonoko*, it is likely that Behn was there during the early 1660s, and that on her return to England, she was married, although nothing is known of her husband. He may have died, or they may have separated, but no contemporary account exists of their relationship or life together. In late 1666 she was involved in spying for Charles II in the Low Countries, and records of her activities and code name exist in the Public Record Office. She used the code 'Astrea', and was commissioned to discover as much as possible from a double agent, Thomas Scott, whom she had probably known in Surinam. During her time in the Low Countries, she ran up large debts, and her spying mission largely failed, since the quality of information she delivered never endangered the Dutch or benefited the English. She returned to England in 1667, in debt, and without a permanent home. She may have undertaken further spying in Italy. Despite the paucity of biographical information, and indeed, the lack of any statements about her own life, it is nevertheless clear that certain patterns may be discerned in this biography which may be said to have informed her writing.

The first is her ability to perform different roles, and adopt different personas according to circumstance. The knowledge that one's place in the world was dependent upon effective performance was one shared by most of her successful heroines. The second, is that despite her relatively humble background, she managed to educate herself, undoubtedly with the help of various patrons, and to read much of the romantic and dramatic literature of the seventeenth century. This suggests a woman of tremendous drive and ambition, as well as talent. Thirdly, she was able to take advantage of the changing and turbulent times in the aftermath first of civil war, then of the republic, and finally of the restoration of monarchy. Many other women in this period took on roles which had hitherto been impossible: wives took over the administration of estates in the absence of husbands or brothers; women went preaching in England and as missionaries abroad in the new climate of religious freedom; the discussion of political freedoms for men during the 1640s engendered an atmosphere in which individual autonomy for men and women became a subject for discussion. Fourthly, during her time as a spy, whether this was solely during her time in the Low Countries, or whether in fact it was continuous between 1659 and 1667, she learned to write in cipher and code. This habit of communication through indirection, whether learned or natural, strengthened her ability as a dramatist to engage and direct her audience. Fifthly, for a young woman of her class, she was widely travelled, and this travel provided her with an intellectual oversight of other cultures, to the extent that she could both perceive and analyse cultural differences.

Such perception is clear in the novel *Oroonoko*, but also in her comic plays, which anatomise a particular kind of Englishness. This developed into a kind of relativism, which she shared with many of

the leading sceptics of the day, such as Hobbes and the Earl of
Rochester. In one of her poems she links this cultural relativism both
to the constraints on women, and to the way in which the bastion of
masculinity is protected and upheld:

> . . . curst her sex and education,
> And more the scanted customs of the nation,
> Permitting not the female sex to tread
> The mighty paths of learned heroes dead.
> The godlike Virgil and great Homer's muse,
> Like divine mysteries are conceal'd from us,
> We are forbid all grateful themes,
> No ravishing thoughts approach our ear;
> The fulsome jingle of the times
> Is all we are allowed to understand or hear.
>
> (*Works*, 1, p. 25)

Finally, if, as some critics and early biographers have hypothesised,
she was forced to marry Mr Behn, perhaps on the way home from
her stay in Surinam, her personal sexual experience may have
strengthened or initiated an antipathy and anger towards arranged
marriages and the supposed natural superiority of men, a view which
is present in almost all her plays. Yet none of these biographical
traces can in themselves alone explain the sophistication of her social
analysis. We must return to her work itself, and the way in which
she evidently understood, learned from and improved on the writing
of others and observed social and political mores, to explain her literary development and success.

11

Restoration Contexts

In the previous chapter we considered Behn's plays in the context of her own theatrical and literary development and environment. In this chapter we shall broaden that approach by discussing in more detail the generic, social and political contexts for her work. We shall first examine contemporary debates about comedy, discussing Behn's own view of such debates, which she expresses in various prefaces and prologues to her plays, and then move on to consider the wider social context in which she lived and worked.

Theories of Comedy

It is a good idea to look at contextual theories of comedy, because it helps us to place Behn's work and thinking within the context of her literary and dramatic peers, and to understand how she approached her drama both practically and intellectually.

During the Restoration period (1660–88), which coincides exactly with Behn's adult years, three identifiable traditions of English comic writing and thinking co-existed, all of which looked back to the drama of Shakespeare's time to find a heritage and justification. These were: the influence from John Fletcher, often termed the comedy of wit; that from Ben Jonson, often termed the comedy of humours and satire; and that from Shakespeare himself, which played a far smaller role, but which had its significant influence on Behn in particular. We shall return to each of these traditions in a

moment, but it is also important to remember that French neo-classical drama, particularly the comic tradition of Molière, had its own
influence on all English comedy during the Restoration. More than
English writers, the French emphasised the neo-classical dramatic
theory of the 'unities', derived from Aristotle via sixteenth-century
commentators. The theory claimed that all drama should conform
to a rigid model, in which time, place and action should have a
unified consistency (the 'unities'). Thus, action represented on stage
should take no longer than the time taken to watch it (unity of
time); the stage itself should only represent one place, since its space
was one dimension (unity of place); and the main characters and
story should be completely integrated (unity of action). Very few
seventeenth-century English comedies conformed to this model
(Shakespeare's *The Tempest* comes closest), although Ben Jonson and
others paid lip-service to its premises. Some of Behn's work does
restrict the fictional time to twenty-four hours – for example, *The
Feigned Courtesans*, whose action takes place over a day and a night –
and *The Rover*'s action takes place over only a few days.

However, let us return to our discussion of Restoration theories.
The first tradition, which looked back to John Fletcher,
Shakespeare's successor with his company the King's Men, was dominated by the poet laureate, John Dryden. Both in his prefaces and
in his *Art of Dramatic Poesy* (1668), Dryden argued that most early
seventeenth-century drama was crude compared with the ideal,
flaunting common or gross characters. Ben Jonson's comic humours
were not elevated enough, and were wanting in 'wit', a term frequently used by Restoration critics and usually meaning a combination of elegant dramatic plotting, with verbal dexterity and skill
amongst characters of elevated status. Dryden additionally argued
that Restoration audiences wanted 'gracious' comedies in which
'making love' was central to the action. Dryden's basic theoretical
premise about the purpose of drama derived from the Roman
Horace, whose *Ars Poetica* argued that poetry's aim was to delight
and teach. Dryden argued, however, that pleasure should come
before instruction, and that the comedy of wit moved audiences to
pleasure first, and consequent emulation of elevated civil virtues.
Dryden's essay melds the theoretical and pragmatic: he criticises

structural and philosophical aspects of Jonson's work, but does this
both from a critical viewpoint, and because the audience profile and
interests had changed.

The second tradition, that which viewed Ben Jonson more posi-
tively, was dominated by the playwright Thomas Shadwell
(?1641–92), who wrote for the Duke's Company. His first play, *The
Sullen Lovers*, was staged in 1668, and many of his plays were adaptations of Molière's plays. In the preface to his first play he explicitly
responded to Dryden's essay, and traced his own comic heritage back
to Ben Jonson. Like Dryden, his basic literary theory was Horatian,
he believed that drama should instruct and delight, but by contrast,
argued that the means to this end should be quite different from
those that Dryden enumerated. He claimed that Jonson's 'wit' lay in
finding 'good humours' (by which was meant a dominant characteristic that could be exaggerated to dominate the action of a single
character), and 'matter proper fit for it', in other words, suitable
action to match characterisation. He decried much of the so-called
witty comedy as illustrating only: 'two chief persons . . . most commonly a swearing, drinking, whoring ruffian for a lover, and an
impudent, ill-bred tomrig for a mistress'. Comedy should render
'figures of vice and folly so ugly and detestable' that the audience
will learn to despise them. This tradition of comedy, where vice is
visibly held up to mockery and punished, encouraged a more satiric
form than that envisaged by Dryden.

The third tradition, far less dominant in theoretical accounts and
prefaces, is the heritage of Shakespeare and the native English tradition. Such plays were far less popular as straight revivals during the
Restoration, although most playwrights indulged in re-writing
them to conform either to the unities or to Restoration social sensi-
bilities (by eliminating the sub-plot, for example). However, the
Shakespearean disregard for the unities, the proliferation of multiple plots, and the engagement with characters from all social
ranks, remained a strong practical influence on English drama. This
comic tradition was silently absorbed by most practising dramatists
of the period, even if the lower classes simply become butts for
political jokes. Behn was one of the few dramatists who defended
and paraded Shakespearean drama as an ideal. Let us turn now to

consider precisely how Behn participated in this contemporary debate.

In many of her prologues or epistles, Behn sets forth views on her place in the comic tradition. In 'The Epistle to the Reader' in the published version of *The Dutch Lover* (1673), she argues that university learning makes for dull drama, and explicitly links such learning with men, thereby suggesting that women playwrights might uniquely be able to provide drama with contemporary relevance. She opposes the classical Horatian defence of poetry and drama (clung to by Dryden and Shadwell), and states:

> I am myself well able to affirm that none of all our English poets, and least the dramatic (so I think you call them) can be justly charged with too great reformation of men's minds or manners. . . . In short, I think a play the best divertisement that wise men have; but I do also think them nothing so who do discourse as formally about the rules of it, as if 'twere the grand affair of human life. This being my opinion of plays, I studied only to make this as entertaining as I could.

Drama's primary aim is entertainment, and entertainment alone.

Her dislike of those who cite and depend on critical theorists is reiterated in the epilogue to *The Rover*, where she addresses critics directly:

> With canting rule you would the stage refine,
> And to dull method all our sense confine.
> With th'insolence of commonwealths you rule,
> Where each gay fop, and politic grave fool
> On monarch wit impose, without control.
> As for the last, who seldom sees a play,
> Unless it be the old Blackfriars way,
> Shaking his empty noddle o'er bamboo,
> He cries, 'Good faith, these plays will never do.
> Ah, sir, in my young days, what lofty wit,
> What high strained scenes of fighting there were writ:
> These are slight airy toys.'

By analogising critical theorists with the restrictions and directives of the Commonwealth (the government under Cromwell), she suggests that critics constrain literary freedom. Monarchy and dramatists also are analogous: both, allowed to rule ('monarch wit'), produce better outcomes. And she is scornful of the critical school who see virtue only in old plays, and those remembered in the critics' youth: thus staking a claim for novelty in theatrical practice.

Yet, over time, Behn developed her views on the significance of her own drama, and moved explicitly to an Horatian view. In the 'Epistle Dedicatory' to *The Lucky Chance*, addressed to Lord Hyde, a member of the Privy Council, for example, she writes:

> The abbot of Aubignac, to show that plays have been ever held most impor-
> tant to the very political part of government, says the philosophy of Greece,
> and the majesty and wisdom of the Romans, did equally concern their great
> men, in making them venerable, noble and magnificent. . . .
>
> It being undeniable then, that plays and public diversions were thought
> by the greatest and wisest of states, one of the most essential parts of good
> government, and in which so many great persons were interested, suffer me
> to beg your lordship's patronage.

She uses this argument as a platform from which to seek patronage, and to assert her loyalty to the King during the Exclusion Crisis. However, it is also clear that these combined economic and political circumstances have served to develop her ideas about the function and place of drama in a social and political framework. She places drama centre-stage as a political and educative tool, arguably one of propaganda, but portrayed by Behn as a form as lofty as philosophy.

In one of her last plays, *The Emperor of the Moon*, Behn wrote a prologue which wittily delineates the fashions in comedies, describing their content and form in a way that makes clear her understanding of her predecessors, and the place of her work within literary history at the end of her career. Although we have not dis-cussed this spectacular play in this book, it is included in the World's Classics edition in which the three discussed here appear. The pro-logue is worth quoting at length.

> Long, and at vast expense, the industrious stage
> Has strove to please a dull ungrateful age:
> With heroes and with gods we first began,

And thundered to you in heroic strain:
Some dying love-sick queen each night you enjoyed,   5
And with magnificence, at last were cloyed:
Our drums and trumpets frighted all the women;
Our fighting scared the beaux and billet-doux men.
So spark, in an intrigue of quality,
Grows weary of his splendid drudgery;   10
Hates the fatigue, and cries, 'a pox upon her,
What a damned bustle's here with love and honour?'
    In humbler comedy we next appear,
No fop or cuckold, but slap-dash we had him here;
We showed you all, but you, malicious grown,   15
Friends' vices to expose, and hide your own,
Cry, 'damn it – this is such or such a one'.
Yet, nettled: 'plague, what does the scribbler mean,
With his damned characters, and plot obscene?
No woman without vizard in the nation,   20
Can see it twice, and keep her reputation – that's certain.'
Forgetting –
That he himself, in every gross lampoon,
Her lewder secrets spreads about the town;
Whilst their feigned niceness is but cautious fear   25
Their own intrigues should be unravelled here.
    Our next recourse was dwindling down to farce,
Then: ''zounds, what stuff's here? 'tis all o'er my –'
Well, gentlemen, since none of these has sped,
'Gad, we have bought a share i'th' speaking head.   30
            (*The Emperor of the Moon*, Prologue, ll.1–30)

This prologue delineates a developmental trajectory for drama,
which Behn's actor claims has been mainly driven by audience
demand (ll. 6–7; 15–20; 28). It begins with heroic tragedy, moves to
satiric comedy, then farce and finally to puppetry (the 'speaking
head'). Whilst this is clearly a parodic view of Restoration dramatic
literary history, it is interesting for two reasons. The first is that it
mirrors fairly exactly the developments in Restoration drama after
1660, and thereby illustrates Behn's active and critical engagement in
dramatic history, and her understanding of her own place within
that. Secondly, she suggests that the intersection of audience and

genre is a crucial and central determining factor in performance and reception. This means that she understood drama as a deeply social and political form, one necessarily responsive to economic and social demands, dependent upon them for its life and performance.

Additionally, she accepts the intersection of fashion and comedy, intimating thereby a symbiotic relationship between contemporaneity and her drama. Such an acknowledgement asks twenty-first-century readers to interpret her plays as commentaries upon such fashions and customs. This attention to both the performance and the context of the performance makes Behn's comic theory distinctive amongst her contemporaries, who often reverted to classical theories, rather than contemporary or personal observation. Finally, she posits the existence of several interpretative and professional communities: the 'we' of the playwrights, and the 'you' of the audience, existing in mutual dialogue, the results of which are performed plays. Although she ostensibly insults her audience's fickle responses, she simultaneously acknowledges her dependence upon them, and the need for playwrights to conform to their demands.

Finally, let us discuss Behn's position as, and views on her status as a woman writer in the comic tradition. Both during her lifetime, and in the century or so afterwards, her writing was often excoriated simply on the grounds of being by a woman. As we have seen in the previous chapter, Behn was conscious of her near-unique status, and it is possible to argue that she exploited that status as a means of encouraging audiences to her plays. However, if we examine the prefaces and prologues to her plays where she addresses her gender, she tends to defend her position rather than use it to titillate. Such defences once again suggest both her necessary dependence on the audience and the limits such dependence will go to in her case.

In the preface to *Sir Patient Fancy*, Behn turns misogynist accusations (about women's supposed natural volubility) made against her, back against the kind of men who criticise her work:

> If they can find any of our sex fuller of words, and to so little purpose, as some of their gownmen [university educated men], I'll be content to change my petticoats for pantaloons and go to a grammar school.

Here she explicitly allies herself with other women, against a retrenched establishment masculinity linked to the institutions of exclusive male education (universities and grammar schools). But in doing so, she also inverts their perceptions of gender: rather than liberating men, she claims, this very education has simply made them slaves to conventional prejudice, and to a wordiness they attempt to displace onto women. In a twist to this insight, she offers to change gender and go to grammar school if she is wrong. This jokily draws simultaneous attention to women's exclusion from such schools, and to her own certainty both that she is right and that few will acknowledge it, and additionally plays on accusations and fears about transgressive women in the theatre.

The Lucky Chance was one of the plays that were attacked as lewd. Behn felt this was only because it was written by a woman. She used the published version of the play as an opportunity to set forth her ideas about both her critics and her own work, and both in relation to her gender. The preface is printed in full in the World's Classics edition, but two parts are worth citing at length. The first part addresses key points about the politics of dramatic reception:

Any unprejudiced person that knows not the author – to read any of my comedies and compare 'em with others of this age, and if they find one word that can offend the chastest ear, I will submit to all their peevish cavils: but, right or wrong, they must be criminal because a woman's; condemning them without having the Christian charity to examine whether it be guilty or not, with reading, comparing, or thinking; the ladies taking up any scandal on trust from some conceited sparks, who will in spite of nature be wits and beaux. . . .

When it happens that I challenge any one to point me out the least expression of what some have made their discourse, they cry, that Mr Leigh opens his nightgown, when he comes into the bride-chamber; if he do, which is a jest of his own making, and which I never saw, I hope he has his clothes on underneath? And if so, where is the indecency? I have seen in that admirable play of *Oedipus*, the gown opened wide, and the man shown in his drawers and waistcoat, and never thought it an offence before. Another cries, 'why, we know not what they mean, when the man takes a woman off the stage, and another is thereby cuckolded'; is that any more than you see in the most celebrated of your plays? As *The City Politics*: the Lady

Mayoress, and the old lawyer's wife, who goes with a man she never saw
before, and comes out again the joyfullest woman alive.

Behn argues, then, that her play has been attacked 'because a
woman's', and that this has been exacerbated by town gossip, particularly that of fashionable women, and because of a piece of lewd
stage business. Her threefold defence argues first that it was casti-
gated simply because a woman wrote it; secondly that the actor
interpreted the role with the action to which critics objected; and
third, that other plays use equally lewd physical gestures or implied
(off-stage) adultery. Behn's own stage directions in the published
version did note that Fainwould opens his gown. Nevertheless, the
third argument is the key and the most valid: other Restoration
comedies were often far bawdier and more explicit than any of
Behn's. Implicitly, then, she claims a right to equality in bawdiness
with male writers, whilst recognising a double standard in her audience's reception of the plays.

The second extract makes this defence far more overt:

All I ask, is the privilege for my masculine part the poet in me (if any such
you will allow me) to tread in those successful paths my predecessors have so
long thrived in, to take those measures that both the ancient and modern
writers have set me, and by which they have pleased the world so well. If I
must not, because of my sex, have this freedom, but that you will usurp all
to yourselves, I lay down my quill, and you shall hear no more of me – no,
not so much as to make comparisons, because I will be kinder to my
brothers of the pen than they have been to a defenceless woman – for I am
not content to write for a third day only. I value fame as much as if I had
been born a hero.

Behn effectively has her cake and eats it here: she wants equality of
access to, and treatment in, the dramatic market-place with men,
but she is prepared to use the self-description of 'a defenceless
woman' to arouse pathos. Yet in fact, what she actually says is more
interesting than this implies: for she talks about herself in bi-sexual
terms. She has a 'masculine part' (her professional writing), linked to
her desire to be a 'hero', but the 'I' who writes is clearly and self-consciously a woman. She thus suggests a radical split between her work

and her private self: the only way a woman can be accepted in the public world as a professional is to claim such a split, and to gender her public self 'masculine'. On a broader canvas, she places her own writing within a tradition of 'ancient and modern' writers, appealing in effect to posterity to judge her work and her defence as worthy of belonging to a canon of dramatists. Although this plea, and her active place in theatrical production in her day, were ignored for nearly three hundred years, her place and worth are now recognised by both critics and historians.

The Political and Social Context of the Comedies

Throughout this book we have discussed Behn's comedies as political, considering the ways in which she raises generalised political and social questions. What do we mean by 'political' here? This does not refer to the narrow sphere of political process, linked to government and monarch, but to the broad nature of relationships between individuals in the public, social and economic sphere, which may include questions of rule and questions of rights. Let us first consider the broad meaning of 'political', and the ways in which Behn may be seen to be in dialogue with her contemporaries on these issues. Questions raised by Behn's plays which may be defined as political in this sense include the following: In what ways is the relationship between men and women dominated or determined by the political, economic and social environment? How and why is marriage bound up with masculine class interests? To what extent, if at all, can women determine their own fates and identity? Does the shift to economic proto-capitalism, and its associated politics of democratisation, reduce women further to economic bartering counters? How far is masculine desire and masculinity bound up in other power structures and relationships? The plays do not answer these questions, but leave the audience with material and ideas for debate and thinking.

What is interesting about Behn's work is how many of these questions pre-empt slightly later philosophical and political debates about these issues. There are three major political works which are particularly pertinent to Behn's drama. The first is John Locke's *Two Treatises of Government* (1690). Although written in defence of James II's deposition and of Parliamentary government, both anathema to Behn, it sets out the founding ideology of contract theory as the basic cement of civilised society. Such a theory, which argued that all social and political action had to be predicated on an implicit contract between two or more parties, in which each had an equal say, was later applied in arguments about equal rights in marriage, and equality for women. Although Behn herself never talks in terms of 'rights', the conversations her heroines have with their lovers explicitly use contractual language, which intimates mutual equality and specifies a voice for women in the public negotiations of a marriage. Plays by many of her male contemporaries, such as Etherege and Wycherley, also often include bargaining scenes between lovers, in which women negotiate their rights within marriage. Contractual assumptions about relationships, and their placing within a social world, were thus part of the discourse of the social and dramatic world before codified by Locke.

The second work which bears a close affinity to Behn's work is that of Mary Astell, who, while a relatively young woman, published *Reflections upon Marriage* in 1700, which quickly went through several editions. Although mainly an analysis of the economic and political constraints of marriage, and advocacy of a single life if women wanted any independence, she articulated a precise programme for women-only educational institutions in order to provide women with the means for independence. Without explicitly naming the system of class and land interest, and its intersection with the naturalisation of predatory masculine 'patriarchy', she comes close to analysing its economic, political and social features. Most of the observations she makes and concerns she raises can be found within the three plays we have studied in this book.

The third work is Robert Filmer's *Patriarcha*, first published in 1680, but actually written during the period of the English Civil War. This was the classic defence of government by absolute monarch. The monarchy was defended and described as modelled on the family, in which the father was 'naturally' head of a domestic unit, over which he had absolute authority because of his superior

status as a man, and a natural wealth earner. This defence of absolutism came just as absolute monarchy was ending in England (since
James II was deposed in 1688), and may be seen as an ideology in
decline. The book was published in the middle of the Exclusion
Crisis, so named because Parliament was attempting to exclude
Charles II's brother James from inheriting the throne, on the
grounds of his Catholicism. The defence of patriarchalism as a combined governmental and domestic theory of rule is never put
forward by Behn, although she supported absolute monarchy, and
during the Exclusion Crisis in particular wrote explicitly political
plays in defence of Tory ideology and the monarch.

In the previous chapter we discussed how Behn's work fitted in
with some of the major political events and controversies that dominated England between 1660 and 1688. Let us briefly review some
of those key events. Charles II was restored to the throne in 1660,
by parliamentary invitation (this was known as 'the Restoration'),
and at the time he was greeted with much rejoicing as a symbol of
order and unification by a country which had been split by civil war
and subsequent difficulties with Republican government. One of the
first plays to celebrate Charles II's return was Nahum Tate's *The
Rump* in 1660, which explicitly satirised the Rump Parliament
(sitting in 1660) through attacking puritans as greedy, self-interested
grandees with lustful wives. The dramatic symbolisation of political
ideology through caricature and through sexuality was a continued
Tory tactic, which Behn shared (as we saw in Chapter 10). Indeed,
this play was the major source for her own play *The Roundheads*, in
1681.

Yet despite Charles II's initial popularity, even by 1661 the court
had gained a reputation for profligacy and recklessness: Pepys
famously described 'the lewdness and beggary of the court'. Charles
II's lack of interest in ruling with the consent of Parliament, combined with his well-publicised sexual adventures and the open
flaunting of successive mistresses and illegitimate sons, paraded the
image of a dandy king, and reminded many of his father Charles I's
disdain for the people he governed. His flirtation with Catholicism,
both through his close association with Louis XIV of France, and
with the religious faith of his own wife, fuelled growing suspicion

that he would lead the country back to both Catholicism and non-parliamentary government. Such fears were reinforced in 1673 when it was clear that, in the absence of any legitimate sons, his heir would be his brother James, who was a fierce Catholic. This came to a head during the Exclusion Crisis of 1679–82, when Parliament successively tried to pass a Bill which would exclude any Catholic from succeeding to the monarchy, and during which period various 'plots' were discovered which supposedly revealed a secret Catholic plot to overthrow many of the aristocrats who supported the idea of an Exclusion Bill.

Charles II had ruled with a single parliament from 1660 to 1679, a further example of his refusal to listen to requests from any parties other than his own close-knit circle of aristocratic supporters. He called a new parliament in 1679, in the hope that it would vote him new subsidies and be less hostile to his brother. The election in this year was the first to follow party lines, the Whigs supporting greater parliamentary powers, and the subjection of the monarch to a more democratic rule, while the Tories supported the status quo. This parliament, known as the Oxford Parliament, the majority of whose members were Whig, refused to acquiesce to new taxes and subsidies, and continually brought in the Exclusion Bill. In 1682 Charles II dissolved Parliament, and ruled without a parliament until his death in 1685, supported by a secret subsidy from Louis XIV, which he had agreed on the condition that the country would convert to Catholicism.

James II inherited the throne in 1685, ruling with increasing disregard for the political opposition to his religion, appointing Catholic supporters to key governmental roles and suppressing dissent. In 1688 he and his wife bore a son, and the arrival of a Catholic heir prompted many aristocrats to turn to Charles II's daughter Mary and her husband, William of Orange, and invite William to invade the country and assume the monarchy. James II fled with his family. This quiet revolution (known as 'the glorious revolution'), in which Whig aristocrats secretly invited the monarch of another country to take over their own, in return for agreements about the power and rights of Parliament, marked the end of absolute monarchy in England.

Aphra Behn died five days after William and Mary's coronation. Politically, during her adult life time, England was riven by party difference and by hysterical fears of a Catholic conspiracy, ruled by a monarch whose sex life was more newsworthy than any political policies, and yet also anxious to avoid a slide back into the chaos of the Civil War years (as is evident, for example, from Behn's epilogue to *The Rover*). During this period London also suffered the ravages of the Plague and the Great Fire of 1666, and the humiliation of the defeat of her navy in the Thames by the Dutch in 1667. Yet culturally, theatre, music, opera and architecture thrived. Despite the crowds and the dirt, there continued to be net immigration to the city.

Social changes included a greater social mobility amongst the middle classes, some of whom became wealthy through trade and financial dealings, and whose views and values began to dominate the Whig party. Economic power was gradually shifting from the land to trade, although land ownership remained a powerful symbol of privilege and power. Many plays of the period express fears about the changing social categories, satirising the nouveau riche for a lack of civility and history: the old city men of *The Lucky Chance* are a good example. Social change included shifts in gender roles and relationships. During the Civil War some women gained greater freedom than hitherto: examples included learning to run businesses or estates in their husbands' absence at war; joining religious sects which practised equality between men and women (such as the Quakers); and acting as religious prophets. A more mobile population also meant more women moved away from their villages, and the controls of family, to the greater freedom of London. Conversely, it has been observed that the Civil War brought about a crisis of a particular model of masculinity: the courtly Cavalier, whose sexual prowess matched his unassailed political power, had literally been defeated. Despite the revival of the Cavalier rake in Charles II himself, his rakishness was, as we have seen, equally followed and reviled.

The philosophical climate, influenced for example by the work of Thomas Hobbes, who argued that all humans were mere matter and passion, reduced both men and women to mechanical bodies, with neither in the ascendant. The family unit itself was changing. Economics, history, politics and philosophy combined to create an atmosphere in which conventional gender roles began to be challenged and sexual autonomy for women was first voiced (as we saw in the beginning of this section). The discussion and representation of gender issues is not something found solely in the plays of Aphra Behn, but is common to most Restoration comedies and tragedies. As with Behn, many plays challenge the rights of older men, fathers or uncles, to make decisions for young women. Fathers are represented as perverse or incompetent. Cross-dressing is used to explore greater freedom for women. Many dramatists, including Behn, make their rakes so self-interested that an audience is forced to be critical of their view of gender relations.

Finally, it is worth reminding ourselves of the broader philosophical climate. We have already discussed the importance of Locke's expression of contract theory to new ideas about rights and gender. Let us turn in greater detail to discuss Hobbes. The Hobbesian philosophy informed much of the language and ideas of the libertine who populated the stage, and Behn herself seems to have sympathised with his expressed materialism. Hobbes described humans as consisting solely of physical appetite (for food, sex, sleep), and their natural condition was to seek for satisfaction in a purely selfish manner, using brute power to do so. Moral and ethical values had no 'natural' basis, and did not inform human action; therefore, he supported absolute political tyranny as the sole means of ordering a chaotic world. This then suggested a radical divide between public conformity and private libertinism. Scepticism, libertinism and political absolutism were thus intimately fused in his world view.

This kind of philosophical outlook can be seen in many plays of the period: the rakes are the mouthpieces for his materialist appetitive theory; the satirical thrust of many of the plays is against hypocritical division between private and public; we are made to see humans as divided creatures, not all of whose needs and desires can be accommodated in social harmony; and a sceptical outlook on the status quo is engendered in an audience through staging and other dramatic devices. What is interesting about Behn's work is that whilst she shares both these views and these dramatic modes with her fellow playwrights, she inserts gender into the equation in such a way as to make the audience see the Hobbesian philosophy within the context of a critical view of domestic patriarchal values, and from women's viewpoints. Yet Hobbes's extreme scepticism contrasted with the scientific spirit of the age: the Royal Society was set up in 1660, and science became both fashionable and a dominant model for explaining phenomena and the world. Scientific certainty therefore co-existed with radical scepticism as philosophical models whereby men and women sought to explain and understand the world.

12

Sample Critical Views and Performances

Literary criticism can be both daunting and impenetrable to students, appearing to dictate a particular approach and discourse to interpreting an author, which students feel obliged to follow. Your own analyses and interpretations, which you have arrived at through the detailed work in this book, will have provided you with a strong and individual understanding. So long as this is based on close readings of the plays, your approach and your own language are as valid as those of academic critics. However, your own interpretations will be stimulated and inspired by other readers and critics, and it is in the context of participating in a shared debate that you should read criticism. If you approach critical argument in this way you will be better equipped to be sceptical and thoughtful about critics' arguments, and be better able to come to your own conclusions about the validity and importance of their views.

Behn has been neglected, by both critics and producers, until relatively recently. Under the impact of twentieth-century feminism, she was one of the first woman writers to be rediscovered, reprinted and reviewed. Yet the total volume of criticism still remains low, and its nature was determinedly biographical until the late 1980s. Such biographical criticism focuses predominantly on Behn's life, from her probable stay in Surinam, her life as a spy, a wit, a woman participating in the London literary milieu, openly taking lovers, to earning her money via professional writing and supporting the

King's policies. This approach to Behn's work began with the first wave of feminism early in the twentieth century with Vita Sackville-West's *Aphra Behn: The Incomparable Astraea* (1927), ground-breaking in its examination of a forgotten woman author, and until the 1980s, further work on Behn continued to focus on biography: George Woodcock's *The Incomparable Aphra* (1948), Maureen Duffy's *The Passionate Shepherdess* (1977), and Janet Todd's *The Secret Life of Aphra Behn* (1996) are the most dominant examples. In this approach, criticism of the drama itself is reduced to finding parallels between the life and the content and themes of the plays, an approach which fails to recognise the complexity of Behn's fiction-making and dramatic abilities. For this reason, the sample views we shall consider in a moment are all much more recent, and take the work rather than the life as their starting point. Students who wish to reconsider the relationship between the scant facts of Behn's life and the drama, should look at any of the four examples above, and decide for themselves how the life helps us to analyse and criticise the dramatic texts we have studied.

The following sample are examples of three slightly different approaches to Behn, all published since 1993. Two are collections of essays, which conveniently bring together much of the seminal and varied work done on Behn since the 1980s, but do so from different editorial perspectives, whilst the third is a full-length study of Behn's plays. Let us consider each briefly in turn.

*   *   *

Our first collection is that edited by Heidi Hutner in 1993, *Rereading Aphra Behn: History, Theory, Criticism*. This collection is a valuable introduction to the state of Behn criticism in 1990: it shows how the impact of political feminism fuelled the rediscovery of Behn as a literary subject in the 1970s and 1980s, as well as how feminist literary theory might be applied to her drama, poetry and prose. The first six essays concern the drama, and had all been previously published in journals, while two of those (by Laurie Finke and Jessica Munns) focus on Behn's literary theory and her prologues. Let us briefly consider the essays which directly relate to plays we have analysed in this book: those by Catherine Gallagher, Jane Spencer and Heidi Hutner.

Gallagher ('Who Was that Masked woman?: The Prostitute and the Playwright in the Comedies of Aphra Behn') argues that masking and feminine masquerade is an essential metaphor for actor, playwright and courtesan, and that Behn self-consciously used the metaphor in her prefaces and prologues as a means of paradoxical empowerment. She writes:

> [Behn] introduced to the world of English letters the professional woman writer as a newfangled whore. The persona has many functions in Behn's work: it titillates, scandalises, arouses pity, and indicates the vicissitudes of authorship and identity in general. The author-whore persona also makes of female authorship *per se* a dark comedy that explores the bond between the liberty the stage offered women and their confinement behind both literal and metaphorical vizard masks. (p. 66)

Behn's writing is thus represented as an extended erotic engagement with the audience, beginning with the invocation of sexual titillation through her teasing prologues, and continued through her representation of ambiguous, teasing female characters. Two important consequences of this argument are that Behn manages to suggest a hidden 'real' identity behind the masks she sets up, albeit one forever postponed ('she managed to create the effect of inaccessible authenticity out of the very image of prostitution'), and that all identity is seen as fluid and constructed. Gallagher argues that Behn's strategy is paradigmatic of all attempts to establish female autonomy and identity in the plays, and indeed for late seventeenth-century women in general. Theories of identity for a woman depended upon her belonging to someone else, her father initially, who then gave her away to belong to her husband.

> This ideal of a totalized woman, preserved because wholly given away . . . Aphra Behn sacrifices to create a different idea of identity, one complexly dependent on the necessity of multiple exchanges. She who is able to repeat the action of self-alienation an unlimited number of times is she who is constantly there to regenerate, possess, and sell a series of provisional, constructed identities. Self-possession, then, and self-alienation are just two sides of the same coin. (p. 70)

Gallagher applies her thesis to *The Lucky Chance*, arguing that despite the apparent comic scenario in which the problem of old men treating women as property will be solved by the women's rejection of such an equation, the overall comic structure does not provide such an unambiguous outcome. Thus, the parallels between the Belmour/Leticia story and that of Gayman/Julia effectively undercut the former plot's conventional comic emphasis on chaste marriage and its concomitant ideology of an intact self given away to a husband. Julia, although proved to be 'nothing' by her husband and Gayman, has herself stage-managed a night with Gayman. Unlike them, her deceit is not discovered: 'Julia has found a way to secure her liberty and her "honour" by maintaining her misrepresentations' (p. 85). For Julia, literal self-possession and future sexual exchange come about through others' mis-cognition and the appearance of valuelessness.

Gallagher's argument is detailed and stimulating, and has influenced many subsequent critics. However, it is worth noting that her basic interpretative premise remains biographical: she continues to make a parallel between Behn's self-conscious and expressed status as author and her fictional women as (feigned) courtesans. However, her approach enables us to make links between fictional strategies and the social history of identity and sexuality, rather than the more reductive equations between life and work of the purely biographical approach.

Jane Spencer's essay in the same collection ('"Deceit, Dissembling, all that's Woman": Comic Plot and Female Action in *The Feigned Courtesans*') argues that Behn adapts the form and structure of the 'typical sex comedy' of the 1670s to three crucial ends. The first is the subjection of the rake to critical rather than celebratory judgement; the second is to link female action and subjectivity directly to the functional workings of the plot's action; and the third is to nevertheless confine the heroines' freedom by a traditional closure in marriage at the end. The value of Spencer's approach is that she integrates an analysis and understanding of how a dramatist may use comic conventions with an understanding of Behn's more political purposes. She shows how conventions are used to non-conventional ends, inverting or diverting the conventional in order to draw an audience's attention to polemical ideas, an approach we have shared in some of our analyses in this book. In summary she writes:

> *The Feigned Courtesans*, then, certainly throws into question the woman's proper role of silence and submission, celebrating women's deceitful, dissembling actions in pursuit of their desires. It does so, however, without really undermining the equation of woman's worth with her sexual virtue. It is an attempt to inscribe women's desire within a patriarchal text, and in our reading of it we need to give weight both to the attempt and to its inevitable limitations.   (p. 100)

Hutner's essay ('Revisioning the Female Body: Aphra Behn's *The Rover*, Parts I and II') argues that through its focus on different female bodies, on the exchange of women as property between men, and on the provisional and constructed nature of femininity, Behn both critiques contemporary models of femininity and posits a utopian ideal celebrating women's bodies as 'other'. She suggests that such celebration occurs most unambiguously in Part 2 of *The Rover*. Her illustrative proof focuses to a large extent on the differences between Behn's plays and their source, *Thomaso*, an illuminating illustration of Behn's radical departure in characterisation and plotting. Hutner analyses how the male gaze on and construction of female bodies, and the men's simultaneous repression and devaluation of the feminine as 'other', is objectified by the play's action and then subverted by both Hellena and Angellica: 'Behn utilises the construction of the sexualised whore to subvert the ideology of passive, self-controlled, and commodified womanhood' (p. 103).

Thus the three writers considered here share a broad feminist approach, although each emphasises different theoretical models. Gallagher utilises French psychoanalytic criticism in emphasising identity as masquerade and provisional; Spencer assumes a model of freedom based on political rights and autonomy, and a historical and political understanding of patriarchy; whilst Hutner combines a political critique of patriarchy with de Beauvoir's analysis of woman as 'other' to man, to analyse Behn's representative strategies.

* * *

Janet Todd, who has edited Behn's complete plays, produced another collection of essays in 1996, *Aphra Behn Studies*. The focus of the collection is overtly contextual, each essay setting Behn's work within a specific context, whether theatrical, political, or historical. Thus whilst many of the critics share a generalised liberal feminism, the content of these essays takes such an approach as implicit, whilst making explicit the Restoration context on which they focus. It includes five essays on the drama, three of which we shall consider briefly here, since only those three relate directly to the plays studied in this book.

Susan Owen's essay ('Sexual Politics and Party Politics in Behn's Drama 1678–83') examines how Behn's plays during the Exclusion Crisis change both their political message and their feminist agenda, directly in relation to actual political events. Thus *The Feigned Courtesans*, early in this period, uses Royalist satire of puritans and ridicules the fear of Popery, opposing Cavalier rakes to hypocritical puritans, whilst still allowing a feminist interrogation of rake masculinity. The later plays, however, make more overtly a simple equation between Cavalier and feminist freedoms, positing a golden age of female sexual freedom in Royalist times. Owen's argument usefully pinpoints changes in Behn's political stance. In times where political crisis was less acute, where party politics perhaps mattered less, Behn was free to analyse more critically both Cavalier and Puritan attitudes to and constructions of women.

In Alison Shell's essay, which also examines *The Feigned Courtesans* ('Popish Plots: *The Feign'd Curtizans* in Context'), she argues that the play's focus on 'plotting' suggests by analogy that as her plotting women are innocent, so are those accused of Popish plots in Charles II's London. Shell argues that Behn's Catholic sympathies are clarified by the play's generous representation of Italian women.

The third essay, by Dawn Lewcock ('More for Seeing than Hearing: Behn and the Use of Theatre'), focuses on Behn's professional use of the space of the theatre and most particularly on the visual effects of performance. She integrates commentary on Behn's plays with an historical account of the development of the theatres, looking explicitly at the machinery available to Behn at the time different plays were produced. Lewcock argues that:

dramaturgical analysis that takes into account the effects of the theatrical elements on an audience, shows how she interweaves the staging with the dialogue to provide a visual commentary to the audience. This is done by several of her fellow dramatists. What is unique to Behn is not only her appreciation of the visual effects of a performance but also the way she uses it to affect the perceptions of the audience and change their conception and comprehension of her plots and/or underlying theme.   (pp. 66–7)

Her main example is the way discovery scenes physically reveal how deceit dominates public and private life, and how they help guide the audience's interpretation, including deceiving us about potential outcomes, most particularly in *The Feigned Courtesans*. Lewcock argues that Behn's dominant dramaturgical impulse is performative: she is continually mindful of the potential audience and their response:

> what appears to govern her staging is not the subject matter nor the style of the play so much as the relationship she wants for any particular piece of action or business with the audience, or how she wishes the audience to perceive the happenings on the stage. She structured her plays to take into account not only the dialogue but also the action bound up with it.   (p. 82)

The strength of this collection is the specificity of its contextual analysis and material.

* * *

The third critical text we shall examine is a whole-book study of Behn, published in 2001, Derek Hughes's *The Theatre of Aphra Behn*. He attempts a revisionist account of Behn, as an antidote to some of the critical feminist commonplaces which dominate Behn criticism. Thus, for example, in his introduction, he argues that Gallagher's analysis of the equation between dramatist and courtesan depends upon a fundamental misreading of the prologue to *The Widow Ranter*, her posthumously performed play. Gallagher makes three mistakes which, Hughes claims, seriously undermine both her argument and other feminist critics who follow in her steps. First, she mistakes the actual sense of the quotation, secondly she does not acknowledge that it was taken from one of Dryden's plays, and thirdly, she doesn't say that it was only the published, not the performed, prologue. Hughes argues that these mistakes typify feminist approaches to Behn in not acknowledging the precise theatrical milieu in which her work was performed, and tending to analyse the drama simply as texts for analysis. Hughes argues strongly and convincingly for a Behn enmeshed in the practices and practitioners of the theatre of her day, and sets out to analyse all her plays in this specific context. Yet despite Hughes's attack on feminist critics, he remains indebted to their focus on gender, as is clear from his summary of a part of his own thesis:

> [Behn] created an integration of verbal and visual signs, exploiting significant scenes and spaces, spatially arranging bodies and props that enforce demarcation of gender: the sword, the document, the watch.   (p. 2)

Hughes's book is structured in an approachable way for students, beginning with an introductory background chapter, followed by ones which organise Behn's plays according to both developmental achievements and political context. Thus, for example, chapters move from 'Experimentation' and 'Maturity' to 'Political Crisis' and 'Political Triumph'.

The background chapter attempts to de-mythologise the feminist hagiographical story of Behn as exceptional woman, by showing how other women wrote plays and had them performed, that actresses were professional working women before Behn produced a play, that the company for which she wrote was managed by a woman, and that many conduct writers as well as other playwrights were questioning the supposed natural basis for male supremacy. These are important contextual and factual observations, although other critics do make similar points. His overall interpretative approach is summarised:

> Her first two plays go back to the origins of male supremacism, depicting feudal societies whose hierarchies and imperatives are those of the battlefield. Memories of the warrior society are generally an important background to her work, but increasingly she examines the transition from military to economic power, and the interaction between the two. At first

she portrays the abuse of power by a wealthy peacetime aristocracy. She then goes further, examining the conflict between the ancient gentry, whose vitality and flamboyance she admires, and the rising commercial classes, who lack the glamour and potency of the old order but give new form to its ways of confining women and ritually exchanging them: however opposed the rival systems of male power are to each other, they can be identical in relation to women. . . . As she moves beyond her simple concern with male military values, she becomes fascinated not only by the power of money, but by that of enumeration: counting, measurement, time-keeping. Increasingly, the power of the sword cedes to that of the clock or watch: Behn was one of the first dramatists to observe that a universe of symbolic forms was being supplanted by one of numerical abstraction.   (pp. 10–11)

Hughes tries to link this interpretative thesis to Behn's theatrical skills: we should not read her plays as ideological texts, but as living theatre. Yet despite Hughes's vocal dissociation from both feminist approaches and the 'ideological' approach, his basic premise remains that her staging strategies are used to reinforce our focus on gender: 'she repeatedly used commonplace stage settings with great care and intelligence, particularly in order to create a sense of gendered space and boundaries' (p. 13).

So does Hughes's work meet his stated aim of integrating staging issues with a textual and contextual analysis? He does draw our attention to specific instances where Behn integrates the physical and visual use of stage props and stage business with the action and themes of plays, in both her early plays and those studied in this book. In addition, by following her career chronologically alongside that of other playwrights such as Dryden, Shadwell, Wycherley and Etherege, we are able to see both what she shares with her contemporaries, and in what ways she is unique. Hughes reminds us that Etherege's *Man of Mode* was far more censorious of rakish masculinity than previous comedies, and that plays after this point 'were more inclined unequivocally to side with the woman' (p. 71), representing the fragility of oaths, trust and friendship. This renders Behn's perspective in *The Rover* less unusual than many feminist critics allow. He also reminds us that *The Feigned Courtesans* was the only comedy staged during the Exclusion Crisis – recognition of Behn's influence and power in the theatrical world.

Hughes's analysis of the plays studied in this book is detailed, and includes commentary on physical stage business and on the use of stage properties and stage space, as well as focusing on actors' bodies as representative of meaning. His account, for example, of the visual and verbal manipulation of the symbolic and physical stage props in *The Lucky Chance* (the sword, the watch and the coin) is compelling and insightful, and is integrated with an account of how exchange and transaction dominate the action. However, unlike Dawn Lewcock's analysis in the Janet Todd collection, Hughes's dramaturgical approach lacks several significant elements. First, he does not explicitly consider how an audience is positioned by both the action and the stage business he discusses, a problematic omission once the visual and physical elements of the theatrical are introduced in an analysis. Secondly, and perhaps consequently, there is a slight sense of a lack of organisation. The reader is not quite sure of the overall direction of his argument as we read the analysis of individual plays, where he skips from point to point without integrating these to a more overarching account. Thirdly, although he is usefully intent upon recording which actors played which roles, he does not convert this to an analysis of what this means about Behn's thinking and working.

Finally, despite his vociferous attack on feminist critics and their lack of contextualisation, he silently uses both the approach and insights of many previous feminists. His analysis of the plays uses much feminist-based theory without acknowledgement, including conceptualising a focus on the physical body, use of theories about the male gaze, and anthropological ones on the ritual exchange of women. He also has a tendency to use terms such as 'male and female principle', suggesting an amorphous idea of a universal masculinity and femininity. This contradicts other evidence Hughes illustrates about Behn's perception of gender as both socially constructed and fluid, that neither masculinity nor femininity are 'natural'. The latter position chimes better with the Behn we have analysed and understood in this book, and is an explicitly feminist interpretative position.

Hughes's strengths are threefold. First he enables us to understand and appreciate Behn's theatricality: her self-conscious use of spectacle, stage business and technical effects. Secondly, he illustrates the integration of such effects with the narrative, plot and conventions of comedy. And finally, his interleaved reminders of the inter-relationship between Behn's plays and their theatrical and political context are an essential counterpoint to modern tendencies to welcome Behn as a post-modernist. His approach is therefore very much grounded in the material world in which Behn wrote and worked. Although other critics have hinted at such an achievement, there is no previous full-length study of Behn which does her justice in this area. However, we need to be conscious that Hughes's work itself is silently indebted to a body of feminist criticism and that his analysis is unanchored to an overall thesis.

*　*　*

Let us now turn to consider how performances of Behn's plays reflect or develop these critical responses. In the past twenty years, after several centuries in the theatrical wilderness, Behn has been reclaimed as a significant woman dramatist. The rediscovery of her work by academics was swiftly followed by amateur and then professional productions of her comedies, although in recent years there have been disappointingly few new productions. We shall briefly consider two such productions of *The Rover* (one by the Royal Shakespeare Company, directed by John Barton, in 1986, and one jointly by the BBC with the Open University in 1996, available on video).

Barton's production is well documented, partly because the production's programme included detailed director's notes, as well as a text which fused Behn's text with that of her source, *Thomaso*. The performed play was self-confessedly a fusion of Killigrew, Behn and Barton, and for many critics, less coherent because of this.

The play's setting was moved to the West Indies, in an attempt to emphasise both its Carnival content and colonial subtext: all the revellers will become slaves again when the play ends. This setting is the kind of decision which looks like a good idea, emphasising as it does the connection between women's status and that of slaves, a connection intimated by Hellena herself. However, both the specificity of

Behn's Restoration world and the very real issue of slavery were thereby lost, and there was no sense of time or place at the end of the performance. This was exacerbated by the manner in which sexual politics were treated as a conventional comic romp. Thus, for example, being undressed in Behn's play is a signifier of danger and threat. In Barton's production, it was a source of titillation: we were asked to admire Jeremy Irons as Willmore by gazing on his body. Blunt was dressed only in a pair of frilly drawers, which undermined his potential threat to Florinda in Act 4. Similarly, Florinda's dress was always half off her shoulder, making her seem sexually forward rather than naïve or threatened.

Carnival was emphasised through costume and technical effects as well: for example masquers danced at the intermission, accompanied by fireworks. Stage business was actively physical and brought out some of the play's farcical moments: Willmore's initial entrance was on a rope, chased by a man with a gun. Choreography emphasised masculine violence: for example, the fight under Angellica's balcony began with Frederick and Willmore kicking Pedro and Antonio in the groin. Willmore's drunken attack on Florinda in the garden had him throwing her to the ground, and ended with him vomiting into Frederick's hat on the forestage, as near as possible to the audience. He used his sword at every opportunity, for example to force Pedro to approve Florinda's marriage to Belvile, an action not present in Behn's original text.

However, whilst stage business in general drew attention to masculine violence, it seemed to apply differently to the women: Angellica fired a gun over her balcony to stop the men fighting, suggesting her power and autonomy. But there was a great amount of stage undressing: for example when Florinda and Hellena got into Carnival disguise; Angellica dressed on stage in her first scene. Florinda's ordeal with Blunt and Frederick combined farce with violence: Florinda, stripped to her underwear, engaged in a struggle with Blunt which somehow combined violence with titillating views of her semi-naked body.

The actors' depictions of their characters pulled interpretation in different ways. Jeremy Irons was a rather playful, swashbuckling Willmore, despite the moments of violence. This exposed a contradiction in the play itself: that despite the violence with which Willmore is associated, we need to believe in him as a desirable consort for Hellena. This production did not really resolve this conundrum, going for both violence as spectacle, rather than sustained critique, and a happy-ever-after conventional ending.

Sinead Cusack's Angellica theoretically provided the gravitas to enable the audience to believe in her assertion of economic independence and her consequent fall for Willmore. However, her adoption of a strange accent rendered her role increasingly comic rather than tragic, thus lessening the play's emphasis on unfinished business, and the power of her final encounter with Willmore in Act 5.

Lucetta was actually enslaved to Philippo, lessening the autonomy Behn gives her. Belvile was played by a black actor, visually enhancing the romantic, egalitarian nature of his relationship with a white Florinda. A post-colonial, utopian, carnivalised world is thereby posited, although the play's end coincides with the ending of Carnival, suggesting their union may be doomed.

Finally, Barton re-arranged and cut Behn's original text quite considerably, in some cases lessening the complexity of her feminist message. Two examples will suffice. He cut Hellena's speech on equality in Act 5, representing her final relationship with Willmore as a conventional submission to wifely duty. But he also gave Florinda an outspoken speech on freedom at the end of Act 5. By contrast Behn's quiescent Florinda, and outspoken Hellena, provide a disquieting and consistent set of questions about what happens to women once they are married. The uncertainty rendered by Behn's darker ending was not present in Barton's production.

Overall, the production's message was messy and uncertain: although stage business and setting emphasised the violent, exploitative nature of masculinity and the business of sex, characterisation and acting emphasised the conventionally comic platitudes of young love triumphant. As we have seen from our own discussions, Behn's text is deliberately and self-consciously more ambiguous.

Let us now turn to the more recent production by Jules Wright. Wright has also directed a production of *The Lucky Chance*, also for the Women's Playhouse Trust, at the Royal Court in 1984, and explicitly wants to draw attention to Behn's 'feminist' message. Does she succeed? The advantage in talking about this production is that you can watch and judge it for yourself, despite the inevitable problems associated with watching it on a flat screen rather than a three-dimensional stage.

Wright attempts to give us a feel for the stage performance by keeping the set completely bare, invoking the Brookean concept of the empty space on which production, text and actors can inscribe their performance. This works well on television, because it enables the audience to focus precisely on content, plot and character. The set and stage enhance this: bare boards or sand are used for all scenes, the sand subtly invoking the play's Carnival/circus metaphor. Where Behn sets scenes indoors (for example, the first scene between Hellena and Florinda, and Angellica's bedroom scene with Willmore), the characters are seated on different coloured cloths. These cloths are coloured symbolically to represent the women's status: white for Florinda and Hellena, and deep midnight blue for Angellica (not the conventional red for prostitutes), to suggest dark passion. Prostitution is thence not simplistically demonised – for example, it is Blunt whose domestic space is represented by a red sheet, linking him symbolically with blood and danger.

Stage properties are kept to a minimum, thereby enhancing their meaning and significance where used. A huge rope climbing net is used to mark the space between the street and Blunt's house in Acts 4 and 5, effectively actualising the play's symbolic suggestion that Blunt is a spider awaiting his prey, and it is then used to hold Florinda captive at the beginning of Act 5, where Behn shuts her in a hidden room. All the characters exit up the rope net at the end of the play, thereby symbolically suggesting that they are all trapped in the nets of marital convention. Rings and swords are used much as Behn directs.

Lighting is also used to great effect in this production: red and orange gels signify the Carnival time outside, and are echoed in the colours of masks, which move from white (in the second scene) to oranges and reds in subsequent scenes, as sexual desire grows and consummation is promised. By contrast, and again unconventionally, moments of particular danger are lit by white and blue gels: Willmore's near rape of Florinda, Angellica's final confrontation with

Willmore, and crucially, Willmore's and Hellena's final agreement to marry. The latter is thus subtly linked to other moments of danger and tragedy, and the darkness of their future is intimated.

Costume is simple, and colour-coded, as are lighting and set. Florinda and Hellena begin in virginal white nehru-type pyjamas, but dress for carnival in red and orange. Angellica also begins in a similar white costume, emphasising her parallel to the two other women. When all the men first appear they too are dressed in white, although in their case in public-school cricket whites, with accompanying panama hats. By contrast to their natty dress, Willmore is dressed in a red army coat, stained white breeches, and only a vest beneath, to which he strips down in the bedroom with Angellica. He wears thick chamois gloves, stained with nicotine and dirt. His visual appearance is thus slovenly, echoing Behn's text, which draws attention to his rakish appearance. After his encounter with Angellica he appears in a clean, long white coat: but this clean-living appearance has in fact been bought by his own act of prostitution: Angellica has given him the money. Wright's visual markers thus aid and complicate dramatic interpretation.

Stage business concretises theme, character and plot: for example, the women go to the Carnival on bicycles, and when in their own characters on stage, perambulate on the bicycles. When acting as gypsies, they walk. Mode of transport and changed dress signal a freedom not given to them at the beginning. The scenes of violence, the sword fights, the duel and the two threatened rapes are well choreographed. They emphasise the violence: men thrown to the ground in the fights, women pulled and pushed in the near-rape scenes and Willmore and Blunt pulling open their trousers in preparation for rape. The potential humour of these scenes (implicit in the language of misapprehension) is downplayed. Music is used strategically in the production: there is a near-constant drum beat, which speeds up and slows down to match action and tension, only occasionally absent altogether, reminding us of the Carnival setting, and of the dangers as well as pleasures it brings. Music plays to Angellica's song, which is delivered as a chant, to which she dances a slow Indian dance.

Casting was important to the meaning: all the women are played by Asian or black actors, and Lucetta and Valeria by the same actor. The women's mixed races give a cosmopolitan feel to their identities: simultaneously suggesting past slavery and future liberation. The Englishmen are all played by white actors, while Pedro and Antonio are by black men. This reinforces the colonial and post-colonial theme which was recognised in Barton's production.

Finally, the acting emphasises a darker interpretation of the overall plot than did Barton's production. For example, when the scene of forgiveness is played after Florinda's identity and her marriage to Belvile are revealed, although asked to forgive Blunt, she does not do so in this production. This acts as a reminder of her ordeal, and refuses to leave the audience with a sense of 'happy-ever-after'. Lucetta's dependence on her gallant Philippo is emphasised, and not any autonomy she might gain by her gulling of Blunt.

*   *   *

Before ending this chapter, it is useful to consider what our critics and the productions share. Remarkably few emphasise or trust Behn's theatrical and dramaturgical skills, the exceptions being Hughes and Wright. This is an opportunity for Behn studies and theatre, which should be addressed. However, critics and producers agree that she stages and figures gender and sexual conflict, and most agree that she problematises Restoration social conventions in a complex, questioning and stimulating way. Greater sensitivity to the way she uses comic and theatrical conventions in unconventional ways, as well as her juxtapositional structural techniques, would produce and memorialise a greater Behn. Consensus thankfully has not been reached, and this makes Behn an excellent choice for future playable drama.

Further Reading

Throughout this book you have engaged in detailed reading of the original texts. You have developed your own independent ideas, reinforced by close, analytical readings. If you read and discuss a play, using the approaches suggested in this book, you should be able to write essays which are original, analytical and convincing. It is best to engage with other critics when you have already formed your own opinions. If you read them before you think about the play yourself, you will find it harder to develop your own personal ideas and feelings.

The suggestions made here for further reading are necessarily curtailed: both by space and by my own selection. All good editions of the plays have additional suggestions for reading, and suggestive introductions to the plays. The catalogue of a good library will guide you to further reading. You will also find that the footnotes and bibliographies of some of the books or articles recommended below, point you to other texts that will interest you.

Reading Behn's Contemporaries

We have mentioned several plays and writers in this book which would give you a good sense of the dramatic context in which Behn wrote. Wycherley and Etherege are good comparisons: in particular *The Country Wife* and *The Man of Mode*, respectively. Congreve wrote most of his comedies in the 1690s, after Behn's death, but his

The Way of the World includes an excellent marriage-bargain scene. All three writers examine gender and politics. Dryden's *Marriage à la Mode* is the first real marriage comedy of the Restoration.

You should also look at Behn's other plays, for example the fourth in the World's Classics edition, *The Emperor of the Moon*, which is particularly spectacular.

It is helpful to look at some non-dramatic contemporary texts which address many of the issues with which Behn was concerned: Hobbes's *The Leviathan* in any edition; John Rochester, Earl of Wilmot's *Poems*; parts of John Locke's *Essay on Human Understanding* and his *Treatise on Government*. Extracts from writers on conduct and femininity are included in Vivian Jones's *Women in the Eighteenth Century*. Read some of Behn's poetry and her short novel *Oroonoko*, in any edition.

Historical and Social Contexts

The Cambridge Companion to English Restoration Theatre, edited by Deborah Fisk (Cambridge University Press, 2000), is excellent on the background to all of the period's drama, and includes chapters on politics, gender, philosophical background and genres. Laura Brown's *English Dramatic Form, 1660–1760* (Yale University Press, 1981) is a clear introduction to dramatic structure and meaning. Bonamy Dobree's *Restoration Comedy, 1660–1720* (Clarendon Press, 1924) is still a reputable account of the period's drama, although Behn takes a minor role in her account. Douglas Canfield's *Tricksters and Estates: On the Ideology of Restoration Comedy* (University of Kentucky Press, 1997) and Harold Knutson's *The Triumph of Wit: Molière and Restoration Comedy* (Ohio State University Press, 1988) are good on political and generic contexts. Elizabeth Howe's *The First English Actresses: Women and Drama, 1660–1700* (Cambridge University Press, 1992) gives a detailed account of the impact of women acting and working in theatre.

Criticism

The critical works which we discussed in Chapter 12 are: Heidi Hutner (ed.), *Rereading Aphra Behn: History, Theory, Criticism* (University Press of Virginia, 1993); Janet Todd (ed.), *Aphra Behn Studies* (Cambridge University Press, 1996); and Derek Hughes, *The Theatre of Aphra Behn* (Palgrave, 2001). We additionally briefly discussed the biographical approaches of Vita Sackville-West's *Aphra Behn: The Incomparable Astraea* (Greenwood Press, 1927); George Woodcock's *The Incomparable Aphra* (Boardman, 1948); Maureen Duffy's *The Passionate Shepherdess: Aphra Behn, 1640–89* (Jonathan Cape, 1977) and Janet Todd's *The Secret Life of Aphra Behn* (Rutgers University Press, 1996).

There is a casebook collection of Behn criticism, edited by Janet Todd, *Aphra Behn: Contemporary Critical Essays* (Macmillan, 1999). If you sample the critical views in this and the above collections, you can then follow up your own interests by reading the extracted books or articles in full.

S. J. Wiseman's *Aphra Behn* (Northcote House, 1996) for the Writers and their Work series published by the British Council is an excellent short and concise account of her life, work and plays. Margaret Rubik's *Early Women Dramatists, 1550–1800* includes a chapter on Behn as well as discussing the theatrical milieu and other early women dramatists. James Redmond's *Drama, Sex and Politics* (Cambridge University Press, 1985) includes some relevant essays, and Katherine Quinsey's collection *Broken Boundaries: Women and Feminism in Restoration Drama* (Kentucky University Press, 1996) looks specifically at gender.

Index